Aditya Malik

Hammīra

Religion and Society

Edited by
Gustavo Benavides, Frank J. Korom,
Karen Ruffle and Kocku von Stuckrad

Volume 83

Aditya Malik

Hammīra

Chapters in Imagination, Time, History

DE GRUYTER

ISBN 978-3-11-135602-0
e-ISBN (PDF) 978-3-11-066279-5
e-ISBN (EPUB) 978-3-11-066163-7
ISSN 1437-5370

Library of Congress Control Number: 2020952717

Bibliographic information published by the Deutsche Nationalbibliothek
The Deutsche Nationalbibliothek lists this publication in the Deutsche Nationalbibliografie; detailed bibliographic data are available on the Internet at http://dnb.dnb.de.

This volume is text- and page-identical with the hardback published in 2021.
Printing and binding: CPI books GmbH, Leck

www.degruyter.com

For M.

As long as you think, there will be existence, person, place and thing,
but when you stop thinking there is no existence,
because there cannot be silence and existence.
Robert Adams

Everything you can imagine is real.
Pablo Picasso

Preface

This book is concerned with two broad themes that are also reflected in the structuring of the book into two roughly equal sections. One section, consisting of the Prologue and Chapters 1, 2 and 4, deals with (a) a series of related historical events that have been profusely written and commented upon through several centuries until the present time and (b) how we perceive relationships between religious communities in India in the past (and also in the present). The events described by different texts and narratives deal with the Rajput chieftain of the impenetrable fortress of Ranthambore and his enmity and ultimate defeat at the hands of the Sultan of Delhi, ʿAlāʾ al-Dīn Khaljī. The text that receives particular focus is the Sanskrit *Hammīra-Mahākāvya*, which was composed by the Jaina scholar and poet Nayachandra Sūri in 1401. The purpose of the *Hammīra-Mahākāvya* seems to be twofold: on the one hand it is about poetry – about rising to the challenge of writing great Sanskrit poetry in the second millennium with all its poetical embellishments and linguistic markers. On the other hand, the poem is commemorative. It commemorates and celebrates the deeds and death of Hammīra, a flawed hero, who is unbending on his word. The poem is therefore both *kāvya* or poetry, and what we would call 'history,' i.e. it aspires to simultaneously contain the signifiers of a literary and a historical work.

The Sanskrit poem, however, is but one of an entire continuum of oral and written Persian, Sanskrit, Rajasthani, Hindi and English works over centuries until the present day, as well as conversations held at the fortress of Ranthambore during fieldwork, that draw out the imaginative fabric of Hammīra's life and heroic death, so much so that this becomes part of Hindu nationalist discourse on the protection of Hindu religion or *dharma* in the 20th century. Thus, a singular moment – the battle between Hammīra and ʿAlāʾ al-Dīn Khaljī – reverberates through centuries vertically to the point of creating a temporal and cultural region, and a 'history' through a crystallization of the event in different texts and languages: Persian chronicles, Sanskrit works, Hindi and Rajasthani poems and songs, and English translations, as well as 20th-century historiography grounded in Hindu nationalist thought.

One critical detail concerning Hammīra's life is that he provides sanctuary to one of ʿAlāʾ al-Dīn Khaljī's mutineering, 'neo-Muslim' rebel generals called Muhammed Shāh (who is later called Mahimā Sāhi) and his followers who then become – more so than the former's own traitorous Rajput generals Ratipāla and Raṇmalla – his closest and most faithful allies and friends, leading, as one can imagine, to wrath of the sultan, and ultimately the tragic demise of Ham-

https://doi.org/10.1515/9783110662795-001

mīra, Muhammed Shāh (aka Mahimā Sāhi) and their families. Yet, it is intriguing that despite the singular fact of Hindu–Muslim friendship and loyalty lying at the core of the Hammīra narrative, in the hands of contemporary, post-independence historiography this fact is glossed over while the story attains the status of a 'national epic' (*rāṣṭrīya mahākāvya*), and Hammīra the status of a national hero protecting India from Muslim imperialists.

Clearly, the text creates a narrative space that allows a series of shared religious, social and political spaces to arise. Is there a set of values that underlie the creation of this shared literary space? Why does a Jain poet write about a Hindu chieftain and his clash with a Muslim sultan, and the accompanying description of gore, treason, violence, bloodshed, weaponry, war and so on? How indeed are religious labels such as 'Hindu' and 'Muslim' or 'Jain' imagined in this context? Evidently, they do not carry the same significance as they would in the contemporary discourse of 'essentialized,' singular, bounded religious identities. Since in the original text they do not carry these meanings, how does Hammīra wind up becoming central to the creation of 20th-century scholarship propelled by Hindu nationalist discourse on the protection and sustenance of Hindu *dharma?* How and why does this shift occur in which shared religious and social spaces shrink? It would seem that modern enclaves of religion and caste also result in a politically charged re-imagining of the past that is both selective and palpably prejudiced in conceiving of discreet religious categories of Muslim and Hindu, rather than, for example, interrelated, rival and yet often mutually beneficial Turk, Mongol, 'neo-Muslim' and Rajput assemblages forged through the expediencies of honour, friendship and power but not necessarily religion or ethnicity.

The other section, consisting of Chapters 3, 5, 6 and 7, arises in particular as a response to the underlying cause that triggers the composition of the Sanskrit work: it is in a *dream* that the dead hero, Hammīra, appears to the poet urging him to write the *historical* poem. Can history begin in a dream? What does it mean to think about the past, and about history and time, through an enquiry into the imagination? Is there a connection between the imagination and thinking about the past? Is history linked to imagination? What, indeed, is imagination? Is time – whether past, present or future – linked to imagination? In other words, does time arise only when there is imagination? Or conversely does imagination arise when there is time? Alternatively, is there a simultaneous arising or rather co-arising of imagination, time and history, and therefore of what we call world? As a corollary to these questions, the book explores the idea that what we call world may be quintessentially nothing more than an enormously intricate 'seemingly real' appearance engineered by the imagination. What are the implications of this perspective for an understanding of history and of time? Is history, as a result, simply a simulation of an apparent reality? Can History ever be *possibility?*[1]

While this book is inspired by the story of Hammīra – a Rajput chieftain who lived and ruled over the impregnable fortress of Ranthambore in south-eastern Rajasthan during the 13th century – the ideas, content and questions in the second section may not immediately appear as belonging to the kind of content and questions one expects of a work of history in the traditional sense. Perhaps at best – given some of the themes it deals with – the second half of the book can be described as an enquiry into the questions that a phenomenology of both history and the imagination would concern itself with. The book is thus about history as it appears in our experience while exploring the idea of what it means to be a historical being, and to write a history from the point of view of the subject who is aware of writing it, and in whom different temporalities and experiences of time are simultaneously intertwined in the here and now.

This book thus attempts to traces the movement of various texts and narratives, spiralling circles of imagination prospectively and retroactively from the 20th and 21st centuries going back to the moment of the *Hammīra-Mahākāvya.* The narratives live forward, backward, and simultaneously in the moment of now and the temporalities of past and future, as a prospective–retrospective field of intersubjective experience. The book endeavours a structure that represents this movement from future back to past, and from past into future in the simultaneity of ever-widening circles of imagination.

1 The understanding of imagination as I am using it is different to imagination as a function of a mental faculty that can conjure and construct and makes sense of past, present and future – it takes us to the realm of sheer possibility and 'clearing' that gives rise to the possibility of imagining as an intellectual or mental faculty of human beings.

Contents

Prologue — 1

Chapter 1 Historical Contexts — 6
1.1 Rajput Identities — **6**
1.2 The Poet — **7**
1.3 The Chieftain — **8**
1.4 The Edition and Commentary — **14**

Chapter 2 Singular Moments — 18
2.1 Modern Formations — **18**
2.2 Narrative Templates — **21**
2.3 Experiencing the Past — **23**
2.4 Cascading Narratives — **26**
2.5 The Subject of History and the Simultaneity of Time — **28**

Chapter 3 Realms of Imagination — 33
3.1 Imagination — **33**
3.2 View with a Grain of Sand — **34**
3.3 The Imagination of Blake — **39**

Chapter 4 Literary Imbroglios — 45
4.1 Medieval Religious and Cultural Sensibilities — **46**
4.2 The Hammīr Rāso — **53**
4.3 The Enchanted Forest — **56**
4.4 Sacrificial Foundations — **60**
4.5 The Sage's Body — **63**

Chapter 5 The Poet's Dream — 69
5.1 Simulated Worlds — **69**
5.2 Future Traditions — **72**
5.3 Real Simulacrums — **76**
5.4 'Mind-Born' Worlds — **81**

Chapter 6 History as Simulacrum — 90
6.1 Thinking about the Past — **90**
6.2 The Empty Sign — **94**
6.3 Mnemosyne and the Desert of the Real — **100**

6.4 History as Possibility? — 106
6.5 History as 'Andenken' — 111

Chapter 7 Interiors of the Past — 114
7.1 Remembering Ranthambore — 114
7.2 Jogi and Pīr — 115
7.3 Battlefields and Tantric Fields — 118
7.4 The Mythical Fortress — 122

Epilogue — 131

Appendix 1 — 134
1 Synopsis of the Hammīra-Mahākāvya — 134
2 Passages in Translation — 136

Appendix 2: Conversations at Ranthambore — 154
1 The Maze of Gates — 154
2 Ritual Landscapes — 169
3 Into the Forest — 172
4 Jogi and Pīr — 186
5 Ranthambore — 190

Bibliography — 195

Authors — 201

Subjects — 203

Acknowledgments

Although I had heard of the *Hammīra-Mahākāvya* during my graduate years at the University of Heidelberg when I was doing my PhD under the guidance of Günther-Dietz Sontheimer[2] and Hermann Kulke, the concrete suggestion to work on the Sanskrit poem came from John Smith of the University of Cambridge more than decade ago when I was invited as a visiting professor to participate in an amazingly productive and inspiring month-long Summer Academy on Regional Sanskrit in Jerusalem. The academy was hosted by David Shulman and Yigal Bronner with the support of the Israel Academy of Sciences and Humanities and the Institute for Advanced Studies at the Hebrew University, Jerusalem. I am grateful to the hosts and the other participants of the Summer Academy, particularly H. V. Nagaraj Rao, for their encouragement and support in clarifying some of the more difficult grammatical aspects of the *Hammīra-Mahākāvya*. However, after returning to the University of Canterbury where I was teaching in the Department of Religious Studies and later in the Department of Anthropology, my research interests turned in different directions that later resulted in the publication of several articles and a book.[3] Many, many years after the Summer Academy, my friend and colleague Ishita Bannerjee asked me to write a book about Hammīra that would be published in a series she was editing for De Gruyter. However, when the series was discontinued, I was fortunate to receive an offer from Sophie Wagenhofer to publish it as a standalone volume. Subsequently, Frank Korom urged me to have the book published in this series. And, since then, Katrin Mittmann has guided me patiently and very ably through the stages of submission and publication. I am grateful to the team at De Gruyter for their enduring support and guidance; to Ben Dare for his meticulous and thorough reading of the manuscript on account of which many ideas in the book became much sharper than they were to begin with; and to Ulla Schmidt for her prompt assistance and friendly co-operation in preparing the manuscript and indexes. I am also indebted to Romila Thapar and Ann Grodzins Gold for their encouraging comments and suggestions during the initial review of the book proposal.

But it was only when I was invited as a fellow at the Max Weber Centre for Advanced Social and Cultural Studies (Max-Weber-Kolleg)[4] at the University of

2 I was probably his only student to work in Rajasthan. Most of his other students worked, as he himself did, in Maharashtra.

3 Malik (2016/2018).

4 *Max-Weber-Kolleg für kultur- und sozialwissenschaftliche Studien.*

https://doi.org/10.1515/9783110662795-002

Erfurt for a period of one year (2016/2017)[5] that I resumed working on the ideas that had initially begun to interest me at the Summer Academy in Jerusalem. The exceptional intellectual space offered at the Max-Weber-Kolleg provided perfect conditions to think, read, write and discuss some of the many ideas presented in this book with colleagues from universities from around the world who had also joined the Kolleg as fellows. The international guest house (IBZ) of the university – located in a 16th-century building that was originally a printer's workshop in which, amongst a few hundred other works, Martin Luther's bible translation was printed – was an ideal place from which to work and walk around the beautiful medieval town of Erfurt in the evenings. The weekly colloquia in which individual fellows' research was rigorously debated gave me a critical platform on which to think about the questions in this book. I am grateful to several colleagues from the fields of sociology, anthropology, religious studies, theology, philology, philosophy, classical studies, history, law and jurisprudence, Sanskrit and Indian Studies, Chinese Studies, and Hebrew Studies at the Max-Weber-Kolleg from whom I received critical and encouraging support: my hosts and friends at the Kolleg, Antje Linkenbach and Martin Fuchs as well as Jörg Rüpke, Harry Maier, Ann Murphy, Saurabh Dube, Ishita Bannerjee, Kumkum Sangari, Asaph Ben Tov, Angelika Malinar, Markus Vinzent, Jutta Vinzent, Avner Ben Zaken, Martin Mulsow, Daniel Boyarin, Michael Staussberg, Julie Casteigt, Richard Gordon and Max Deeg. I am also grateful to Oliver Schmerbauch, Diana Blanke, Diana Pueschel and Bettina Hollstein, who untiringly and generously provided many other kinds of support and assistance at the Max-Weber-Kolleg. As I was writing it, parts of the book were presented in the form of lecture presentations at the University of Leipzig, and at an enormously creative international workshop I organized together with my colleagues in the School of Historical Studies at Nalanda University that was entitled *Imagining Histories, Writing Pasts*. I am grateful to my colleagues and students at these institutions for their observations and comments: Ursula and Sadashiv Rao for their invitation to visit Leipzig and give a lecture at the Institute of Anthropology; my colleagues at Nalanda – Samuel Wright, Sraman Mukherjee, Murari Kumar Jha, Kashshaf Ghani, Pankaj Mohan, Ranu Roychoudhuri, Abhishek Amar and Christine Vial-Kayser; and my students at Nalanda – Aditya Chaturvedi, Annalisa Mansukhani, Shikhar Goel, Shashi Ahlawat, Pritha Mukherjee, Sanjivani Dwivedi, Azad Hind Gulshan Nanda and Pavni Sairam. At the fortress of Ranthambore in Rajasthan where I conducted fieldwork, I was fortunate to have extended conversations about

5 This project has received funding from the European Union's Horizon 2020 research and innovation programme under the Marie Skłodowska-Curie grant agreement No. 665958.

the history of the fortress with Wahid Mohammed, Manohar Lal Mina and Naresh Gujjar.[6]

While the idea for this book was first conceived in Jerusalem, different parts of it were written in Christchurch, Erfurt, Nalanda and Delhi. Wherever I happened to be, I was constantly accompanied by the love, support and encouragement of my parents, Zarine Malik and Subhash Chandra Malik. I am grateful to my father, Bhashiji, for reading through the draft of the book and offering many valuable and critical observations. My daughters Renuka and Ambika have always been patient about the vast distance there is between India where I now work and live, and New Zealand which is their home. They are a constant source of strength and inspiration. My aunts Usha Malik (Ushaji), Kapila Vatsyayan (Kapilaji) and Anjali Capila (Anjuji) have brought depth to my own thinking through their prodigious creativity in so many areas of the arts and scholarship.

This book is dedicated to Meethu, who is the embodiment of brilliance, tenacity and compassion, without whom I would not have endeavoured to undertake and complete many things, including this book.

Aditya Malik
22 May, in the First Year of COVID-19

Note

While this book substantially, though not solely, draws on the content of the Sanskrit poetical work, the *Hammīra-Mahākāvya*, in which the life and deeds of the Rajput king Hammīra Chauhan and his ancestors are described, it does not contain a full length translation of the *Hammīra-Mahākāvya*. To do this would be to alter the size, direction and character of the book. Instead, some translated passages of the poem along with the original Devanagari text have been included in the main body of the text, while other translated sections that I found relevant to the broader purpose of the book are contained in Appendix 1.

Here I would like to express my gratitude for the assistance I received in the translation from scholars of Sanskrit literature and language: Rakesh Das (Ramakrishna Mission Vivekananda University, Belur Math), Abirlal Gangopadhyay (Central University of Hyderabad) and Aneesh Raghavan (Pondicherry University).

6 The bulk of these conversations are included in Appendix 2.

In addition to the translated portions of the Sanskrit text featured in Appendix 1, Appendix 2 incorporates translations of several longer conversations in Hindi concerning the history, architecture and the ritual and religious significance of the fortress of Ranthambore, which is the site of the siege laid by 'Alā' al-Dīn Khaljī against Hammīra. These conversations were recorded during a short period of fieldwork conducted at the fortress and nearby locations. Excerpts of these conversations are also included in the chapters of the main text.

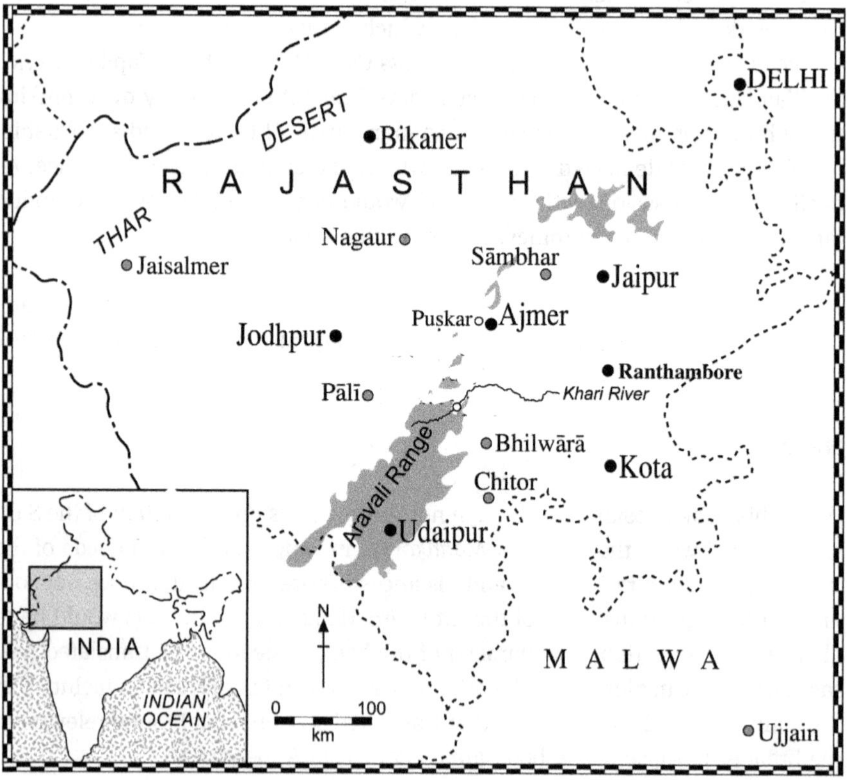

Map 1: Map showing location of Ranthambore in relation to other cities and towns in Rajasthan.

Prologue

Imagination is more weighty than fact.
Thomas Moore

Fig 1: Outer wall of the fortress

Fig 2: The rampart built around the fortress

Fig 3: An outer wall and rampart

https://doi.org/10.1515/9783110662795-003

Imagine the following scenes:

Hammīra, the chieftain of the great desert fortress of Ranthambore in Rajasthan, realizes that defeat is imminent by the enemy forces that have laid siege of his fortress for months. He turns to his most loyal commander, Muhammed Shāh (aka Mahimā Sāhi) and tells him to leave the fortress because he is a foreigner,[8] and therefore should protect himself and his family before it is too late. The loyal commander is inwardly enraged but seems to happily agree with the chieftain's request. But when he returns to his quarters, he draws his sword and unflinchingly slays his wife and young children.[9] Then he informs the chieftain that his wife was grateful for the latter's concern and care. The chieftain insists on visiting the commander's home only to find his wife and children's corpses afloat in pools of blood. The chieftain swoons and falls to the ground upon apprehending the ultimate loyalty shown by his 'foreign' commander. He praises the commander calling him "O Upholder of the Kāmboja[10] Tribe!" "O Dwelling Place of the Glorious Tribe!" "O Bearer of the *kṣatriya* Vow!" "O beloved of humanity!"[11] Not long after this the chieftain bids farewell to his own wife, Āraṅgīdevī, and leaves his young daughter, Devalldevī, in a poignant embrace before they and scores of other women of the fortress leap into a terrible, all-consuming fire pit, committing *jauhar.*[12] Then the chieftain together with his loyal commanders rides out to face the superior army of his enemy only to die in dramatic yet heroic fashion. The chieftain, who is struck by a hundred arrows, beheads himself before the enemy can take him captive. The loyal commander, Mahimā Sāhi, is injured and taken prisoner. The enemy king, 'Alā' al-Dīn Khaljī, offers to spare his life in return for his loyalty. When the commander refuses to betray the dead chieftain, the enemy king has his head placed under the foot of an elephant and crushed.[13]

---

8 Skt.: *vaideśika* i.e. someone belonging to another country (*videśa),* a foreigner, or stranger.
9 See the movie *The Usual Suspects* (1995) in which the mysterious, main character *Keyser Söze* is rumoured to have murdered his own family who were being held hostage by Hungarian mobsters after which he massacres the mobsters and kills their families. I am grateful to Eli Franco for pointing out this comparison.
10 A tribe thought to have its origins in Afghanistan or even further north-west in Tajikistan and Uzbekistan.
11 The king also calls Mahimā Sāhi "O Person of Matchless Virtue!" "O Blessed Courage!". Sanskrit: "*Hā Kāmbojakuladhāra!*" "*Hā Kirtīkulamandira!*" "*Hā Ananyajanyasaujanya!*" "*Hā Dhanyatamvikram!*" "*Hā Kṣaitravratāgara!*" "*Hā Viśvajanavātsala!*"
(*Hammīra-Mahākāvya Sarga* 13.163–164ab)
12 While the etymology of *jauhar* remains uncertain, the term refers to a collective or mass self-immolation of women belonging to the Rajput or warrior communities. This act of sacrifice and bravery was undertaken when it became clear that the women's male relatives (husbands/fathers/brothers) would inevitably lose or die in battle leading to the captivity and enslavement of the women. *Sati*, on the other hand, represented the self-immolation of an individual woman subsequent to the death of her husband either in battle or of natural causes.
13 This detail is found in Kirtane's introduction. It is not in the text of the *Hammīra-Mahākāvya*. There is reference to this also in the *Khazā'in al-futūḥ* of Amir Khusraw. See Appendix 1, for the translation of excerpts from *Sarga* 13.147–226 and *Sarga* 14.17–21 of the *Hammīra-Mahākāvya*, which contains the scenes described above.

Exactly one hundred years later, the dead chieftain appears in the poet Nayachandra Sūri's dream. In the dream the chieftain urges the poet to write a poem called the *Hammīra-Mahākāvya*[14] about the history of the chieftain's lineage, and the series of incidents leading to his heroic death and the defeat.

Dreaming History

Can history begin in a dream? What does it mean to write a history – an account of *factuality* – from a seed planted in a dream?[15] A seed, vision or an urge planted in the subconscious that bubbles over into a cascading poem? What sorts of reverberations and ripples in space and time does the poet's dream set off once it has been birthed in material form as written language? How can or do spirals and whorls of meaning emanate from an ephemeral dream? Can the subject of a historical work direct the writer of the work in a dream? The dream I am talking about here is one that a poet and scholar from the 15th century had of a warrior king from the sandy tracts of Rajasthan who died dramatically in the 14th century. The whorls of meaning are literary and historical accounts of the events the poet wrote about elaborately in his poem that have found their way into different languages – Persian, Rajasthani, Hindi and even English – in different genres – ballads, royal chronicles, translations and scholarly essays across vast regions of space and of time.

How does the inception of time, region, history and literature flow from the poet's dream? It is not uncommon for poets and writers to be inspired by the things that they are going to write about. The inspiration may come from the

14 See below for further details about the *Hammīra-Mahākāvya*. The siege of Ranthambore is comparable to the siege of Constantinople by the Ottoman Emperor Sultan Mehmed II (Mehmed the Conqueror) on May 29, 1453. Both sieges become narratives of persistence, betrayal, loyalty, the shortage of grains, the slaying of traitors by the victorious king, close relatives turning against the defending ruler and joining the attacking kingdom, and so on. Many historical details of Sultan Mehmed's siege and assault on the unconquerable and impenetrable city of Constantinople, which had stood firm even after 23 attacks in the past, are similar to the details of the attack, defence and siege of the impenetrable, unconquerable fortress of Ranthambore. Is there, perhaps, a template into which historical narratives concerning sieges of impenetrable fortresses are inserted and woven around?

15 This, of course, would seem to be at odds with the so-called 'evidentiary protocols' of the modern discipline of History. Dreams can be both private and public, inside and outside, revealing the past or the future. In the case of the composition of the *Hammīra-Mahākāvya*, the dream seems to have the place of an 'authenticator,' legitimizing the truth-claims of the author.

past, or it may even come from the future.[16] The poet in question is no exception, except that the warrior king that he will write about appears to him – like apparitions sometimes do in people's dreams – with a request, perhaps a directive, decree or even royal command that he cannot turn down. A command that lodges in the poet's mind an unusual but urgent desire, possibly a demand: to compose a poem about the warrior king, a poem that recounts his ancestors' deeds, his own birth, his reign as a king in a remote, sprawling, impenetrable fortress atop a flat hill surrounded by barren, dry land, speckled with thorny green shrubs, thickets of tall yellow-green grass and the occasional precious shimmering, shallow lake. The warrior king directs the poet to write a poem – not just any poem, but a poem that runs to a thousand and five hundred verses in the most complex and difficult Sanskrit verse, embellished with all forms of alliteration, rhythm, metres and grammatical twists for knowledgeable readers of high culture to decipher and relish. The warrior king commands the poet to write a story, a compilation of facts put to wonderful verse about how the stubborn and strong king gave refuge to enemy generals who had mutinied from the army of their commander-in-chief, the Sultan of Delhi, and how after defeating the sultan's armies, the warrior king's fortress was besieged by the sultan himself for months, even years. Some say that the siege lasted so long that mango kernels the sultan's soldiers had thrown away after eating the delicious fruit had grown into shady fruit bearing trees themselves. In the end the warrior king was slain, after being deceived by his own trusted generals. Only the mutineer generals who sought refuge by him remained close. The warrior king's wife and daughter, and all the other noblewomen of the fortress, dressed in bedazzling jewellery and the finest, flowing garments, burnt themselves alive in a flaming pit. The king and a handful of remaining loyal friends then rode out of the fortress to confront the camping sultan's army only to die in flamboyantly heroic ways – the warrior king, struck by a hundred arrows, severed his own head lest he be taken captive.[17]

The warrior king's generosity in giving enemy generals refuge but also his steadfast – indeed stubborn[18] – adherence to a code of Rajasthani (Rajput) war-

---

16 Kurt Vonnegut (2005) in his novel *A Man without a Country* writes: "Is it possible that seemingly incredible geniuses like Bach and Shakespeare and Einstein were not in fact superhuman, but simply plagiarists, copying great stuff from the future?" See Bowie's (2004, 13–28) reflections on 'remembering the future'.

17 See Appendix 1 – translated portions of *Sarga* 13 and 14 of the *Hammīra-Mahākāvya.*

18 Sanskrit: *haṭṭa*. Hammīra has been described in the *Hammīra-Mahākāvya* and in other sources in varying ways, not always positive. But one feature that does consistently characterize him is his indomitable will to keep his word regardless of the circumstances. He is called *Haṭṭa-*

rior's code of honour, his impossible defeat of the sultan's armies and his audacious pursuit of bravery in death creates a spiralling imagination through literary forms, languages and epochs both pre-modern and modern in India. How and why does this spiralling of meaning and its sedimentation in literary and historical genres take place? How do different literary and historical moments look back, appropriate and refashion the events that were first inscribed in the poet's dream of the warrior king? How do different narratives and the events they speak about create a future time and a time past? What does the poem itself say about the dramatic events of the 14th–15th centuries? Who is the warrior king here and who is he in the Persian chronicles of the victorious sultan? Who is he in the ballads and songs of the Rajasthani countryside? And, finally, who does he become in the writings of 19th- and 20th-century Indian historians moulded now in the tradition of empirical history, and the nationalist fervour of a young independent, post-colonial republic? How does the hero of our poem transform from a stubborn, honour-driven local chieftain and hero in Sanskrit and Rajasthani poems and songs, to vanquished enemy chieftain in Persian chronicles, and then back to iconic figure of Hindu national identity in Hindi and English scholarly writing? How does the poem with its inception in a dream-like vision slide like a piece on a carom board from being a poetical work of historical and factual significance composed in the pattern of *kāvya* in the 15th century, to becoming a non-historical work of poetical and imaginative significance in the 19th–20th centuries? What sorts of shifts in the ideology of historiography – of writing history – can we glean from this movement? How are we supposed to read and listen to the poem inside the swirls of meaning that have spun around it from its beginning up until close to the present moment?

Hammīra or stubborn, staunch, unbending Hammīra. This characterization of Hammīra is key in some ways to understanding the unfolding of the narrative in *Hammīra-Mahākāvya*.

Chapter 1
Historical Contexts

1.1 Rajput Identities

The period between the 8th and 11th centuries witnessed the emergence and rise of different Rajput clans and lineages in Rajasthan and Gujarat. This was also a period when there were several invasions, raids and clashes with Muslim chieftains and rulers (for example, with Muhammed Ghori, 1175 CE). It was also the time when the Delhi sultanate under the so-called slave kings (for example, Qutb al-Din Aibak, ruled CE 1206 – 1210) and the Khaljī dynasty was established. This was also a time of interchange, allegiances, victories and defeats that occurred between Rajput rulers themselves and Muslim sultans. It was a time when the culture of valour, heroism and self-sacrifice – a particular kind of Rajput martial ethos – begins to emerge. Not only are a number of heroic narratives composed during this time in Rajasthani and Sanskrit, contemporary oral epics in Rajasthani such as those of Pābūjī and Devnārāyaṇ also situate themselves in that period, i.e. 10th–11th centuries.[19] One of the main themes of these oral narratives is the self-sacrificial deeds of the heroes. These oral narratives, as well as written compositions from the period, celebrate heroic death. Death and dying is seen as a kind of victory. Indeed, in all its complexity, the *Hammīra-Mahākāvya* celebrates this idea in a fundamental manner.[20]

One of the central narratives that we also find evidence for during this period through inscriptions and also written texts is the so-called *agni-kula* origins of certain Rajput clans. According to this narrative, of which there exist a number of tellings, Rajput clans, in particular the Chauhans or Cahamanas, arose either directly out of the fire or from the sun during the performance of a *yajña* (Vedic fire ritual) by Brahmā.[21] Their prime purpose was the protection of the *yajña* from marauding groups of *dānavas*, *daityas* and possibly *Mlecchas*. The narrative of Brahmā's *yajña* and the origin of the Chauhans is also retold at the beginning of the *Hammīra-Mahākāvya*.[22]

The period preceding the composition of the *Hammīra-Mahākāvya* is therefore one in which various new *kṣatriya* (warrior caste) and Rajput identities,

---

19 See Smith (1991) and Malik (2005).

20 See Blackburn (1985).

21 See also Malik (1993) for an analysis of the *Puṣkara-Māhātmya* which contains a description of the ancient pilgrimage place of Pushkar, the origin of which is a *yajña* performed by Brahmā.

22 See *Hammīra-Mahākāvya, Sarga* 1.13 – 18.

https://doi.org/10.1515/9783110662795-004

clans and dynasties are being forged. The formation of these new clans and dynasties was taking place in the context of allegiances and conflicts amongst Rajput clans themselves as well as between them and the Muslim rulers of the time. One of the most well-known and powerful clans that emerged was that of the Chahamanas or Chauhans. The *Hammīra-Mahākāvya* is a narrative about one of the most celebrated leaders of this dynasty.

1.2 The Poet

Perhaps it is time now to turn from this rather enigmatic mode to introducing the reader to the poet and the warrior king who appears in his dream. The poet's name, as mentioned earlier, is Nayachandra Sūri. The warrior king, we already know, is Hammīra.

Nayachandra Sūri is of the Jaina faith. He is a poet with a remarkable scholarly pedigree: he is the disciple and grandson of Jayasiṃha Sūri, a scholar and poet who knew six languages and composed three important works – the Nyāya Sāraṭika, a new grammar of Sanskrit and a poem on Kumāra Nṛpati. But he was famous also because he is supposed to have vanquished Sāraṅga (dhara) in a disputation and was considered to be a master of logic, grammar and poesy. Nayachandra himself was court poet to the Tomara ruler King Vīrama. Hammīra, the hero of the poem he composed, apparently visited him not once but several times in a dream instructing him in the content of the narrative. But there is more to this fascinating story of how the poem got written – not only did Hammīra instruct him in what to write, but Nayachandra also rose to a challenge put forth in King Vīrama's court that no poet could compose *kāvya* of the same high order as did Kalidāsa, Bilhana and so on over a thousand years prior. Writing Sanskrit poetry, it seems, had come to a standstill or was at best only mediocre subsequent to the epoch of these grand poets. The king is supposed to have gestured with his eyebrows towards Nayachandra Sūri as the poet in his court who would be capable of composing a poem comparable in poetic depth to the earlier 'classical' poetry. Nayachandra thereupon composed this poem about Hammīra that contains *sṛṅgāra*, *vīra* and *adbhuta rasa*.[23] Nayachandra's vision thus encompassed

---

23 See Chapter 6 and Appendix 1. The *Hammīra-Mahākāvya* consists of 1500 verses divided into 14 *Sargas*. The initial *Sargas* deal with the origin of the Chauhans and with reigns and deeds of early Chauhan rulers, including Pṛthvīrāj Chauhan III. The *Sargas* 5, 6, and 7 contain descriptions of the seasons [*vasanta* and *varṣā*] as well as *sṛṅgāra rasa*. The latter half of the poem is dedicated to Hammīra, his birth, his *digvijaya* and *koṭi yajña*, various deeds of his generals, his brother, allies and his battles against ʿAlāʾ al-Dīn Khaljī. The poet has used a variety of me-a twofold dream, one about Hammīra, and the other about writing a poem that would match the bygone golden age of Sanskrit poetry. He traverses different worlds in following his creative impulse: the worlds or states of dreaming and being awake, the world of the past that seems to represent a closure, and the world of the future that presents novel possibilities through his investiture of a new age of poetical effort.[24]

1.3 The Chieftain

The poem is about Hammīra, whose name itself suggests Arabic influence. This is not uncommon amongst Rajputs who carry names such as Zalim Singh, Bahadur Singh, Iqbal Singh and so on. In fact, Hammīra is a Sanskrit form of the Arabic title '*Amir*,' meaning chieftain or commander. This title was conferred upon early Ghaznavid rulers before the title of 'Sultan' was used.[25] Indeed, these early Ghaznavid rulers adopted the Sanskritized version of Amir, namely Hammīra or its variants such as *Hamira*, *Hambira*, and *Hamvira*. In fact, several north Indian dynasties refer to the latter series of titles when describing their political adversaries.[26] For example:

tres, twenty-four in fact, and a number of sometimes rare and occasionally difficult grammatical forms (for example, *red. aorist*). The predominant *rasas* are *sṛṅgāra* and *vīra*. Figures of speech such as *rūpaka*, *upamā*, *virodha*, *atiśayokti*, *parisaṃkhyā*; a variety of *alaṃkāras: utprekṣa*, *arthānataranyāsa*, *aprastutapraśaṃsā*. *Virodha* seems to be the chief *alaṃkāras*.

24 Several other important works focusing not only Sanskrit grammar and poetry but also Rajput histories) were composed by Jaina scholars and poets during this period (12th–15th centuries). This raises the question of the relationship between the Jaina and Rajput communities and the intention behind the composition of texts by Jainas. Romila Thapar (2005, 107) points out that the relationship was marked by both kinship as well as the desire to elevate the Jaina community: "Much of the intention of these works was to edify the congregation and demonstrate the might of the Jaina Sangha. There was nevertheless a demarcation between the Rajput aristocracy and Jaina elite, although some members of the latter claimed Rajput origin. The demarcation was not merely between a warrior aristocracy and a powerful segment of society espousing a philosophy of non-violence. Cultural differences arose more effectively between an aristocracy of landed magnates connected through a vast network across the region based on lineage links, and an elite drawing status primarily from the acquisition of wealth primarily from commerce and, to a lesser extent, from land." Thapar (2005) refers to the relevant works composed by Jaina authors in Chapter 5 of her book.

25 The Ghaznavid dynasty ruled over large parts of Iran, Afghanistan and north-west India between 977 and 1186 CE.

26 See Flood (2009, 255).

> *Hambira* is [...] mentioned in an eleventh- or twelfth-century inscription from Bada'un while several copperplate inscriptions issued in the name of the Gahadvala rajas of Kanauj between Vikrama 1165 / AD 1109 and Vikrama 1232 / AD 1175 refer to *Hammīra*. Similarly, a Chauhan inscription of 1167 refers to Hansi fort being protected against *Hammīra*. Over the following decades, an inscription in the name of the Chalukya Raja Bhima II (1178–1239) at Veraval on the coast of Gujarat records the defeat of *Hammīra*; around the same time, a Yadava inscription from Patna dated ca. 1209–10 makes a similar claim [...] by the second half of the thirteenth century the term *Hammīra* had come to denote a series of formidable Turko-Persian adversaries who had menaced the Rajput kingdoms for almost three centuries [...] In all these instances, Hammīra is portrayed as a ferocious opponent, *an enemy by virtue of strength rather than religious affiliation* (Flood 2009, 255–256; emphasis added).

Since Hammīra is used to denote a chieftain or great warrior it is to be distinguished as a title from other Sanskrit labels that signify Muslim ethnicity such as Tajika, Turuska and Yavana – as well as Mleccha, which is a more general category to denote stranger, foreigner or barbarian that was also used to refer to non-Vedic communities and cultures such as those belonging to the Kambojas, Śakas, Hunas, Kushanas and so on (Flood 2009, 256). Hammīra thus did not necessarily designate a personal name. For example, Mahmud of Ghazni is conferred the epithet/title Hammīra in a number of places (Flood 2009, 256 and Chattopadhyay 1998). Subsequent to the establishment of the Delhi sultanate, this Sanskritized version of the Arabic *Amir* "was adopted as a personal name by a myriad of northern Indian Hindu rulers. In an ironic twist, for example, the last scion of the Chauhan royal house was named Hammīra" (Flood 2009, 257).

Hammīra's name itself suggests a relationship to Mongol/Mughal rulers of the time that may not necessarily have been anchored in resistance. If resistance to Mongol 'colonial' rule was foremost in the list of his clan's aspirations, would they have chosen an appellation derived from the language and culture of their oppressors? Rivalries certainly did exist between Rajput clans and Mongol rulers just as there were rivalries between different Rajput clans. But to adopt a name used by one's enemies also indicates a kind of admiration and mutuality. Moreover, the 'Mohammadan' enemies of Hammīra that Kirtane mentions, are, in fact, never referred to with that particular religious signifier; rather, they are called Yavanas/Śakas/Turks/Mongols/Mughals, even Mlecchas, but not Muslims or 'Mohammadans.'[27] 'Mleccha' as a term of exclusion has a long and differentiated pedigree denoting 'non-Vedic' communities, foreigners or barbarians. Mleccha, but even more so Śaka, Turk or Mongol, alludes to an ethnicity or a place of origin, along with its accompanying insinuations of divergence from the norm and

27 Several epithets are used in the text for ʿAlāʾ al-Dīn including King, Lord, and Leader of the Yavanas, Śakas, and Mlecchas.

of 'otherness.' Furthermore, as Romila Thapar points out, "much space is given in the *Hammīra-Mahākāvya* to Hammīra's conquests of neighbouring kingdoms and his plundering of many cities. As in the case of the Turko-Persian chronicles, battle, plunder and loot were the hallmarks of a heroic king in the literature of the courts" (Thapar 2005, 120). Hammīra's early conquest are therefore directed to other Rajput kingdoms, it is only toward the latter sections of the poem that his conflicts concern ʿAlāʾ al-Dīn Khaljī and his generals. Here again the matter is not a simple one of Hindu king versus Muslim sultan. As the sultan lays siege of Hammīra's fortress, Ranthambore, it is his own Rajput generals who betray him in the hope of being rewarded by being given control of his kingdom by ʿAlāʾ al-Dīn. In striking contrast to the treachery of the Rajput commanders is the unflinching loyalty of the Mongol/Mudgal/Mughal or so-called 'neo-Muslim' rebel generals of ʿAlāʾ al-Dīn Khaljī to whom Hammīra has granted refuge after they revolted against the former on account of a misunderstanding over the amount of tax they were supposed to hand over to the royal treasury. According to Baranī, these insurgent generals were "neo-Muslims who had taken service with the Khaljīs and settled in various part of Delhi and some had also been granted villages. They were central Asians more recently converted to Islam" (Thapar 2005, 121). The narrative that emerges here is more complex and multifaceted than an uncomplicated story of clear-cut allegiances between groups organized around their religious or quasi-national identities. Instead power, wealth, control and loyalty seem to be the common denominators around which are ordered the actions of Hammīra, ʿAlāʾ al-Dīn and their respective commanders involving different Rajput clans, Śakas, Turks as well as Mongols.[28]

Hammīra was a descendant of another great Chauhan king, Pṛthvīrāj III, who ruled from about 1160 CE. Pṛthvīrāj III is the subject of a number of narratives himself, particularly the Sanskrit *Pṛthvīrāja-vijaya* and the *Pṛthvīrāja-rāso*, which is also a Sanskrit composition describing Pṛthvīrāj's reign. Pṛthvīrāj fought a number of battles against Muhammed Ghori but was finally captured and killed by him in 1192 CE. His death and defeat are not mentioned in the *Pṛthvīrāja-vijaya*. Our knowledge of Hammīra is derived from a number of sources, one being the *Hammīra-Mahākāvya* itself, but also through inscriptions (from Balwan and Gadha) and other narrative and textual sources such as the *Khazāʾin al-futūḥ* of Amir Khusraw, the *Taʾrīkh-i Fīrūz Shāhī* of Ẓiyāʾ al-Dīn Baranī, the *Surjanacar-*

28 Two questions seem to emerge: one, if the complexity of relationships between Rajputs themselves, and Rajputs and Turks, was not unique why does this particular configuration acquire so much attention as to be retold in different languages through centuries? And two, why, if the relationships are indeed so complex and multihued, lacking in clarity, is this image rearranged into monochrome shades in recent 20th-century historiography?

ita, the *Prākṛta-piṅgala* and *Sāraṅgadhara-paddhati*, as well as later Hindavī and Rajasthani works such as the *Hammīra Rāso* of Jodharāja, *Hammīrahaṭṭa* of Candraśekhara and *Hammīrāyan* of Bhāṇḍauvyās.[29]

After ascending the throne in 1282, Hammīra set out on a *digvijaya* (conquest of the cardinal directions) which is also described in the *Hammīra-Mahākāvya*. The *digvijaya* led him through towns and principalities in south-eastern Rajasthan and Malwa (Madhya Pradesh) including Mandalgarh, Ujjaini, Dhar, Chittor, Abu, Vardhanapura, Pushkar and so on. After completing the *digvijaya* he performed a *koṭi yajña* under the direction of his Purohit, Viṣvarūpa. In the meantime, in 1290 ʿAlāʾ al-Dīn Khaljī ascended the throne of the Delhi sultanate. In 1298, according to the *Taʾrīkh-i Fīrūz Shāhī*, ʿAlāʾ al-Dīn conceived the idea of founding a new religion like the prophet Mohammed and conquering the whole world like a second Alexander. He gave up his first idea quite quickly, considering it to be arrogant. However, he translated the second idea into first conquering Ranthambore, Chanderi, Dhar and Ujjaini. Ranthambore received his attention partly because of its pre-eminent stature as one of the strongest and wealthiest Rajput fortresses, and partly because of an incident involving a mutiny amongst some of his soldiers and their being granted refuge by Hammīra.[30] While the details of the mutiny do not seem to be mentioned in the *Hammīra-Mahākāvya* the the *Taʾrīkh-i Fīrūz Shāhī* describes the uprising and its grotesquely brutal suppression by the sultan with some thoroughness:

> After th'roughly ravaging and plundering Gujrāt Ulugh Khān and Nuśrat Khān set out on their return loaded with immense spoils, and on the way back, in order to collect their fifth share of the body; and in searching after and scrutinizing the amount of the spoils, they inflicted various penalties and punishments, and carried their investigation to the extreme; for they placed no credence whatever on what the soldiery put down in writing, but persisted in calling for more. By dint of persecution (*banamak āb*) after they endeavoured to exact the gold, silver, jewels, and all other valuables and used to put their troops to all kinds of torture, till at last the soldiery were unable to bear such tyranny and ill-usage any longer.
>
> The number of newly converted Amīrs and horsemen in the army was very considerable; so having entered into a combination, some two or three thousand horsemen assembled together, and mutinied. They first slew Malik A'azzuddin, the brother of Nuśrat Khān, who was Amīr Hājib to Ulugh Khān; and with a great uproar forced their way into Ulugh Khān's pavilion; but the Khān dreading their fury, escaped out of his tent, and conveyed himself by stratagem to Nuśrat Khān's quarters. The nephew (sister's son) of Sulṭān 'Alauddin, however, happened to be sleeping below Ulugh Khān's quarters; and the mutineers

29 See Bednar's (2007) impressive study in this regard of Persian and Sanskrit sources.
30 Hammīra and ʿAlāʾ al-Dīn are not unlike each other in that they both aspire to a kind of universal conquest of different regions of the subcontinent.

imagining that he might possibly be the Khān, put him to death under this misapprehension. The mutiny extended at length throughout the army, and the camp was very nearly becoming the scene of indiscriminate not and pillage; but as the good fortune of 'Alauddin was in the ascendant, such a tumult as this even was speedily quelled. The cavalry and infantry of the army formed up in front of Nuśrat Khān's pavilion, and the recently converted Amīrs and horsemen dispersed, such of them as had been the chief actors and confederates in the mutiny fleeing away and gaining the disaffected and rebellious Rāis. After this, the search after the booty in the army was abandoned, and Ulugh Khān and Nuśrat Khān reached Delhi with all the wealth, elephants, slaves, and other spoils they had got possession of from the pillage of Gujrāt.

As soon as the news of the mutiny among the new converts reached Delhi, Sulṭān 'Alauddin, under the influence of the haughty pride which had now inflated his brain, directed that the wives and children of all the mutineers, both high and low, should be seized and imprisoned. This system of seizing upon the wives and children for the fault of the men dates its commencement from this period; for previous to this at Delhi, they never laid hands on women and children on account of the crimes of their male relatives, nor used they to seize and incarcerate the families of any delinquents.

Besides this tyrannical system of seizing women and children, a still more glaring piece of injustice was committed in those days by Nuśrat Khān, who was the originator of numerous acts of oppression at Delhi; for it was publicly witnessed that in revenge for his brother's death, he brought infamy and dishonour on the wives of those who had pierced his brother with arrows, by delivering them over to sweepers to be violated like helpless victims, while the infant children were ordered to be cut in pieces in presence of their mothers (Baranī 1967, 24–25).[31]

Furthermore, the translators Fuller and Khallaque in a footnote to the above description of the mutiny and subsequent merciless acts of vengeance, single out an important detail from a later source:

---

31 The uprising is supposedly not mentioned in great detail in *Khazā'in al-futūḥ*. However, the sultan's siege and victory over Ranthambore is described in the following passages: "When the celestial canopy of the Shadow of God cast its shade over the hill of Rantambhor and the conqueror of the world emitted his heat like the sun over the unlucky inhabitants of that place, the days of their life began to decline. The towering fort, which talked with the stars through its lofty pinnacles, was surrounded by the troops ... When the celestial sun had ascended the steps of honour and sat in the sign of Aries to hold the festival of the New Year's Day (*nauruz*), *tankas* of gold were showered on the earth like falling leaves, and it became finer than a garden. After the *nauruz*, the Sun of Justice (the Sultan) shone full on the Rantambhor hill and every day its heat and light increased, till finally the lofty fort, which drew its water supply from the azure sky, became a desert from lack of vegetation and water. The world seemed smaller to the Rai (of Rantambhor) than the prison within a rose-bud. So in his desperation one night he lighted a high fire, which rose like a mountain-tulip on the hill, and threw into it the rosy-coloured young maidens who had grown up in his arms" (Habib 1931, 38–41).

> Firishtah[32] calls the leader of the rebels *Muhammad Shāh.*[33] He says, the mutiny took place at *Jālor* (Jodhpur), but the editions of Badāonī have Alwar, which lies nearer to Rantanbhūr and Jhāyin to the chief of which place, Hamīr Deo (Ed. Bibl. Indica, Hambar Deo), the mutineers ultimately retreated (Baranī 1967, 25 fn. 14).

Here, Muhammed Shāh (Mahimā Sāhi) is clearly named as is the place of his refuge, namely Ranthambore, and its chieftain, Hammīra. This act of protection ultimately leads to ʿAlāʾ al-Dīn Khaljī laying siege of the fortress and to the deaths of Mahimā Sāhi and his refuge-giving Rajput king, which is described in the *Hammīra-Mahākāvya* in an extraordinary manner befitting great warriors:

> Seeing that Mahimā Sāhi had collapsed after being struck by arrows, Hammīra himself entered the battlefield.
>
> Hammīra alone slaughtered hundreds of thousands of soldiers. With his sword he sliced off enemy-heads making the sky seem like a [vast] lake of lotuses.
>
> Surrounded by Hammīra's blazing arrows, the Śaka fighters felt as though they had entered the sun's orb.
>
> Hammīra cut through the bowstrings and the archers who were capable of competing with Arjuna.
>
> The battleground that was littered with the heads of enemies severed by the king appeared as though death itself had harvested a field of sesame seeds.
>
> This hero slaughtered enemies in such a way that the abode of Yamarāj was overflowing [with the dead].
>
> The one who performs fearsomely in war, the jewel in the crown of the heroes' clan, wounded in every limb by the onslaught of enemy arrows, honoured by the entire earth, King Hammīra, thinking that the Yavanas would capture him, slit his own throat and carried on toward heaven becoming a guest of the gods![34]

In sheer contrast, however, the *Taʾrīkh-i Fīrūz Shāhī* seems to reluctantly devote a few lines to the victory of the sultan, and the unspectacular, forced death of the Rajput chieftain and the 'new converts.' This brings to surface the starkly divergent fashion in which Hammīra is imagined in different textual sources each claiming to be 'historical' but at the same time representing disparate political and cultural ideologies:

---

32 Firishtah (Ferishtah) or Muhammad Qasim Hindu Shah (1560 – 1620) was a historian of Persian origin who was in service of the Deccan sultanate in Bijapur.

33 Emphasis added.

34 *Hammīra-Mahākāvya*, *Sarga* 13.209, 211, 212, 218, 220, 223, 226. See Appendix 1.

> Some time after Hājī Maulā's[35] revolt, Sulṭān 'Alauddin succeeded with immense toil and difficulty in capturing the fort of Rantambhūr, whereupon he put Rāi Hamīr Deo, and the new converts, who had fled from the Gujrāt insurrection and taken shelter with him, to death. Rantambhūr, together with the surrounding country, was given to Ulugh Khān, and whatever was in the fort became his.
>
> The Sulṭān then returned from Rantambhūr to Delhi, and being greatly incensed against the inhabitants of that city, sentenced many of the chief men to be exiled from it; and he himself would not enter the town; but took up his quarters in the suburbs (Baranī 1967, 69–70).[36]

1.4 The Edition and Commentary

Nayachandra Sūri's poem becomes known to us in the modern era through the *editio princeps* prepared by Nilkanth Janaradan Kirtane in Bombay in 1879. In his brief but illuminative introduction Kirtane begins by gathering evidence of texts that are either similar or the same as the *Hammīra-Mahākāvya* before commencing with an analysis and summary of the *Hammīra-Mahākāvya's* contents. The first set of texts Kirtane refers to is a work called the *Hammīramardana* ("*The destruction of Hammīra*") which is mentioned by the famous Indologist and associate of Friedrich Max Mueller, Georg Bühler in the initial pages of his edition of the great Sanskrit poet Bilhana's eulogy of King Vikramaditya, the *Vikramāṇka-kāvya* or *Vikramāṇka-carita*. The edition by Bühler was published in 1875. In his introduction Bühler states that a manuscript of this work existed about ninety years prior to the publication of the edition in the Jaina Bhandar (Jaina Library) of Jaisalmer in Rajasthan. Kirtane assumes that even though the two works have different titles, they contain the same narrative "since it [i.e. the *Hammīra-Mahākāvya*] ends with the death of Hammīra and a lamentation over the events" (Kirtane 1879, i). Kirtane also mentions two other works that Col. James Tod ([1832] 1920) writes about in his *Annals and Antiquities of Rajasthan*. These include a work with the same name, i.e. the *Hammīra-Mahākāvya* and a work called the *Hammīra Rāsa*. Though Tod asserts that both these works were composed by Sāraṅgadhara,[37] Kirtane cites evidence that this is not the case and that the text that Tod refers to with the same name is in all likelihood another work:

35 Hājī Maulā is one the several 'neo-Muslim' commanders to have rebelled in the sultan's army.
36 The sultan's annoyance with the inhabitants of Delhi again refers to a series of revolts led by Amīrs and Maliks who had influential administrative and military positions.
37 According to Tod, Sāraṅgadhara was Hammīra's bard.

"there must be some other poem in Sanskrit bearing the name of Hammīra Mahakavya; but it may be doubted whether it has any reference to the history of the hero of our poem" (Kirtane 1879, i). While Tod mentions Hammīra, his reference, according to Kirtane is not to a particular chieftain of that name, "but is a jumble of anecdotes relating to several distinct personages bearing the same name" (Kirtane 1879, ii). This fact is interesting and important in itself since the name Hammīra functioned as a generic title for a brave, indomitable warrior belonging to Ghaznavid and Rajput dynasties alike, rather than a personal pronoun during the 10th–12th centuries. The copy of the manuscript of the *Hammīra-Mahākāvya* that Kirtane used for the *editio princeps* was obtained by him from Govinda Sastri Nirantar of the town of Nasik in Maharashtra. Kirtane translates the colophon of the manuscript as follows: "The present copy was made for the purpose of reading by Nayahaṃsa, a pupil of Jayasiṃha Sūri, at Firuzpur, in the month of Śrāvaṇa of the Saṃvat year 1542" (Kirtane 1879, ii).[38] Kirtane continues his introduction to the edition by praising Nayachandra Sūri's work while underlining its poetical and historical significance:

> as a poetical composition [that] has considerable merits, and deserves publication as a specimen of the historical poems so rarely met with in the range of Sanskrit literature. Though the author did not live, like Bāṇa and Bilhana, in the reign of the hero whose history he celebrates, yet his work is not of less historical importance than theirs [...] The present attempt to place the English reader in possession of the historical information contained in the Hammīra Mahakavya will, I presume, be acceptable to those who are interested in the advancement of our knowledge of Indian history (Kirtane 1879, ii).

In the final chapter of the poem, which proceeds after Chapter 14 in which Hammīra's death in battle is described, the author recounts his own lineage and also the motivation and reasons for his composing the work. Kirtane's translation of sections of the final chapter are, in part, reproduced here:

> In the circles of the Sūris, whose actions are the homes of wonders, in time, Jayasiṃha Sūri was born, who was the crowning ornament of the wise; who easily vanquished in disputation Sāraṅga, who was the leading poet among those who were able to write poetical compositions in six languages, and who was honest among the most honest; who wrote three works, – (1) *Nyāya Sāraṭike*, (2) A New Grammar, (3) A Poem on *Kumāra Nṛpati*, – and who

38 saṃvat 1542 varṣe śrāvaṇe māsi śrīkṛṣṇārṣigacche śrījayasiṃhasūriśiṣyeṇa nayahaṃsenātmapaṭhanārthaṃ śrīperojapure hammiramahākāvyaṃ lilikhe | kalyāṇamastu | bhadraṃ bhūyāt saṃghasya | granthāgraḥ 1564 | The year Samvat 1542 equals 1496 CE. Nayahaṃsa thus supposedly copied the poem 95 years after it was composed, given that the commonly agreed upon date of its composition by Nayachandra Sūri is 1401. 'Sri Perojpur' or Ferozpur is a town in Punjab on the banks of the River Sutlej. It was founded by Firoz Shah Tughlaq (r. 1351–88) who was one of the principal rulers of the Tughlaq dynasty and of the Delhi sultanate.

> hence became known as the chief of those who knew the three science of logic, grammar, and poesy.[39]
>
> To the lotus-like Gadi of Jayasiṃha, Nayachandra is like the life-giving sun; who is the essence of the knowledge of the sciences, who is the exciting moon to the sea of the races of the poets. This poet, his spirits raised to the height of the subject by a revelation imparted to him in a dream by the king Hammīra himself, has composed this poem, which gratifying to the assembly of the kings, and in which the heroic (*rasa*) is developed.[40]
>
> The author in lineal descent is the grandson of Jayasiṃha Sūri, the great poet, but in that of poesy his son.[41]
>
> Let not good readers take into much account the faults of expression that I may have fallen into. How can I, who am of mean capacity, escape stepping into that path which even poets like Kalidāsa were not able to avoid? But a poem that is replete with good matter loses none of its value for a few common-places of expression[42] (Kirtane 1879, iii).

These lines represent a self-reflexive turn in the composition in which the author not only lays down his biological and creative lineage as two different genealogies,[43] but also the motivation for the poem. It is here that he reveals that it is in a dream in which he is instructed by Hammīra. The poet's "spirits" were "raised to the height of the subject by a revelation" granted to him by the Chauhan chieftain.[44] The poem is treated as a revelation that shows itself in a dream. Poem, dream and revelation thus come together as intertwined realms of the imagination that open the space for truth and history. The poet does not, as a modern historian or even writer of historical fiction might be expected to do, mention his search for archival or material sources such as archaeological remains. He does not mention the time spent painstakingly sifting through old manuscripts or hunting for inscriptions or recording oral histories. Such familiar sources for establishing a historical narrative are nowhere to be found in notes or appen-

---

39 tasmin vismayavāsaveśmacaritaśrīsūricakre kramāt jajñe śrījayasiṃhasūrisuguruḥ prajñālacūḍāmaṇiḥ | ṣaḍbhāṣākavicakraśakramakhilaprāmāṇikāgresaraṃ sāraṅgaṃ sahasā viraṅgamatanod yo vādavidyāvidhau ||23|| śrīnyāsasāraṭīkāṃ navyaṃ vyākaraṇamatha ca yaḥ kāvyam | kṛtvā kumāranṛpateḥ khyātastraividyavedicakṛīti || 14.24||

40 The Sanskrit text and a slightly different translation of this verse is offered at the beginning of Chapter 6.

41 pautro'pyayaṃ kavigurorjayasiṃhasūreḥ kāvyeṣu putratitamāṃ nayacandrasūriḥ | navyārthasārthaghatanāpadapaṅktiyuktivinyāsarītirasabhāvavidhānayatnaiḥ || 14.27 ||

42 prāyo'paśabdādikṛto'pi doṣo na cātra cintyo mama mandabuddheḥ | na kālidāsādibhirapyapāste yo'dhvā kathaṃ vā tamahaṃ tyajāmi || 14.38 ||

43 While the poet belongs to the lineage of the Sūris, he owes his creative abilities and aspirations to his grandfather, thereby skipping the generation of his father.

44 See Chapter 6 for an analysis and meaning of the poet's dream.

dices. The source for the series of events that the work describes is the poet's dream that is concretized and instrumentalized by the slain hero of the poem. The dream does not have the character of randomly juxtaposed events, people, places and moods of ordinary, everyday dreams. It is ordered, sequenced to the point of becoming a convincing narrative. A witness of past events composed and presented in poetic Sanskrit.

Chapter 2
Singular Moments

2.1 Modern Formations

The Hegelian view that historical consciousness, the nation state, and modernity arise together is mirrored in V. S. Naipaul's statement about contemporary India: "To awaken to history is to cease to live instinctively. It was to begin to see oneself and one's group the way the outside world saw one; and it was to know a kind of rage. India was now full of this rage. There has been a general awakening." [45] But what kind of rage is this? What kind of awakening? And, particularly, what kind of history?

Recent studies on religion in India tend to focus justifiably on the pressing problems of collective religious identities and their ensuing conflicts by debating issues of religious fundamentalism, religious nationalism, and the phenomenon of 'communalism' and its resultant violence. It is certainly important for scholars to investigate disturbing and divisive aspects of religion in the context of modernization, secularization and the nation state. However, there is the danger of losing sight of alternative ways of imagining religious identities that in fact facilitate social cohesion and the mutual participation of religious communities. Thus, contrary to the popular political imagination current in certain segments of society in India today, and in the Indian media, there has been and continues to be an intermingling of religious spaces and relationships that challenge the popular antagonistic view. This book asks various questions within an interdisciplinary framework: What allows shared religious spaces and relationships to emerge, thrive, and inform various personal and social identities? What notions of 'selfhood' emerge from the locative and social identifications that go beyond the everyday, commonplace representations that are informed by religious, ethnic and other affiliations, including nationality and ethnicity? How are shared spaces created, negotiated and maintained? What are the mechanisms through which shared spaces are negotiated in ritual and architecture, in religious, historical and poetical texts, and at sacred sites? How are the shared relationships – including friendships – enabled by various aesthetic, ritual and textual media related to these shared spaces?

Some recent academic studies have begun to probe the fluid boundaries of religions, but this book focuses on the relationship between shared social and

45 V. S. Naipaul, cited in Chakrabarty (1995, 3374).

https://doi.org/10.1515/9783110662795-005

literary spaces, and shared relationships in a historical and contemporary perspective while suggesting that there are ideological, historiographical and sociological forces that support both the expansion and contraction of these spaces. In other words, such shared spaces are in constant competition with powerful narratives that push toward rigidity and fixity. They may be expressed through the historiographies of various interrelated oral 'texts,' including epics, ballads, and written poetical and historical narratives. Such narratives and ritual spaces challenge nationalist and imperialist accounts that attempt to constrain the existence of fluid movements. As Dipesh Chakrabarty (1995, 3375) points out, the imperatives of modernity and the legacy of imperialism in India have sought to create "a quasi-modern public sphere in India" by instituting fixed and standardized "collective identities (such as caste and religion)."

The main focus of this book, as mentioned earlier, is on the story of 13th-century legendary Rajput chieftain Hammīra, and the shifting religious and political meanings that narratives concerning Hammīra achieve in different textual, historical and historiographical contexts, medieval as well as modern. While the primary text that the book relies on is the 1500-verse Sanskrit poetical work *Hammīra-Mahākāvya* that was composed by the Jain poet Nayachandra Sūri under the patronage of Tomara rulers in western India, other later works in Rajasthani and Hindi are also taken into account along with more recent oral accounts concerning Hammīra and the fortress of Ranthambore that are gleaned from interviews conducted at the site during fieldwork.

According to some sources, Nayachandra Sūri composed his poem in 1383 CE or 1401 CE, i.e. exactly 100 years[46] after the hero of the poem's – Hammīra's – death. Hammīra was the ruler of the fortress of Ranthambore (Sanskrit: *Raṇasthaṃbapura: "City of the Battle Post"*) in southern Rajasthan. He ascended the throne in 1282 CE and died in 1301 CE after a momentous battle against ʿAlāʾ al-Dīn Khaljī, the sultan of Delhi who lays siege to the fortress after Hammīra grants refuge to two 'neo-Muslim' rebel generals of the former.[47] The purpose

46 The figure of one hundred years possibly also has a particular poetical and commemorative significance. The gospels of Christ, for example, were supposedly also written within the space of one hundred years after his death. I thank Jörg Rüpke for pointing out this possible implication.

47 Ranthambore continues to be the focus of political conquest even after the sultan's annexation. Thus, for example, the Mughal Emperor Akbar lays siege of the impregnable fortress on February 8, 1568. During the siege he make use of specially designed narrow-barrelled cannons that were between 6–8 metres long to damage the fortress from the position of a steep angle on the hillside below the ramparts. This strategy of using extremely long-barrelled cannons to damage and penetrate thick fortifications was also put into use by Sultan Mehmed II during his siege of the medieval city of Constantinople in 1453.

of the *Hammīra-Mahākāvya*, as mentioned earlier, seems to be twofold: on the one hand it is about poetry – about rising to the challenge of writing great Sanskrit poetry in the second millennium with all its poetical embellishments and linguistic markers. On the other hand, the poem is commemorative. It commemorates and celebrates the deeds and death of Hammīra, a flawed hero, who is unbending on his word. The poem is therefore both *kāvya* or poetry and what we would call 'history,' i.e. it simultaneously contains the signifiers of a literary and a historical work.

A reading of the text(s) indicates that it creates narrative spaces that allow a series of shared religious, social and political spaces to arise. Is there a set of values that underlie the creation of this shared literary space? Why does a Jain poet write about a Hindu chieftain and his clash with a Muslim sultan, and the accompanying description of gore, treason, violence, bloodshed, weaponry, war and so on? How indeed are religious labels such as 'Hindu' and 'Muslim' or 'Jain' imagined in this context? Evidently, they do not carry the same significance as they would in the contemporary discourse of 'essentialized,' singular, bounded religious identities. Since in the original text they do not carry these meanings, how does Hammīra wind up becoming central to the creation of 20th-century scholarship propelled by Hindu nationalist discourse on the protection and sustenance of Hindu *dharma?* How and why does this shift occur in which shared religious and social spaces shrink?

It would seem that modern collectives of religion and caste also result in a politically charged re-imagining of the past that is both selective and palpably prejudiced in conceiving of discreet religious categories of Muslim and Hindu, rather than, for example, interrelated, yet rival, Turk, Mongol, 'neo-Muslim,' and Rajput assemblages forged through the expediencies of honour, friendship and power but not necessarily religion or ethnicity. Thus, far from the politically motivated segregation of religious communities the religious sharing in identifications and relationships (which are not to be reduced to notions of syncretism), the historical and literary spaces that will be examined here reflect and invite interreligious participation based upon a range of values including mutual respect, loyalty, honour and friendship. However, that these assemblages should be viewed as emerging solely based on the expediencies of power and its resulting theatre of dominance, submission and counter-allegiances, would seem to arise out of the categorical imperative of modernity and imperialism in India. Both Kirtane and Muni Jinavijaya[48] are caught in the trajectory of warped, yet on-

48 Muni Jinavijaya (1968) is the editor of the volume containing the original edition of the *Ham-*

going encounters with modernity and its mission in both a pre- and post-independence context of the Indian nation state.

2.2 Narrative Templates

In attempting to answer some of the questions posed above, this book examines how the singularity of Hammīra's particular circumstances are embedded into a historical narrative template that inserts meaning into the text and the events it describes. The template is informed by an emerging regional culture that celebrates valour, heroism and self-sacrifice – a particular kind of Rajput martial ethos. Not only are a number of heroic narratives composed during this time in Rajasthani and Sanskrit, contemporary oral epics in Rajasthani such as those of Pābūjī (Smith 1991) and Devnārāyaṇ (Malik 2005) situate themselves in that period, i. e. 10th–11th centuries.[49] One of the main themes of these oral narratives is the self-sacrificial deeds of heroes. Following Jan Assman, this is what Rao, Shulman, and Subrahmanyam call *mnemo-history*, i. e. "how a theme, or an event, or [...] an individual is remembered and continually refashioned or systematically re-narrated as an entire tradition of memory is slowly formed. Mnemo-history allows us to observe the multiple crystallizations of past processes [...] in widely diverse media of remembering: Sanskrit epic, *purana*, living folk-epic" (Narayana Rao *et al.* 2001, 13). Thus, one could claim that both history and folklore are, first and foremost, exercises in *imagination*. Both imagine the past in a way that is relevant for the present otherwise they would cease to be read or told. The boundaries between these two modes of imagining the past (one written, the other usually spoken or sung), however, are at best vague, perhaps even non-existent. At most they are a matter of nomenclature decided by people who engage in such narratives through writing and reading or listening and telling. Even so, the narratives that are told by history and by folklore are *real* in that they convey meaning. Nevertheless, the contours of meaning shift as new readers and listeners emerge bringing new political and social contexts to bear on the otherwise skeletal framework of a narrative. The poetical history of Hammīra written by the Jain poet Nayachandra Sūri begins, as do many seminal insights, in a *dream*. The dream is then transformed both through the metrics of Sanskrit poetry but also, in this case, the poignant and dramatic *facts* of historical events:

---

mīra-Mahākāvya by Kirtane. The volume includes lengthy introductory sections written in Hindi by the Muni and the well-known historian Dasharath Sharma.

49 See also the Telegu oral epic of Palnādu (Roghair 1982).

Hammīra's protection of the rebel general Muhammed Shāh (aka Mahimā Sāhi) and their subsequent heroic deaths (and also of their families) in an uneven battle against the Sultan of Delhi, ʿAlāʾ al-Dīn Khaljī. While these are the facts, the events themselves are saturated by an ethic of valour, loyalty, friendship, honouring one's word and more. Death itself is the culmination of maintaining such an ethic unstintingly until its unbending conclusion. But this kind of death (the heroic one) is not confined to the poetical text of the *Hammīra-Mahākāvya*. It is found everywhere in all the narratives which commemorate and remember violent, premature deaths of heroes (men and women). Thus, the oral epics of Pābūjī and Devnārāyaṇ from Rajasthan both bespeak of and commend conscious sacrifice and death without which there would be no 'folk-heroes' or for that matter 'folk-deities.' The point is that the historical series of events involving Hammīra and ʿAlāʾ al-Dīn Khaljī seem to be automatically embedded in a pool of significance and meaning that simultaneously also frames so-called folk and oral narratives from the region creating siblings out of history and folk narrative. Similarly, a new template of meaning derived from nationalistic and religiously motivated political aspirations is overlain on the same series of facts to give them novel, albeit controversial, significance in terms of resisting centuries of perceived and actual colonial rule in India (conceived as a Hindu nation) first by Muslim dynasties and then later by the British.

To respond to the perception that the poem primarily enunciates a cleavage between Hindu and Muslim identities, it is important to pay attention to the adoption of a particular historiography that accompanies the arrangement of the social and religious world into sets of discreet categories that are the cherished substratum of modernity, imperialism and nationalism. It seems evident that the historical analyses of the *Hammīra-Mahākāvya* by Kirtane and Muni Jinavijaya from the 1870s and 1960s are selective in their emphasis of the heroic (read: striving for independence by resisting Muslim rule) nature of Hammīra's actions. Muni Jinavijaya thus prefaces his analyses of *Hammīra-Mahākāvya* with an account of India's independence from British rule on 15 August 1947. The introductory passages are highly celebratory, describing the rise of a free and independent India (*bhārat*) as a nation (*rāṣṭra*) that, in a sense, had always existed but had been suppressed by succeeding centuries of colonization. Jinavijaya (1968, 29) continues with a report of Islam's origins in Arabia under the inspiration of Mohammed who sought to redress the social and economic inequalities of this region. Later he recounts the expansion of Arabian political power towards the Indus River and beyond into northern India, beginning with the raids and plundering of early Central Asian invaders culminating in the establishment of the Delhi sultanate. The responsibility of protecting India and preserving its cultural and religious heritage rested, he then emphasizes, with the Rajputs who were filled with a sense of duty toward the defence of territory and tradition. These opening pages frame his subsequent analysis of the role of Hammīra within the context of resistance against Muslim dominance. It is precisely because of this particular quality of the poem – the heroic quality of defence and protection of the country or nation – that the *Hammīra-Mahākāvya* is not simply a "great poem:" it is a "*great national poem*" (*rāṣṭrīya mahākāvya*):

> The *Hammīra-Mahākāvya* is a national poem of the highest order. To my knowledge there is no comparable Sanskrit "great poem" of this superior quality that expresses such noble sentiments. This is not an ordinary narrative in the style of the puranas that simply describes the *rasa* of love. This is a historical narrative of the utmost degree of a heroic nation which is filled with the inspiration that raises the sentiment of Bharat [...] The *Hammīra-Mahākāvya* praises the qualities of our nation's historical warriors and contains their glorious, patriotic story, therefore, it is a great national poem (Jinavijaya 1968, 29, *trans.* from Hindi by the author).

2.3 Experiencing the Past

This book is about remembering Hammīra. But how can I remember someone or something that I have no experience of? And, this it seems lies at the crux of historical knowledge: how can I know a past or the past without having experienced it?[50] Experience is about here and now but it also about accumulation and about retention and protention. History, as a concern about a past which may never have been experienced by the historian, must concern itself with intentionality, that is, it concerns itself with the mind that intends toward an object even though that object may not exist in the here and now. The object of history, therefore, must therefore take on the contours of an object in the mind or in the imagination, and the relationship of the mind to the object that it intends towards or creates within itself. In order for the past to exist it must be carried forward into the present-now otherwise it has no existence that we can know of.

50 See Gadamer (1960). Gadamer lays emphasis on understanding via conversation which is always mediated by language. Understanding is therefore always occurring or happening in language. But what if there is a kind of understanding or knowing that begins prior to or after language? Where does silence as the possible source of language fit into this scheme? Where is the experience of no-thought and therefore no-language (and therefore no world and no self) located? What would a philosophy that begins and ends prior to language and thought look like? A philosophy of emptiness or meaninglessness because meaning and understanding can only be given by language. Imagination is that from which world begins to appear, arise. Imagination is thus prior to world. But what is Imagination grounded in? No-thingness?

Therefore, there must be an element of an event or object or person that carries forward into the present-now. The so-called 'past' must have an existence in the present-now for it to qualify as 'past.'[51]

2.3.1 The Field of Experience

What does all of this have to do with history as a particular understanding of, or rather 'access' to, the temporal dimension we call 'past'?[52] Whatever we call the past or for that matter whatever we call 'history' as an 'authoritatively'[53] constructed and selected idea of the past (that is, of what happened in the past) must happen or rather occur in the field of our experience, since nothing exists outside of this field. We are both anchored in time (or rather in temporalities) that in turn exist within the field of our experience which (in an arguably circular manner) is given by the fact that we exist temporally (that is, as temporal beings). What does it mean to say the past (or for that matter any temporal dimension) occurs within the field of our experience? What is the field of experience? The field of experience is all that lies in front of us that we experience – tables, chairs, houses, cars, people we know and don't know, chalk boards, water bodies, sky, emotions, ideas and more. The field of experience is not limited by any particular object; rather, all objects and potentialities exist within this field. In fact, the field itself is not an object; rather, it is that inside of which objects occur to the experiencer of those objects. The field may expand or contract and it may be filled by more objects and persons, ideas, thoughts, actions, etc., or by less objects and persons, ideas, thoughts, actions, etc. This expansion or contraction of the field cannot be caused through any particular kind of action or practice; it occurs when there is a shift of the point of view. A shift in the point of view entails a shift in the very being-ness of a person since a person is – as an entity that is definable as a point of view of the field of experience – given by his or her point of view. It is the point of view that a person or human being *is* that determines the possibility of thought, action and indeed experience of self that that person has and is. Thus while a human being is a being that is temporally anchored, the temporal anchoring is given by the point of view that a person *is* of

---

51 See Heidegger (1967, 372–436).

52 "Your brain is locked in silence and darkness inside the vault of your skull and its job is to figure out what's happening outside but it has to do a lot of editing tricks." "Time is a psychological construct" (Eagleman 2019). (See Carr 2014 on history and experience.)

53 By authoritative I mean through the 'authority' of a community or individual whether religious or secular.

the field of experience that potentially contains all objects, knowledge, action and thought. Hypothetically (and indeed even in actuality) the field of experience contains not only all objects, actions and thought – all knowledge – but also all possible temporalities that exist individually and collectively. The past as one possible temporality invariably entails a partitioning off of time and of not-time as it stands in the field of experience. This partitioning off is uneven depending on the point of view that an individual or community *are*. There are therefore as many pasts as there are potential points of view of the field of experience. These points of view slice up and partition off the possibility of time, of an existence given by both time and not-time, or thought and not-thought or of action and not-action and so on.[54] This is not to repeat the important, though perhaps now trite, statement that there exist multiple pasts depending on one's interpretation of the past, but that the past itself arises as a function of the point of view that a person *is* of the field of experience. *Everything*, in the perspective outlined, occurs or appears within the field of experience and a human being *is* that field of experience albeit limited so to speak by the point of view.[55] Another way of saying this that the field of experience and a human being are not distinct from one another. In other words, the field of experience is the awareness of time, space and objects in time and space, but it is not the passing of time and disintegration of objects in space. What occurs with the field of experience is given by the point of view which in turn gives what a human being *is*. Thus the 'past' or 'history' is not separate from the field of experience that a human being *is*. The past is therefore an ontological category inasmuch as all objects, entities, etc., which appear within the field of experience are ontological categories by virtue of being themselves and being given by the being-ness of a human being. This is to say that there is no occurring of time (whether past, present or future) that is outside or distinct from the being of a human being that itself is given by the point of view of the field of experience. The general field of experience as possibility and the particular experience of the field of ex-

---

54 See Heidegger's (2001) idea of the bridge which he sees as the location for the fourfold gathering together of earth and sky, divinities and human. See also the idea of the electromagnetic field and electron field in quantum physics. It is 'excitations' in the field that give rise to what we call photons and electrons. The electromagnetic field itself is vast.

55 This 'limitation' of the experiencing of the field of experience is what gives rise to the entity we call a 'person' or an 'individual' (which we are familiar with in our everyday lives), a limitation which as a 'persona' clouds or conceals the unlimited nature of a human being as a being that is concomitant with the field of experience. But where does the point of view arise from? I do not see an answer to this question. The point of view is part of the 'thrown-ness' so to speak of the condition in which we find ourselves. It is there just like body, thoughts, space and time arise the instant the subject is aware of itself.

perience given by the point of view together with a human being that *is* a particular point of view and the possibility of temporality is, in fact, one seamless whole. Therefore, there is no objective 'access' or, for that matter, certainty about the past. This does not mean that the past is 'subjective'[56] since both the possibility of the subject and of time arise so to speak within the field of experience. Time and the so-called subject arise simultaneously as ontological entities (categories) that are given so deeply by each other that separation is only an illusionary surface twist. However, saying that time and the subject arise simultaneously also suggests that both subside or disappear simultaneously. They return so to speak into the fundamental substratum of possibility which is the field of experience. It is with the arising of thought and language that the possibility of time and subject are brought into existence. In other words, thought and language complete the fourfold nexus of time and subject through which a manifestation of the world becomes possible. Without thought and language there is no time and subject but without these there is also no world. There is therefore a simultaneous arising and subsiding of the subject and the world. I am not saying that the world arises for the subject in terms of her/his knowing of the world, rather that the world arises for itself since the world, its arising and the subject are all linked in such a way that the one brings forth the other into the horizon of manifestation and the awareness[57] of that manifestation.

2.4 Cascading Narratives

This book has been ignited by the story of Hammīra and the many ways that this story has been told and retold over hundreds of years. Yet, if I look deeply into the materials I have read, there is, in fact, no single 'authoritative' story about

---

56 By subjective I do not mean here the common understanding of the term that implies a judgement, evaluation, interpretation or conclusion about some aspect of the world that is engendered or even obscured by an individual's culture, religion, ethnicity, history or personal circumstances. This common meaning of the word is almost always used in contrast to 'objective' that suggests an apprehension of an aspect of the world that is somehow 'true' or at least closer to the 'truth'. I am using 'subjective' in the sense of that which *belongs* to the 'subject', that beneath the layers of cultural, social, biological, political, historical and economic conditioning of an 'already-always', 'thrown' existence is *not knowable* in the same way we might think we know objects and facts that that exhibit a relative degree of measurability. (Heidegger, for example, uses the phrase 'being-in-the-world' to bridge the divide between 'subjective' and 'objective'.)
57 That is, the possibility of investigating, enquiring and reflecting upon the subject and its relationship to the world.

Hammīra.[58] Therefore, strictly speaking, there is no re-telling either, since which story would be retold if there is no single source from which we can derive re-tellings? Hammīra exists as an object that has been created in our consciousness through multiple perspectives expressed through multiple narratives that cascade over different centuries, in different languages and extended genres. It is this cascading and continuous re-appearance of Hammīra in our conventional structures of time as a forward movement of years and centuries that is puzzling. It is not puzzling because of the question of why writers, reciters, readers and listeners would think and imagine Hammīra at all, but because the temporal sequence in which I would normally be compelled to frame my analysis of the narratives is itself doubtful, questionable; it is at best a socially agreed[59] upon structure that falls apart once someone moves away from convention and embarks on another, alternate imagining of time and of memory. Thus while the usual manner in which Hammīra would be presented in a study of the kind that this book represents is one in which, for example, the interconnections between different narratives and the historical conditions inside of which they arose would be investigated, examined and analysed. In other words, as a historian or someone interested in understanding how narratives are situated in their cultural contexts, I would trace a sequence of one text or narrative following the other whether consciously or unconsciously – a kind of domino effect with its implicit inevitability to trigger a forward movement encapsulated here in different stories told in different genres over long stretches of time. This is, at least in part, what I am doing here. But the narratives surrounding Hammīra and in particular the self-reflexive character of the *Hammīra-Mahākāvya* has led me to ask questions about time, imagination, history and the subject who seems to know and experience all of this. The cascading of narratives has led me to think of an upward or reverse flow of events rather than solely in terms of a downward or forward flow. While simultaneity is one possible and indeed powerful, yet rarely sought after, rendering of time, so are retroactive and proactive movements and imagined causalities of events and thoughts in the form of the spoken and the written word. If the experience of time in the narratives or of the authors of those narratives about Hammīra is not the same as mine or my contemporaries' experiences of time, since the experience of time is a function of the formation of the subject

58 We know Hammīra through layers of interpretation and new contexts that create new meanings. We do not and cannot know Hammīra as he 'really was'.

59 What we call 'reality' itself can be considered to be a function of social agreement which in turn also creates notions of continuity and coherence in what is a discontinuous 'multi-verse' in which nothing is repeatable. What exists is a transformation of energy into multiple manifestations and forms.

and vice versa, do I not do injustice by forcing their experience of time (to which I barely have access) into my experience of time, which albeit is an often implicit or unexamined notion of temporality in relation to equally unexamined notions of language, memory, body and self?[60] What if the *Hammīra-Mahākāvya* was written not only with an awareness of a particular past but also of a particular future? What if the political developments of the 20th century and historical interpretations surrounding Hammīra within that particular political climate were already somehow embedded in the 15th-century text? What if the text had been written by virtue of being brought forth by a future possibility that existed in the mind of the author – by a possibility that was pulling toward a particular future that shaped the contours of the text?[61] I am suggesting that not only this text but all texts and narratives come into existence not just in terms of a rich intertextuality and conversation with other texts but also in terms of an 'inter-temporality' which is ultimately given by the simultaneity of time in the present moment yet also by the flows and eddies of the imagination that are both forward and reverse looking.

> *"Life's more interesting phenomena," he replied, "probably always have this Janus face toward the past and the future, are probably always progressive and regressive in one. They reveal the ambiguity of life itself."*[62]

2.5 The Subject of History and the Simultaneity of Time

While all history seems to be retrospective, that is, the view of temporal events offered in a historical account of the past is one that moves from the present into the past, rarely or perhaps never is history considered to be retroactive, that is, events that took place in the past are not considered to originate 'because' of what is happening now, because of what is happening in the present. The present is not considered to be the source of the past; rather, the past is considered to be the source, in causal terms, of the present. Thus, sequences of events do

---

60 See Carr (2014).

61 I am distinguishing possibility as something (an idea) that 'lives' in the temporal domain of the future. Possibility *and* future are generated through/in language. It is the future as a creation in language which in turn affects our experience of the present.

62 From Thomas Mann's novel *Doktor Faustus*. Cited in Bowie (2008, 13). All history must therefore be understood not only in terms of what happened in the past but also how that past was shaped by forward-looking future possibility, that is, by experience, and anticipation and expectation; conversely the past too is shaped by present possibility thus becoming a 'future past' (see Koselleck, 2004).

not propel themselves backward rather they propel themselves forward. The past in the conventional view espoused by historians is neither retroactive nor prospective. It is grounded in neither a reverse causality nor a future one – in which events occur 'because' of which they are already tethered however firmly or loosely to a future set of events or occurrences. While it may seem counterintuitive or even irrational to claim that events in the past originate or are shaped by what is happening now – since the temporal vector of sequenced events seems to move forward even though this forward movement may not be 'straightforward' – there may be divergences, loops, dead ends, repetitions, vanishing points, zigzag branching patterns and so on in this forward movement that seems to arrive at the doorstep of the present. Of course, this forward movement does not stop at the present but continues to rush forward such that the present can only be 'halted' or 'caught' by the conceptual apparatus of thought in its translation and re-formation of experience into memory. Thus, the moment up to which the zigzagging sequence of past events seems to lead cannot be grasped or held onto. It is ephemeral and subversive in that it disintegrates before one can touch it with understanding and knowledge; indeed it disintegrates at the very intention of touching or grasping it. Only the past as a conceptual edifice can be grasped. It too cannot be grasped as a 'presence' in the moment of the now. The same idea applies to the future. It too can only be grasped and comprehended by the conceptual apparatus of thought. Past and future are connected and mirrored in each other as structures of thought. Not only are they structures of thought, they (as in time) are the condition or context inside of which thought arises, and vice versa thought is the condition or context inside of which time arises. The present as the third mode of thinking about time *should* be the most accessible mode of time available to us since it is in 'front' of us, so speak, yet it remains elusive since it can be only 'known' through direct, unmediated experience. Yet direct, unmediated experience of '*what is*' is itself rare since experience seems to present itself to us through a variety of filters including prejudices, perspectives and points of view provided by language,[63] culture, religion, geography, education and history. The past then 'leads' to something that cannot always be directly grasped. In other words, it 'leads' to something that can only be known without mediation. But then unmediated experience does not have substance in the sense that is does not carry the meanings and interpretations inherited through the filters that make up our perception of the world. In that sense unmediated or direct experience is 'meaning-less' or simply devoid of significance and interpretation. 'Meaning' seems to emerge only when

63 See Wittgenstein (1958).

the conceptual apparatus and filters of thought 're-arise' after a brief gap in which the apparent division between the subject that experiences and the world that the subject experiences collapses leaving what can be termed 'direct experience.'[64] Thus the past rushes toward something that cannot be grasped or perhaps can only be grasped as a fleeting '*presence*.' The past therefore only 'leads' to itself and not to the present. This is because the present moment is re-directed through the conceptual apparatus of thought that 're-forms' direct experience into memory that is the past. The past is known as the past and the present is also known as the past.

While 'common sense' tells us that time moves from past to present to future, the sequence of events leading from past to present and the implicit or explicit understandings of causality seem at best to be constructed and are, as mentioned earlier, a matter of social agreement.[65] These twin formations of implicit or explicit construction and social or community agreement lend historical causality with the appearance of uniformity, clarity and reason. In fact, however, historical causality may in reality be a shifting, unstable, perhaps even vague proposition. What would be the value then in proposing a kind of sequence that works retroactively, that moves from the present into the past and then perhaps back into the future-present? By present I do not mean the unmediated, direct present of experience, but rather again an agreed upon notion of a conceptually structured idea of the present given by thought. Thought here finds a variety of expressions through either different texts and narratives; or buildings

---

64 Can there be direct experience of anything? See the critique of Hume, Locke and others in Carr (2014). Furthermore: "*Events are important because of what comes later, and observation would reveal nothing about their true significance and be no help at all.* Examples abound: Columbus and his crew had no idea they were discovering America. Anyone observing Martin Luther, nailing his 95 theses to the church door in Wittenberg in 1519, would have no idea he was launching the Reformation; indeed, Luther himself did not know this. Those angry Parisians storming the Bastille in 1789 couldn't know they were setting off the French Revolution. The assassin of the Archduke Ferdinand in Sarejevo, in 1914, did not know he was starting World War I—and on and on. No doubt these events were important, in some cases matters of life and death, to those participating in or observing them. But their historical significance – our reason for including them in the historical account – was hidden from them because the future was hidden. It was not available to observation" (Carr 2014, 57; emphasis added).

65 See the 'block universe theory' in which space–time – in contrast to the big bang theory of an ever-expanding universe – is imagined as an immense 'block' in which past, present and future exist simultaneously in the now. This does not mean, however, that we, as human beings who represent a particular point of view or exist within a particular horizon of knowledge (and action), have the same epistemological access to the future as we have to the past and present. This imbalance of epistemological access itself poses a philosophical and existential conundrum.

including temples, shrines, monuments and dwellings; philosophical treatises; art; political manifestos; ritual compendiums; chronicles; technology and machinery; and virtually all forms of work involving the human body. The experiment of working backward could therefore begin from a narrative text or scholarly work or even from a social and political context that has been captured in a text or fragments of writing and speech. Retroactive causality suggests that the effect precedes the cause. The effect does not 'cause' the cause but does precede it and affect it. Therefore, while the cause must be temporally prior to the effect, and the effect must lie in the future, the effect must have (paradoxically) already occurred. But if the effect does not 'cause' its own cause or set of causes in what sense can we say that it precedes the cause? Supposing for the sake of argument we do away with the notion of cause and effect and think of the present moment as a context or as a framework that is pulling or drawing past events into a particular future. A context or a framework is different to the substantive notion of a cause as in, for example, 'x' chemical causes a chemical reaction to take place in the 'y' chemical or 'z' metal, etc. How can a future context give shape to the past? A context must be understood to represent a possibility that exists in the future. Thus, for example, the idea of a nation state in the 20th century and all its associated elements of territoriality, uniformity, the dynamics of insider and outsider, perhaps even citizenship and democracy exists as a context for events, situations, political formations and allegiances that take place in the 14th and 15th centuries.[66] Again a context is not a cause and yet it determines the meaning and movement of events and actions. How would a history look if it were written and explored in a retrograde manner moving 'backward' from a text or narrative or any other expression of thought in the present to a text or narrative in the past? Can a history be written both with a retrograde movement and a forward

66 See Husserl's (1990) idea of *protention* or anticipation of a future. Can we think not only of individual experience as inhabiting a protention but also historical events as anticipating a future? Thus in terms of a simultaneity of time, all events – past, present and future – must be 'entangled' so to speak with one another. Was Nayachandra Sūri already imagining a future, even in the slightest unformed manner, in which his poem would become embedded in a nationalist discourse? Or was he already imagining that scholars would write and think about his work in the 20th century, or poets in the centuries preceding it? This is quite possible since he was also writing as a response to an awareness of the literary past of *kāvya* composition that his writing belonged to. Thus he could imagine that some future writer or scholar would compose something as a retroactive response to an awareness of the intention and meaning of Nayachandra's composition. A history of Hammīra can be written where readers recognize which parts are scholarly and 'historical' and which parts are 'non-historical' and poetic, literary and philosophical. For example, Borges style of writing produces the effect of a historical account although his short stories are actually 'fiction'. See Narayana Rao *et al.* 2001.

movement? Would these two historical narratives meet somewhere and merge like the black-and-white and colour, non-linear sequences of the movie *Memento?*[67]

67 There are two parallel scenes running in *Memento.* One that moves forward in time in a chronological sequence and other that moves in a reverse order until both sequences meet. See also Markus Vinzent (2019). Causation, which is one of the central ideas of history (and of science) in understanding and explaining how one event is succeeded by another, must also be relegated to the world of appearance or phenomena like all other aspects of sensory and conceptual experience. What is the meaning, indeed substantive nature, of cause and effect (the idea of causality) in a world of which we have only access to appearance? Cause and effect are always considered to be 'real,' somehow more concrete and more justified than our experience that is always mediated through language or hidden contexts and frameworks. In what way then are cause and effect as a mode of *interpreting* circumstances and events itself an outcome of implicit, unreflected structures of thought, language and perception?

Chapter 3
Realms of Imagination

The description is not the described.
J. Krishnamurti

3.1 Imagination

It seems that the series of historical events and the narratives that subsequently describe them cannot be understood without comprehending the imagination.[68] They cannot be understood (in the sense of knowing their inner logic and workings) without realizing that they arise and come into existence because of the imagination. Imagination is at the very root and substance of how the past is both ordered, thought of, manifested and retrieved – releasing memory from a constant state of forgetting. Imagination is the path by which the past, and history as a study of the past and indeed as a peculiar construction of the past, is sought after and returned to us as a seemingly concrete and yet at the same time intrinsically ephemeral object. The object that is history is thus at once abstract

68 Did the text arise in the 15th century 'because' it 'retroactively anticipated' the configurations and ideas of the nation state, nationalism and a history tied up with national identity? In other words, can we claim that the *Hammīra-Mahākāvya* was somehow 'living into' a future of such political, social and philosophical constructions? What is this movement from future back to past, and from past to future from the location of the present or rather moment of now? Take, for example, the *paṛ* or pictorial and narrative 'scroll' used in night-time performances of the oral narrative of Devnārāyaṇ (Malik 2005). The *paṛ* illustrates the simultaneity of past, present (also 'presence') and future. It is an extremely complex spatially and temporally organized visual 'presence' of the deity along with the history of his ancestors and the achievements and events of his own life. The *paṛ* is a 'flat' scroll measuring over nine meters with the god and his brothers in the centre. It contains hundreds of scenes, images, objects, people and geographical locations. The images to the left of Devnarayan are located in the past (with reference to the deity) and the events to his right are located in the present (and also future) with reference to his own life. Past, present and future are simultaneously depicted on one continuous 'flat' surface of the scroll. The spatial and temporal features of the scroll can only be distinguished through the telling of the narratives that unfolds in a seemingly linear fashion, although this too is ambiguous since in the actual performances of the narrative the audience and singers may choose to single out episodes that they want to hear in a non-sequential fashion. Thus on one day a part of narrative may be told that is followed by another episode that precedes it on the following day. See also Borges (1964) and Vonnegut (2005).

https://doi.org/10.1515/9783110662795-006

and open-ended only giving an impression of solidity as it moves through phases of surfacing and receding inside of the imagination.

The past cannot be pinned down, in the same way that the present and future are shimmering replicas of an apparent reality. Reality is apparent because it defines itself in an inherently contradictory manner by being real only to the extent that perception and experience are contextually determined. Reality resides in the imagination that by virtue of the changing, capricious nature of thought shifts its contours and shape moment by moment. Thus, the apparent concreteness of historical fact is yet but a singular frame in what is ultimately a series of moving frames, each of which have the potential to branch off into an alternative series of narrations and stories. Since the physical and spatial location human beings occupy – the Earth – has no real up or down or east or west or setting or rising sun[69] or any real position in the vastness of empty outer space, how can there be a time that moves in a succession of straight-lined events in a universe that isn't 'going' anywhere? Time itself must be circular like the curve of the Earth, bendable, reversible, a whirling series of events that perhaps converge one upon the other – events that create precarious and entangled arches and loops that are meant to be only partially grasped by the intellect, leaving the issue of understanding to more fluid, intuitive faculties that engender intimacy and truth through listening and telling, through narration and speaking, through a thinking that is to be distinguished from the uncontrolled and uncontrollable, incessant stream of thoughts that arise and subside in the mind. Both the ordering and the bringing into existence or bringing forth of things that happened, of things that no longer have the substance of what is happening in the present moment lies in the imagination. The imagination manifests what is no longer present in conversation and in language.[70] It is also that through which sequences of events that even though only vaguely remembered seem bitingly sharp, utterly precise and irrevocably tangible, and are given sense, meaning and order.

3.2 View with a Grain of Sand

Sequences themselves are stitched together in the imagination. Imagination holds Time together. To paraphrase W. B. Yeats: *time falls apart; the centre cannot hold*

---

69 This idea is borrowed from the deeply innovative thought and work of the inventor and genius, Buckminster Fuller.

70 Imagination in this sense stands in contrast to 'non-imagination' or 'facts'.

without imagination; mere anarchy is loosed upon the world of events. Imagination, however, is not fantasy; it is a faculty, a sense through and in which the world in its spatial and, above all, temporal dimensions comes into being. *The world is being imagined.* Without imagination and thinking there is emptiness, an unfathomable void that retreats into a silent self accompanied by a disappearance of world. Imagination transforms this emptiness into a cornucopia of visions, tastes, sounds, memories, smells, into a body that moves, changes, grows, desires, decays into being born and dying.[71] As the following poem tells us:

View with a Grain of Sand

We call it a grain of sand,
but it calls itself neither grain nor sand.
It does just fine, without a name,
whether general, particular,
permanent, passing,
incorrect, or apt.

Our glance, our touch means nothing to it.
It doesn't feel itself seen and touched.
And that it fell on the window-sill
is only our experience, not its.
For it, it is not different from falling on anything else
with no assurance that it has finished falling
or that it is falling still.

The window has a wonderful view of a lake,
but the view doesn't view itself.
It exists in this world
colorless, shapeless,
soundless, odorless, and painless.

The lake's floor exists floorlessly,
and its shore exists shorelessly.
The water feels itself neither wet nor dry
and its waves to themselves are neither singular nor plural.
They splash deaf to their own noise
on pebbles neither large nor small.

71 What is a thing without a name or description? In other words, is it possible to think about a thing or person without a name or without words? Without a name or words, the thing neither exists nor not exists. A thing and its constituent properties can only be assumed to exist outside the world of words. Even the elementary particles and processes of fundamental physics exist within the world of words and description within language. They have no independent existence in the *world as it appears to us* except as a description in words that we provide. See Rorty (1989, 5) "The world is out there, but descriptions of the world are not." and Wittgenstein (1958).

> And all this beneath a sky by nature sky-less
> in which the sun sets without setting at all
> and hides without hiding behind an unminding cloud.
> The wind ruffles it, its only reason being
> that it blows.
>
> A second passes.
> A second second.
> A third.
> But they're three seconds only for us.
>
> Time has passed like courier with urgent news.
> But that's just our simile.
> The character is invented, his haste is make-believe,
> his news inhuman.
>
> *Wislawa Szsymborska*[72]

The world seems independent of us, but is it? It is independent of our words and descriptions and yet the only way we know 'it' is through words and descriptions. Things acquire existence and meaning for us only when we give them names and descriptions.[73] What are things and persons outside of those words and descriptions? Can we know what they are? Do they cease to have existence outside of our descriptions? Or do they become neither existent nor not existent? What are the implications of saying, as the poem above does, that objects, things and even time only exists for 'us,' that is, only exist the way they show up for us because of the way we describe them in language? A stone is neither large nor small, nor for that matter is it a stone for itself. Water is neither wet nor cold nor hot nor a liquid for itself. The sky is neither blue nor above nor empty. But what of events that have taken place in the past. What are they? Are they anything other than what we say they are? Do they have any existence independent of our calling and naming them as something? If we do not describe them, what are they? Do they too neither exist nor not exist? Do they begin to disappear if we do not name them? Is their appearance and existence therefore contingent on our describing them? But then how do we describe something we haven't ex-

72 Wislawa Szsymborska was a Polish poet and writer who was awarded the Nobel prize for literature in 1996. She died in Krakow in 2012.

73 But more so we perhaps generate the world through a kind of projection that has its source in imagination, subsequently crystalizing or 'solidifying' through language.

perienced? Is there a pre-existing 'trace-description' from which our current description emerges?[74] How do descriptions come into existence in the first place?

Does the past even exist outside of language?[75] If it is hard or indeed impossible to think about objects or people or even oneself without language, then how do we, or can we, think about time outside of language – language not only in its capacity to describe but more pertinently in its capacity to generate distinctions, abstractions, theories, interpretations and contexts that provide the conditions and contours of human existence?[76] Once language is removed and along with it thought, then these contours disappear. Human existence does not disappear – the descriptions and interpretations we have of existence and experience disappear. What is it that remains when our experience is bereft of such generative acts through which both experience and the world as we know it subside or disappear? Perhaps Nothing? Or Presence? Presence without words and therefore without time or self-description. Presence that is the condition for the arising of language, interpretation, sound, symbol, self and time past, present and future.

> What this means is that my experience of time is a function of the events that I live through, the events, that is, that are meaningful or significant for me. It is these events, not abstract points on a scale, that are ever receding into an indefinite background and make up the horizon of my past. And it is the events that figure in the immediate sphere of protention or anticipation, and not some abstract empty spaces to be filled in, that make up the horizon of my future. For the individual, events can be meaningful or significant such that I not only live through but also remember them – and here we come to Husserl's distinction between primary and secondary memory or between retention and recollection. Likewise, future events can be of such importance that I explicitly look forward to or dread them, that I plan for them or seek to avoid them. This is the horizon of "secondary expectation" which is somehow a counterpart of recollection. The point of all this is that these primary and secondary horizons of past and future form the complex background against which the "now" stands out and from which it derives its significance. Like a single note in a melody, the

74 See Heidegger's (1967) notion of 'already-always' ('schon-immer') and the idea of the 'disclosure' of a world. Speaking and listening are the instruments of unconcealment. See also Gadamer (1960) on the nature of a dialogue or conversation.

75 How is the use of language here different from *Begriffsgeschichte?* Is the latter to be subsumed under language as that which manifests and invents the world including temporality and spatiality amongst others?

76 Included in this list is also the 'I' or 'me' which can be said to exist as linguistic and socio-cultural entities that gain substance through memory, which in turn arises or is embedded in the structures of thought. This raises the question of whether there is an entity independent of thought and memory that can referred to as 'I' or 'me'. In the space of now, in which thought or language is absent, the 'I' or 'me' is also absent even while the generative substratum of existence persists.

> present is nothing by itself; it is what it is thanks to its "place" (a spatial metaphor again) in the melody, its role in the unfolding whole of which it is a part (Carr 2014, 179).

The question is: where does this unfolding take place? In time or space? Or is it in fact solely in the imagination? Protention and retention must exist in the conditions provided by generative language and imagination. *In fact, imagination is generative language.*

Presence in the now distances itself from itself to create presence in the past and presence in the future, although these triple sensations of presence all exist simultaneously in the now.[77] Only the projections, stretchings and generative plasticity of imagination loosens a movement in time that compels us to believe in the actuality of different, successive moments speeding away from and speeding toward the present like a temporal *Doppler* effect.[78]

Where does this sensation of speeding away from and moving toward come from? If all there in actuality is the now then this now cannot speed away from itself nor move forward toward itself. It can only remain 'here' in itself, in the 'now.' The quality or colouration of the now for an individual or for a community can, however, be dependent on the bringing into the now a possibility that is 're-hauled' and 're-created' from the past or a possibility that lives in the future that is 'brought forth' in the now which in turn determines the quality of the present in one's experience. Thus while human beings and the world are anchored in the now – in fact not only anchored but do not have a choice about this anchoring – there is the movement of thought or imagination that 'impacts' and 'fills' the present moment which without thought or imagination is both empty and meaningless.[79] Why do I say human beings do not have a choice about being-in-the-now?

---

77 "The parallelism of lived space and lived time leads us to the very heart of subjectivity itself. Just as the spatial 'here' is absolute, representing the 'zeropoint of orientation' around which all of space arranges itself, no matter where I am, so the 'now' is absolute as well, the 'place,' as it were, where I am always located, even though the content of the now is always changing. Just as the space of my surroundings extends indefinitely in all directions, so time, with its two-fold horizon, extends indefinitely into the past and the future. Opposed to the here is the there; to the now the then. The present, which is both spatial and temporal, stands out against its background: the absent, in the case of space, the past and future, in the case of time" (Carr 2014, 176).
78 The Doppler effect or shift "is an increase (or decrease) in the frequency of sound, light, or other waves as the source and observer move towards (or away from) each other. The effect causes the sudden change in pitch noticeable in a passing siren, as well as the red shift seen by astronomers."
79 I am using 'thought' here in the sense of 'deep' thought that as Vedic texts state is the origin or source of the manifestation of the world. This equates with language as speech that has the power to create, and can also be compared to the understanding of the 'word' or 'speech' (San-

Because no matter what one thinks or does or whether one resists feeling or thinking or doing, all that happens is happening in the ungraspable moment of now. We cannot escape this fact even though thought is perpetually attempting and also succeeding in obscuring this moment by all kinds of shielding mechanisms including work, play, talk, illness, regret about the past and anxiety about the future, and on and on. Why do I say the present moment is 'ungraspable'? Because even though we recognize and seem to 'know' the present moment, this knowing is given by what we already know, which is conditioned by the past. Yet a knowledge of the present that arises from memory (that is, from the past) is insufficient to know the present moment which in fact is 'new' and requires an un-knowing. The present moment cannot be fully known since some significant or perhaps even total dimension of it escapes our horizon of knowledge. The presence of the present moment can only be glimpsed out of the corner of one's eye, like something flashing swiftly by in our peripheral vision; something the contours and shape of which are blurred; only to be briefly felt and seen like an idea in the mind that quickly subsides to be forgotten.

Since it is empty and meaningless, the present moment which is also the sole or primary location of Being is also *the source of all possibility.* Thus, in this respect being-in-the-now is empty and without significance. And, yet it is being-in-time that gains meaning and significance. Since our everyday experience of self is one of being-in-time, this obscures the meaninglessness and 'insignificance' of the present moment and therefore also of Being. Underlying, or rather parallel to, the meaning we attach to experience is its fundamental meaninglessness.

3.3 The Imagination of Blake

But what is the imagination? According to William Blake: "The principle of all creation is mind; or as he called it Imagination [...] All Things Exist in the Human Imagination" (Blake, cited in Raine 1991). Blake defines imagination in the following manner:

> This world of Imagination is the world of Eternity; it is the divine bosom into which we shall all go after the death of the Vegetated body. This World of Imagination is Infinite &

---

skrit *Vāc*) as in the biblical notion: *In the beginning was the Word, and the Word was with God, and the Word was God* (Gospel according to John 1.1). This is in distinction to the discursive, personal thought or rather 'thoughts' and 'internal dialogue or commentary' or incessant and automatic stream of judgements, opinions and evaluations of people and circumstances that we are occupied by in our everyday lives. See Chapter 6.1.

> Eternal, whereas the world of Generation, or Vegetation, is Finite & Temporal. There Exist in that Eternal World the Permanent Realities of Every Thing which we see reflected in this Vegetable Glass of Nature. All things are comprehended in their Eternal Forms in the divine body of the Saviour, the True Vine of Eternity, the Human Imagination, who appear'd to Me as Coming to Judgment among his Saints & throwing off the Temporal that the Eternal might be Establish'd (K. 605–6) (Blake, cited in Raine 1991, 15).

For Blake thus "the world of Imagination" is the source from which the phenomenal world of things (including humans) arises and returns.[80] Time, space and body also have their origin in imagination, which is not limited by time and space, that is, by the dimensions of temporality and spatiality or by creation and destruction. In this sense, the idea of the field of experience outlined earlier is co-terminus with Blake's idea of imagination. The phenomenal world is, according to him, a reflection of the "Permanent Realities of Every Thing" that are housed, so to speak, in the imagination. This notion of original 'templates' or 'moulds' from which is derived the multiplicity of objects in 'this' world, or as Blake calls it the "Vegetable Glass of Nature," is of course, close to Plato's theory of 'Ideas' or 'Forms.' Things have Eternal Forms that are not subject to decay. These undying forms are understood to be 'in' or 'part of' or 'located within' the "divine body of the Saviour" which is the imagination. It is in the imagination that the eternal is established and out of which all objects that are anchored in time and space emerge. As Kathleen Raine (1991, 17), in her insightful appraisal of Blake, points out: "Imagination is in its nature a world of immortal life; being incorporeal, not located in space or in time, and not therefore subject to change, generation and decay. Blake affirms without doubt that it is the world 'into which we shall all go after the death of the Vegetated body'." Imagination is to be equated with Consciousness – not an individual or particular consciousness but Consciousness with a capital 'C'. This Consciousness is prior and beyond measurement. While it cannot be contained by a definition, it is the condition, so to speak, from which time, space and the possibility of measurability and therefore of birth and decay arises.[81] As Raine (1991, 18) further elucidates: "We must remember at all times that a 'world' for Blake is situated not in Cartesian space but in consciousness; therefore, every change of consciousness changes the

---

80 The phenomenal and noumenal worlds are not two distinct entities that are opposed to one another. Rather the phenomenal world is a 'shadow' of the noumenal. But the 'shadow' is an indicator of the original source or 'Imagination' which itself is beyond words. (S. C. Malik, personal communication).

81 Descartes' famous dictum on which most of modern structures of thought and action seem to rest, *I think, therefore I am*, must therefore be rephrased: *I am, therefore there is thinking.* (I am indebted to S. C. Malik for these ideas.)

world. The positivist scientific ideology shrinks man from the unbounded being of Imagination into mortality." The world arises in the mind, is affected by the mind and returns into the mind. This idea again is echoed in Vedic conceptions of creation and the role of the mind therein. As David Shulman points out:

> The mind is also the only one in the series to be qualified in terms of its somewhat ambiguous reality-status; as such, it seems to be equated to the initial "this," neither real nor unreal, that is existence itself, or the living cosmos seen as a whole. Such equations of an internal aspect of the person with some external correlate are common enough in the Brāhmaṇa sources. Yet, the assertion in this passage that mind and cosmos are similarly balanced on a fine, somewhat precarious existential point is far from trivial. The mind is clearly capable of yielding worlds no less tangible and crisply contoured than the one we normally inhabit or the ones we are capable of putting together, in externality, by ourselves (Shulman 2012, 10).

The mind as it is elucidated in this text that Shulman outlines is, like the imagination in Blake's thought, prior to time and space; it occupies a status in the "initial 'this'" which is neither real nor not real; a state of being that is prior and beyond the dual categories of thought once it has entered the more 'solidified' spatio-temporal realms of person, body, identity and limitation. Furthermore, this prior state of being-ness or mind from which objects or the world emerge is equated with imagination. Thus, the text under consideration also says:

> Whatever these living beings imagine in their minds is performed (*tad yat kiṃ cemāni bhūtāni manasā saṅkalpayanti teṣām eva sā kṛtiḥ*). [...] The verb is *sam-√kalpaya*, which can mean "to conceive, to think, to construct [mentally, in some integrated manner], to intend, to determine." It can also mean "to imagine" – which is to say that imagining is, in some contexts, a process of using the mind to bring something together or to construct something that belongs initially to the world of thought (Shulman 2012, 11).

The imagination is an instrument through which we gather and bring something into reality. The imagination is an active faculty that produces or rather generates a reality that is as solid as a brick. As Shulman points out, imagination here is definitely not concern "flights of creative fancy or [...] the conjuring up of some hitherto undreamt-of reality. On the other hand, it is quite likely that, like the Vedic ritualist, each day of our lives we are busy imagining ourselves into some kind of mentally appointed reality, one built up of mind-born bricks" (Shulman 2012, 11). Imagination or mind in the contexts that Blake and Vedic thought occurs is something prior to the parameters and limitations of body, space and time as expressions of a dimensioned reality. It is the faculty which engenders experience and the world as a reflection of that experience.

Imagination in the view of Blake and also in the Vedic context (which will be discussed in more detail in section 5.4) is not simply a mental act or an act of thought in the more modern understanding of the term, something that an individual engages in their personal inner world. Imagination or thought in the former sense is free, in a sense, of the individual and her or his personal history, circumstances, set of values, cultural context, etc. Imagination here is not linked to creativity as it is understood in the contemporary world, as an expression of a particular kind that is limited to the extent of knowledge that an individual acquires within the course of a lifetime. Imagination in the sense that both Blake and Vedic thinkers use it is linked to creativity by way of being the very source of the creation of the phenomenal universe. Imagination and thought here are the background against which the multiplicity of form and its experience arises. It is the 'clearing' or 'lighting'[82] (to use Heidegger's vocabulary) or possibility, not only for the existence of things but for existence itself. Imagination thus seen is not something that occupies the phenomenal world; it is not something that emerges or 'belongs' to the author of a work of art or literature or of an invention. Rather, it is distinct from all this. Imagination in Blake's understanding is 'Experience,' not my or your 'experience' which is ultimately only a shadow, replica, reflection or repetition of what is true or real. So-called individual experience conceals or veils what is real, i.e. what is not limited by time and space, by masquerading as that which is real, inducing the individual to believe they are also limited by time, space and body. The phenomenal world is therefore an apparent, or rather an '*as if*,' world that does not have any solid substance even though it appears to have a ground. It is, in fact, a 'conceptual world.' The phenomenal world is thus taken to be real, although what is real and true is the source from which all this arises and emerges. The source is imagination or mind or thought. Imagination is not only the source of things, objects, entities, sentient beings, etc., but also the source of the ability to conceptualize time and space in their varied forms understood philosophically, scientifically and culturally. Yet the understandings of time and space, however complex and refined, are still occurring within the limited parameters of the idea of a beginning and an end. Thus, the idea of a time past, present and future, the idea of history, of historical events, and of linear and cyclical time are also all ultimately emergent from the imagination. Time and history are thus not just being imagined by the individual or collective intellect; rather, they are first the product of imagination and second a product of a 'misrecognition' or rather 'misapprehension' of the intellect of the limitation of the world as a collection of entities caught up in and at the effect of, so

82 German: *Lichtung.*

to speak, the apparent parameters of time and space.[83] The misapprehension of the 'unlimited' nature of imagination and Being leads us to think in terms of a succession of events with a beginning, middle and end, of birth and destruction, and of history as a structuring of time past that grants meaning to terrestrial, human existence. The understanding of imagination as I am using it is different to imagination as a function of a mental faculty that can conjure and construct and makes sense of past, present and future.

The meaning of imagination takes us beyond (limited) human intellect and faculties to the realm of sheer possibility and 'clearing' that gives rise to the possibility of imagining as an intellectual or mental faculty of human beings. Within this intellectual faculty is the capacity to reflect inward or backward into the source of this faculty and into the source of existence. What then does history as a function of imagination in the sense of the intellectual or mental faculty or capacity mean in the context or from the perspective of imagination from which the very possibility of the phenomenal world of entities, things, subjects, bodies and intellect arises? Imagination, in the sense I am using it collapses time past, present and future into an eternity that cannot be grasped by the intellect that is irrevocably situated and defined by succession and linearity. History as an explication or even celebration of succession and linearity ceases to exist. It is at best a second order understanding of what is real, a shadow presented to the intellect in order to be able grasp something that is not graspable by this faculty. Events, insofar as they exist, collapse either into no-thing-ness or at the most into simultaneous array of almost infinite pathways and entanglements. One thing may seem to lead to another or in fact it may not lead to anything except a swirling, criss-crossing series that appears and disappears like reflections in a powerful whirlpool. This simultaneous criss-crossing of events in the second order of apparent reality undermines the linear, causal imagination that history in its dominant mode depends upon. Neither cause nor linearity are ultimately real; they only represent one possible mode of organizing temporality once it has come into existence in the shadow world of apparent or 'as if' reality. Imagination can also be considered to be the source of the dream in which we pursue our everyday lives, in which we pursue knowledge, in which we pursue art and literature and architecture. In other words, the world of the dream is the world we consider concrete, tangible, real and even true, although it is a shadow or rather a simulacrum of the world of 'Experience' (Blake). The world that appears

83 By using the phrase "at the effect of" I mean the experience that human beings have of being 'victims' of their circumstances rather than being the 'source' or the 'clearing' for what happens in their lives.

real, and the historical sequence that appears to have happened while bringing us to the present moment through a meaningful causality, is, in fact, the world of the dream; a simulation that goes undistinguished and unknown for what it is by virtue of its forceful, compelling hold on our senses, our intellect and our desires that seek satisfaction and meaning in the unreal.[84]

84 This book, as mentioned in the preface, is an attempt at a phenomenology of history, that is, history as it appears in our experience or rather history as appearance and the past as an '*as if*' past. What is the idea of historicity, that is, what does it mean to be a historical being from this perspective? Can I write a 'history' of Hammīra from the point of view of the subject who is writing it, that is, from my point of view as a subject who is exploring what it means to be a historical being in whom different temporalities and experiences of time are simultaneously intertwined in the here and now?

Chapter 4
Literary Imbroglios

As it is the case with other Sanskrit compositions but also later oral epics from Rajasthan,[85] the the *Hammīra-Mahākāvya* begins with an all-important invocation and salutation of several deities. The author employs a subtle linguistic style to create two meanings with one word or phrase. This mechanism of dual meanings (Sanskrit: *dvayārtha*) is applied to the invocation series which can be understood as either denoting Hindu deities or Jaina spiritual leaders. For example, the second verse of the opening lines refers to Nābhibhū (Skt.: 'navel-born') which can be an epithet for Brahmā or can refer to the progeny of Nābhi, the first Tirthaṇkara of the Jaina lineage. The third verse uses the name Śrī Pārśva to refer either to Viṣṇu or to Śrī Pārśvanāth, the 23rd Tirthaṇkara of the Jainas. The next verse invokes Śaṃkara Vīravibhu which can refer either to Śiva or Mahādeva or to Mahāvīra, the 24th and most significant Jaina Tirthaṇkara. The fifth verse addresses Bhīsvān Śānti, which according to Kirtane, is an epithet either for the Sun or a name, Śānti, of the 16th Tirthaṇkara. Similarly, the sixth verse refers to Samudra Janman, which may mean either the Moon, or point to Nemināth, son of Samudra, the 22nd Jaina Tirthaṇkara.[86] Kirtane interprets this modus of dual meanings as an indication of "freedom of thought so characteristic of the age in which the author lived, when the narrow and bigoted intolerance even of the Muslim had begun to appreciate the beauties of the allegorical language of the Hindu popular religion" (Kirtane 1879, iv). Indeed, the poet's artistic credentials and the theme of the poem he wrote do signify a kind of cosmopolitan culture in which religious identities were not so sharply contoured as they seem to be in the late 19th and certainly 20th/21st centuries. However, Kirtane's comment regarding the "narrow and bigoted intolerance of the Muslim" must be critically re-evaluated. 'Muslim' culture needs to be seen as part of this emerging cosmopolitanism, specially since the narrative themes of the poem are not built around conflict arising from fixed religious identities but rather allegiances fashioned around moral qualities such as loyalty, steadfastness, friendship and protection.

---

85 See Malik (2005, 18).
86 *Hammīra-Mahākāvya Sarga* 1.1–8.

https://doi.org/10.1515/9783110662795-007

4.1 Medieval Religious and Cultural Sensibilities

This compartmentalized view that "freedom of thought" was the hallmark of 'indigenous' culture marked by Hindu and Jaina sensibilities that supposedly existed during the author's time is further emphasized when Kirtane explains that Hammīra "is one of those later heroes of India who measured their swords with the Muhammadan conquerors and fell in defence of their independence" (Kirtane 1879, iv). This perspective is repeated in Aziz Ahmed's scholarly article published much later in the *Journal of the American Oriental Society* in 1963. The article's main focus is the birth of literary genres that reflect "Muslim conquest" in India and its resistance through Rajput rulers and chieftains. Ahmed, in his introductory sentences, points out that

> Muslim impact and rule in India generated two literary growths: a Muslim epic of conquest, and a Hindu epic of resistance and of psychological rejection. The two literary growths were planted in two different cultures; in two different languages, Persian and Hindi; in two mutually exclusive religious, cultural and historical attitudes each confronting the other in aggressive hostility. Each of these two literary growths developed in mutual ignorance of the other; and with the rare exception of eclectic intellectuals like Abu'l Fazl in the 16th century, or the 17th century Urdu poets of the Southern courts of Bijapur and Golconda, their readership hardly ever converged. The Muslim and the Hindu epics of Medieval India can therefore hardly be described as "epic" and "counter-epic" in the context of a direct relationship of challenge and response. Yet one of them was rooted in the challenge asserting the glory of Muslim presence, and the other in the response repudiating it. In this sense one may perhaps use the term "counter-epic" for the Hindi heroic poetry of Medieval India as I have done (Ahmed 1963, 470).

Ahmed's description of the historical and political circumstances out of which texts such as the *Hammīra-Mahākāvya* is born, is more explicit and forceful than Kirtane's assertion cited earlier. The literary genres that arise because of early medieval political configurations are not only in themselves separated by language, but the bearers of these literary traditions belong to different religious communities and cultures. It seems that there is no common ground for a mutual literary, cultural or historical conversation to occur within this black-and-white case of exclusion that is supposedly taking place at several, if not all, levels. Ahmed's first account is that of the type of literature he identifies as "Muslim conquest" literature. Here he cites two works of Amir Khusraw, the well-known scholar and poet writing in Persian.

> Amir Khusrau's Miftah al-futuh is the first war-epic (*razmiya*) written in Muslim India. It celebrates four victories of Jalal al-din Khaljī (1290–96), two of them against Hindu rajas, one against the Mongols and one against a rebel Muslim governor [...] The next historical narrative of Amir Khusrau, Khaza'in al-futuh, was written in prose, but the epic style

and formulae were retained as well as the thematic emphasis on the glorification of the Turk against the Hindu. The concentration is on style in the tradition of Hasan Nizami's Taj al-ma'athir rather than on history; and the stylist's effort to make use of the artifices of prose composition Khusrau had recommended in his treatise on rhetoric, I'jaz-i Khusrawi, is manifest throughout the work as a continuous tour de force, unfolding itself in extended images, parallelisms, stylistic deductions, conceits and analogies. For instance:

"[...] the Rai became *hot* at their words and thus disclosed the *fire* that *burnt* in his breast: 'Our old and respectable *fire-worshippers*, the *lamps* of whose minds *burnt bright*, have said clearly that never can the Hindu stay before the Turk, or *fire* before water."

In the Khaza'in al-futuh, the glorification of the Khaljī's conquest of the Deccan exults in irrepressible bravado of iconoclasm:

"There were many capitals of the *devs* (meaning Hindu gods *or* demons) where Satanism had prospered from the earliest times, and where far from the pale of Islam, the Devil in the course of ages had hatched his eggs and made his worship compulsory on the followers of the idols; but now with a sincere motive the Emperor removed these symbols of infidelity [...] to dispel the contamination of false belief from those places through the muezzin's call and the establishment of prayers" (Ahmed 1963, 470).

Here in the translations of the Persian sources there is a reference to Hindu ritual being identified with "fire" and "fire worship" that could be an oblique allusion to Vedic practices but also more 'popular' forms of worship using oil lamps in the daily veneration of deities. The Turks are, interestingly, represented by the cooler element of water that ultimately extinguishes fire. Furthermore, the second citation identifies the locations of 'devil' worship as the capitals of Hindu deities (*devas*; wrongly classified as both gods and demons). These capitals are presumably temples, but perhaps also cities or kingdoms that had certain divinities as their tutelary gods which in the discourse of the text are described as 'eggs hatched by the Devil' in a plan spreading over hundreds or thousands of years. The sultan now took it upon himself to purify the conquered land of these symbols of infidelity. It is clear from these excerpts that the two Persian texts under consideration are composed within the framework of eulogizing the deeds of the sultan as he propagates Islam but also while defeating the Turk's rivals, the Rajputs. Even though the texts seem to clearly highlight these motives, Ahmed points out that the 'English translator' of the texts emphasizes that the

Deccan expeditions had no clear object – the acquisition of horses, elephants, jewels, gold, and silver [...] Of course the name of God was solemnly pronounced. The invaders built mosques wherever they went [...] This was their habit. Of anything like an idealistic, even a fanatic religious mission the Deccan invasions were completely innocent (Ahmed 1963, 470–471).

In addition to the motivation provided by the desire to defeat local rulers and destroy the symbols of "infidelity," Ahmed discusses other lesser mentioned, but equally important reasons for Muslim or Turk conquests: the rescue and protection of Muslim women from the imprisonment and abuse by local kings and chieftains. This literary motif is stressed in other Persian texts:

> The motif of a war waged to protect or avenge the honor of Muslim women, similar to the motif "rape of Helen" in Greek epic and historiography, originally an epic theme, lends itself again and again to Muslim historiography in India. The official casus belli in the case of Hajjaj ibn Yusuf's expedition against Sind reads in al-Baladhuri very much like the first few pages of Herodotus; the expedition was claimed to have been in response to the appeal of Muslim women captured by the pirates of Debal, and since their release could not be obtained by negotiation, it was accomplished by war and conquest. One of the expeditions of Sultan Bahadur of Gujarat (1526–37) against a Hindu chieftain was to avenge the dishonor of two hundred and fifty Muslim women whom he had captured. Sher Shah Suri's expedition against Puran Mal, the Raja of Raisin, was undertaken on the complaint of some Muslim women: "he has slain our husbands, and our daughters he has enslaved and made dancing girls of them." Puran Mal was defeated and slain and his daughter was given away by Sher Shah to some wandering minstrels who might make her dance in the bazars (Ahmed 1963, 471–472).

This motif, though lesser known, strongly matches and also reverses the more well-known narratives of Rajput women committing *jauhar* to escape imminent defilement at the hands of victorious sultans and their soldiers who are depicted as plundering and rapacious marauders.

Ahmed goes on to discuss the historicity of events surrounding Hammīra's life and deeds in the *Hammīra-Mahākāvya* and other works as an example of epics or narratives concerning 'Hindu' resistance to Muslim dominance and conquest. The works in question and their depiction of Hammīra are, according to the Ahmed, "unhistorical," containing fantastical details that do not match up to historical evidence:

> The unhistorical epic legend of Raja Hammīr Dev's (c. 1300) gallant fight against 'Alā' al-Dīn Khaljī, and his heroic death, was celebrated in bardic literature of several Indian languages. Chief among these are Hammīr Rasa, and Hammīr Kavya by Sarang Dhar, a bard of mid-fourteenth century.
>
> In the middle of the 15th century Nayachandra Sūri rewrote this legend in his Hammīr Mahakavya. Though a Jain, he invoked the blessings of Hindu gods on this epic, because of its Hindu chivalric theme and because of its anti-Muslim content. The epic weaves in the heroic history of the Chauhans from Prithvi Raj to Hammīr, and has a section of Prithvi Raj's exploits. Rajput rajas gather in gloom round Prithvi Raj to tell him of Ghuri who is accused of burning Hindu cities and defiling Hindu women, and who is said to have been sent to this earth "for the extirpation of warrior caste." Then follows the legend of Prithvi Raj taking Muhammad bin Sam Ghuri a prisoner in Multan, presumably after his victory at Tara'in,

and later setting him free. Unable to defeat Prithvi Raj in open battle, the Ghuri invader has recourse to a ruse; he sends some Muslim minstrels in disguise in the Rajput army, who enchant the Rajput hero's horse Natyarambha with their music, and Prithvi Raj himself so enthralled with the dancing of his horse that he forgets to fight and is taken prisoner by the Muslims.

Another anti-Muslim hero in Nayachandra Sūri's epic is Viranarayana who turns down Jalal al-din Khaljīs offer of alliance, – alliance with the mlechchas would have been disgraceful betrayal of Rajput chivalry – as also does Vagbhata who seizes the throne of Malwa, and whose son Jaitra Siṃha has a beautiful queen Hira, Devi, who is at times "possessed with a desire to bathe herself in the blood of Muslims" during her pregnancy, "a desire which was often gratified by her husband." The child she gave birth to was the last great hero of the Rājpūt epic, Hammīr.

The Hammīr epic narrates the legendary story of ʿAlāʾ al-Dīn Khaljī's expeditions against Hammīr, the Raja of Ranthambore, who had ceased to pay tribute to the Muslim Sultan. Bhoja, a formerly vanquished foe of Hammīr takes refuge in ʿAlāʾ al-Dīn's court. The first Khaljī expedition led by the Sultan's brother Ulugh Khan wins an inconclusive victory because of the treachery of a Rajput noble, the second is defeated by the Rajputs, who also capture some Muslim women who are forced "to sell buttermilk in every town they pass through." Significantly, the Mongols are in alliance with Hammīr against the Khaljī Sultan, though Hindu chiefs all over India ally themselves with him against Hammīr. ʿAlāʾ al-Dīn offers three alternative terms for peace to Hammīr, to resume paying tribute, or to hand over the four Mongol chiefs who had taken refuge with him or to give his daughter to ʿAlāʾ al-Dīn in marriage. As Hammīr rejects all the three alternatives, ʿAlāʾ al-Dīn personally undertakes the siege of Ranthambore. One of ʿAlāʾ al-Dīn's (Hindu) archers kills by an arrow a Hindu courtesan Radha Devi defiantly dancing on the wall of the fort, but Hammīr gallantly forbids his archers to shoot at ʿAlāʾ al-Dīn when they have a chance. Finally ʿAlāʾ al-Dīn wins over Hammīr's minister Ratipāla, by permitting him to seduce his younger sister – humiliation of Muslim women being a recurring theme in the Hammīr cycle of epics. Ratipāla as well as Hammīr's wives urge bestowing the hand of Hammīr's daughter on ʿAlāʾ al-Dīn to put an end to the hostilities, and the girl herself requests her father to "cast her away like a piece of broken glass," but Hammīr regards giving his daughter away to an unclean mlechcha "as loathsome as prolonging existence by living on his own flesh." Hammīr's womenfolk, including his daughter, throw themselves into flames to escape dishonor at the hands of the Muslims, and Hammīr himself performing jawhar throws himself on the Muslim army, but "disdaining to fall with anything like life into the enemy's hands, he severed, with one last effort, his head from his body with his own hands."

Neither this, nor other legends about Hammīr have any sound historical foundation. Another equally fantastic Rajput heroic legend describes Muhammad bin Tughluq's defeat and imprisonment at the hands of Hammīr (Ahmed 1963, 473–474).

Again, Ahmed asserts that Nayachandra Sūri, the author of the *Hammīra-Mahākāvya*, includes Hindu deities in his composition because of its 'chivalric' theme but also because of its anti-Muslim sentiment. However, the inclusion of Hindu deities in the text also significantly in this and other texts relates to the overlaps and rivalries between Jaina and Hindu notions of ritual, divinity and salvation. Thus, for example, the Jaina author of the work entitled *Dvayśraya-mahākāvya*, Hemachandra,

> was challenged by the courtiers to worship the icon of Śiva. This he did with the appropriate rituals as prescribed in the *Śiva Purāna* to the astonishment of those assembled. After the consecration of the temple, Kumarapala dismissed the courtiers and the chief priest and, together with Hemachandra entered the sanctum. Here he asked Hemachandra who was the true deity to guide one to moksha [...] Hemachandra decided to use his spiritual powers to call upon the deity of the temple, Śiva, to manifest himself. With this is mind, he meditated and so powerful was his meditation that he was able to invoke Śiva. When Śiva appeared before the king as a resplendent ascetic [...] Kumarapala was so overwhelmed by this miracle that, instead of its strengthening his faith in Shaivism, he was converted to Jainism [...] The focus here is again on the superior power of Jainism. The Shaiva *acharya* would not have been able to perform the miracle and it required the power of the Jaina *acharya* to do so. And so great was the power of the Jaina *acharya* that he could even invoke Śiva (Thapar 2005, 110–111).

One detail in the *Hammīra-Mahākāvya* is, however, interesting and would seem to corroborate Ahmed's claim: the insistence of Hammīra's mother, Hira Devi, to be bathed in the blood of Śakas during her pregnancy.[87] The text goes on to state that Hira Devi's husband often fulfilled her macabre desire. Although this image could be taken to be symbolic rather than literal, representing a desire for revenge and the decimation of one's enemies, it is, of course, a violent image saturated with aggression that at the same time confers power on Hira Devi and her soon to be born son. The image also represents a foreshadowing concerning the kind of ruler Hammīra will be, namely, one who is likely to slaughter his enemies. Thus, as Romila Thapar (2005, 118) suggests, the *Hammīra-Mahākāvya* and other "epics of resistance" as Ahmed calls them do record "Some anti-Mus-

---

87 svakarāmbhojakīnāśadāsīkṛtaśakāsṛjā |
garbhānubhāvato rājapatnī sisnāsati sma sā ||
(*Hammīra-Mahākāvya* Sarga 4.141). "Vagbhata was succeeded by his son Jaitrasimh. His queen was named Hira Devi, who was very beautiful, and in every way qualified for her high position. In course of time Hira Devi was found to be with child. Her carvings in this condition presaged the proclivities and greatness of the burden she bore. At times she was possessed with a desire to bathe herself in the blood of the Muslims. Her husband satisfied her wishes, and at last, in an auspicious hour, she was delivered of a son ... The astrologers predicted, from the very favourable conjunction of the stars that presided over the child's nativity, that the prince would make the whole earth wet with the blood of the enemy of his country, the Muhammadans. Hammīra (for that was the name bestowed on the child) throve and grew up a strong and handsome boy. He easily mastered the sciences, and soon grew up an expert in the art of war. When he attained a proper age, his father had him married to seven beautiful wives" (Kirtane 1879, xxi).

lim sentiment [...] since the Turk was the enemy, but this does not annul the contrary sentiment of friendship with the Muslim, or indeed the loyalty of the Muslim to the Rajput where such loyalty is recorded and narrated."

The conflict between Hammīra and the Sultan of Delhi is, therefore, not solely one driven by defending the former's independence from 'Muslim dominance;' rather, it is propelled by other concerns such as those mentioned elsewhere regarding providing shelter to seekers of protection who themselves can be labelled as 'Muhammadan' or Mongol/Neo-Muslim. Kirtane, anticipating the kind of resistance marking a subaltern history further states: "Even the history of the conquered is not without interest. The man who fights against hope, – fights because he thinks it his duty to do so, – who scorns to bow his neck before the oppressor, because he thinks such a course opposed to the ways of his ancient house, deserves our sympathy and our admiration. Hammīra is such a character" (Kirtane 1879, iv). Kirtane thus sets up a binary and subsequently common contrast between 'tolerant,' 'open-minded' Hindu culture which is often equated with 'Indian' culture and the stereotypical view of a more 'bigoted,' 'intolerant' Islamic culture which sought to repress indigenous cultures while seeking to forcibly proselytize their populations. Hammīra is portrayed here as an 'underdog' in the larger constellation of the powers that existed during his reign, one who acquires the coveted and enduring status of a hero through his act of self-sacrifice but also observance to the moral code that defines, in a sense, the 'heroic age' that in turn defines not only a chronological space but also the regional and cultural space. The author in his capacity as a writer and poet thus occupies, according to Kirtane, a creative, 'liberal' space of cosmopolitanism in terms of the intermingling of ideas, narratives, languages and the like, whereas the protagonist of the text occupies or rather embodies and celebrates a nexus of values that underpins or perhaps even allows such admixtures, interchanges and hybrid cultural forms to flourish. It is the loyalty to a code of keeping one's word and providing sanctuary that ostensibly transcends religious and regional boundaries that in turn cultivates an ethos of 'equality' that is not biased toward ethnicity, 'caste' or 'religion.' This represents a form of universalism that engenders ethical behaviour that is sensitive to overarching human concerns such as the need for safety from perceived or real forms of injustice. These needs and the character of Hammīra as representing a warrior's quintessential response, it may be argued, are 'context free,' operating, so to speak, regardless of a person's inherited social, economic, or religious status and identity.[88]

---

88 See Bednar's (2007) important work on Rajput identity as a conglomeration of values that is not *varṇa* or ethnicity based.

Furthermore, as Romila Thapar (2005, 120) points out:

> Much space is given in the Hammira-Mahakavya to Hammira's conquests of neighbouring kingdoms and his plundering of many cities. As in the case of the Turko-Persian chronicles, battle, plunder and loot were the hallmarks of a heroic king in the literature of the courts. In the last third of the epic, his confrontations with Ala al-Din Khalji are narrated. This becomes a litany of the duplicity and disloyalty of fellow Rajputs, including his ministers and generals, some of whom joined Ala al-Din. A noticeable exception was his adviser, Mahimasahi, who was loyal to him till the last [...] Hammira had other Mudgal courtiers loyal to him and hostile to the Turks.

This scenario complicates the simplified notion that the political situation in the 15th century was one driven by notions and realities of 'religion' or even 'ethnicity,' not only because such categories and therefore their corresponding concreteness in the social world did not exist,[89] but also because the interrelationships on the ground were motivated by a range of other concerns determined by qualities such as loyalty, but also the desire to gain power and control in the territorial assertions of northern Indian kingdoms and principalities.

Kirtane adds that the poet, moreover, compares Hammīra with the great heroes who represent not only battle prowess but above all moral steadfastness at its pinnacle: Yuddhiṣṭhira and Rāma. But Kirtane water downs the comparison, which according to him, is no doubt a matter of "poetical exaggeration." But it

89 See Boyarin (2016). Boyarin argues for a non-essentialized understanding of the meaning of words based on their usage. He refers to Wittgenstein's ideas of language concerning the convergence of usage and meaning. For example, with regard to the 'word' Judaism – which raises similar questions as does the category or 'word' Hinduism, primarily a 19th-century colonial construction that assumes the 'unity' and historicity of the 'religion' called Hinduism – Boyarin asks:

"How does one show that a beloved term, such as 'Judaism' is an anachronism? First, obviously, by simply showing that word for it does not exist in several central Jewish languages. Notably, the argument that the very rare Second-Temple Judaeo-Greek word, *Ioudaismos* does not mean anything like later 'Judaism' has already been made. Second by arguing that without a word, it borders on the impossible to identify a concept. For this we need a bit of theory. Ludwig Wittgenstein wrote: 'Philosophy must not interfere in any way with the actual use of language, so it can in the end only describe it' (PI 124). In contrast to some Wittgenstein scholars, I take him at his word here. The project of the *Philosophical Investigations* is, I am convinced, to produce an actual description of language as a means of communication, nothing more, nothing less. Wittgenstein famously remarked: 'For a *large* class of cases – though not for all – in which we employ the word "meaning" it can be defined thus: the meaning of a word is its use in the language' (PI 43). This basic statement is what underlies the significance of Wittgenstein's contribution: a change from a conception of meaning as representation to a view which looks to use as the crux of the matter".

may well be pertinent to ask why the poet saw it fit to compare Hammīra with epic heroes that are paragons of righteousness and integrity, in some ways individuals who are beyond comparison. Is it a particular quality of Hammīra's that leads the poet to state this comparison? Or does the poet want to situate both his hero and his work in a larger framework of literary networks just as he attempts to compose a poem that is comparable to the poetry written during the 'classical' age of Sanskrit poetry? Similarly, it would be worthwhile asking whether the poet sought to portray a narrative of resistance against 'Mohammedan conquest,' perceived as a kind of Central Asian colonization prior to the British. Or was this a narrative of bravery, of fearlessness, and the ethics of honouring one's word? After all, the poet is a Jaina, under the patronage of a Tomara king – not even a Chauhan king, who would have perhaps had a vested interest in eulogizing an ancestor. Was there, in the midst of all the internecine struggles between Rajput clans, such a sense of nationalism as to warrant the composition of a work praising another clan? Would a Jaina poet feel so aligned to an apparent Hindu 'cause' that he would compose a poem out of such motivations? Or was it really the dream that drove him?

4.2 The Hammīr Rāso

The *Hammīr Rāso* is another text or rather poem written in Hindi concerning Hammīra, his life and deeds.[90] The *Hammīr Rāso*, or *Rāsa* as it also called,

90 What are the reasons for re-telling/re-composing the story of Hammīr at the beginning of the 18th century? What is the historical and social context that motivates the re-telling? Is the re-telling of the story an example of what Jan Assman calls "cultural memory" that is created through what he calls "figures of memory"? See Assman and Czaplicka (1995, 129–133): "cultural memory is characterized by its distance from the everyday. Distance from the everyday (transcendence) marks its temporal horizon. Cultural memory has its fixed point; its horizon does not change with the passing of time. These fixed points are fateful events of the past, whose memory is maintained through cultural formation (texts, rites, monuments) and institutional communication (recitation, practice, observance). We call these 'figures of memory.' The entire Jewish calendar is based on figures of memory. In the flow of everyday communications such festivals, rites, epics, poems, etc. form 'islands of time,' islands of a completely different temporality suspended from time. In cultural memory, such islands of time expand into memory spaces of 'retrospective contemplativeness' [retrospective Besonnenheit] ... In cultural formation, a collective experience crystallizes, whose meaning, when touched upon, may suddenly become accessible across millennia ... The concept of cultural memory comprises that body of reusable texts, images, and rituals specific to each society in each epoch, whose 'cultivation' serves to stabilize and convey that society's self-image ... The content of such knowledge varies from culture to culture as well as from epoch to epoch. The manner of its organization, its media, and its institu-

was composed by the court poet Jodharāj in 1701 CE. Jodharāj composed the poem, much like Nayachandra Sūri, on the behest of the ruler to whose court he belonged. Similar to the *Hammīra-Mahākāvya*, the *Hammīr Rāso* also contains a brief autobiographical section that makes both these works important as self-descriptive or even self-reflective exercises in composition. The *Hammīr Rāso* begins with 'author's preface' that outlines the social context and genealogy of the poet Jodharāj.[91] The poet states that he belongs to "Gaur Brahmans" who are descended from the Ṛṣi Attreya and born in Bijawar in the province of Rat. He states his father's name as Balakrishna, and also that he (Jodharāj) is an accomplished astronomer and astrologer besides being a pandit and a poet. It is because of these qualities and accomplishments that the ruler of the royal court, Raja Chandrabhan, has gifted him with property, clothes, wealth, horses, houses and so on while requesting him to write an account of the battles fought between 'Alā' al-Dīn Khaljī and Hammīra. Raja Chandrabhan is himself a descendant of the great Rajput and Chauhan warrior Pṛthvīrāj. Raja Chandrabhan reigns in the town called Nimrana that lies in the district of Alwar in Rajasthan. The king's "name," according to the poet, itself "is religion" (*dharma?*). His kingdom is one marked by the well-being and prosperity of his subjects who consist of all four castes. The king having inherited all the heroic qualities and virtues of his noble ancestors expresses a passionate interest in the deeds of Hammīra, and requests Jodharāj to write a *history* of the Rajput hero.

The opening chapter of the poem begins with a series of well-known events leading to the origin of four central Rajput clans, particularly the Chauhans, from the Vedic ritual fire pit (*agni-kula*). The story which is embedded in *puranic* narratives, describes the slaughter and massacre of 21 generations of *kṣatriyas* by Paraśurāma who takes revenge on the warrior caste after his father has been murdered by a *kṣatriya* king. It is only after there is no one to protect the sages and priests from marauding and destroying demons (*asuras, rākṣasas*) that the four clans unexpectedly arise from the fire pit of a ritual that a large group of sages including Gautama, Lomaharśana, Bhṛgu, Atteriya, Bharadvāj, Garg and Vasiṣṭha are performing while chanting hymns from Sāma Veda.[92]

tions, are also highly variable ... One society bases its self-image on a canon of sacred scripture, the next on a basic set of ritual activities, and the third on a fixed and hieratic language of forms in a canon of architectural and artistic types ... Through its cultural heritage a society becomes visible to itself and to others."

91 The following excerpts from this work are derived from Brajnath Bandyapadhyaya's (1879) translation of the *Hammīra Rāsa*.

92 The Sāma Veda is the 'Veda of songs' or the 'Veda of chants and melodies.' It consists of 1549 verses the majority of which are from the Ṛg Veda. It dates back to c. 1200 – 1000 BCE.

The warrior after whom the Chauhan clan of Rajputs was named had four arms, each carrying a weapon (sword, dagger, knife and bow). He was blessed by Śakti, the Goddess who carried ten weapons in her ten hands and rode on a lion. Brahmā instructs the warrior to brave "all dangers for the cause of your religion."[93] As the warrior fights the demons he continues to seek the blessings of the Goddess who subsequently becomes the clan goddess or *kuladevī* of the Chauhans and is named Asapurī.[94] The text goes on to state how after many generations a Chauhan ruler named Raja Jeyat Chohan (*sic*) was born in the village of Barbagao. It is Jeyat Chohan who establishes the fortress of Ranthambore over which Hammīra later rules. The story of the founding of the fortress deserves attention, and is as follows:

> Once the Rao was out in a forest on hunting-excursion, accompanied by all the skilful huntsmen in his territories. He saw a white boar and pursued it very closely. It ran into a dense jungle, which was full of windings. He was separated from his train. The figure of an ascetic met his view. Rishi Padam, the best of all sages, sat there, engaged in deep contemplation. The prince left off chasing after the game. He fell prostrate before the sage, joined his hands and thus began to pray: "I am very fortunate, that I am able to see thee [...] Protect me, bless me [...] I bow down before thee [...] Place thy hand on my head, O lord! And bless me!" The sage was greatly pleased with the Rao's prayers. He blessed him. "Build a fort yonder on the hill, my son," said he, "dwell there and worship Śiva."
>
> When Raja Jeyat returned to his capital, he called a council of his ministers and vassals and consulted all the learned astrologers of his court. A lucky hour was fixed to lay the foundation-stone of a town and that of its fort [...]
>
> The newly built town of the Rao was full of temples and squares. It resembled Amaravati, the city of Indra. The temples were very beautiful. Lofty, and decorated with screens of lattice work [...] Perfumes of various kinds filled the air with fragrance. All the four castes and Asramas lived there in happiness, each following its own profession. The people were all of a forgiving nature, kind charitable and hospitable to strangers. The splendid town was named Ranthambor.
>
> All the Bhils, inhabiting the mountain fastness, readily acknowledged the power of the Rao and recognized in him their sovereign [...]

---

93 Presumably the translator is using the word and category of 'religion' for the Hindi/Sanskrit term '*dharma*.' The translation of *dharma* into religion represents and interesting and longstanding conundrum regarding the existence of an Indic category that distinctly means 'religion' with its particular connotations derived from European linguistic and theological usages. See Boyarin (2016).

94 Interestingly the Chauhan warrior is called 'the Hindu champion' in the text accompanying his birth and bloody defeat of demons.

> A very curious story is told of the erection of the fort. The wall of the portico fell down as often as it was raised. The Raja was struck with wonder and was extremely anxious to find out the cause of this mysterious occurrence. At last, finding all resources fail, he summoned up all his courage, and said – "Let me die, for my death alone can give stability to the wall." He seated himself at the foundation, ready to carry out his desperate resolution, when Ravana and Basava, two warlike and loyal Bhils exclaimed – "Rao Jeyat, the fort is emphatically ours, although you have nominal title to it. You are but our guest. The fort is emphatically ours. It behoves you, therefore, to cut off our heads and raise the wall upon them." Ravana said, "Only look after my son Bhoj." The brave Bhils were beheaded, their heads placed as foundation-stones, and the wall built thereon became as firm and lasting as a rock. [...] It stands to this day in all its majesty, a monument of the martial tact and skill of the ancient Rajputs.

> The austere penances of the Sage Padam greatly frightened Indra. His throne shook. In fear he sent Cupid to allure the sage [...] The apsaras danced, and Kinnaras sang [...] The forest became full of flowers and bees, cuckoos and peacocks [...] But the soul of the sage could not be moved [...] it remained firm as a rock [...] Spring failed [...] Summer failed [...] The rainy season failed [...] Then came with fury the severe winter [...] Then came with pride the season of dew and bowed before Cupid [...] He [Padam] saw the nymph and became greatly delighted [...] and felt a fever of love [...] but the nymph vanished, triumphant at her success. Stung by separation he breathed his last in the month of Magh in Samvat 1140, the moon being in the sign of Adra.

> *The body of Ala-uddin was made of his head, that of Hamir of his breast, and those of Muhammad Shah and Mir Gabru of his hands.*[95]

4.3 The Enchanted Forest

These passages are important for a variety of reasons which are not limited to their outlining the origin of the fortress called Ranthambore which is Hammīra's city and also the location of the unfolding of the series of events that the work written by Jodharāj, but also the composition by Nayachandra Sūri and others describe. The origin story is embedded in a recurrent motif or theme involving a king on a hunt who gets lost in a dense forest after detaching himself from his hunting entourage. As the king penetrates the middle of forest he usually arrives at a kind of clearing[96] represented either by a source of water – a pond, waterfall or lake – or as is the case in this story, the hermitage of a sage from whom he goes to receives blessings in one form or another. The encounter in the clearing in the middle of the forest is usually revelatory or transformational, leading

95 Emphasis added.

96 See also Chapter 6 for Heidegger's notion of 'clearing' or 'Lichtung' as a space that "encircles all that is."

the king to become the architect of a historic and profound destiny. The moment of being lost and alone, and being separated from his royal accoutrements, bereft of the signs and symbols of authority and status, results in a deep regenerative and creative turn that the king experiences in the presence of a sacred or holy object or person. In a sense, the relatively brief sojourn in the forest represents a substantive shift in which the king *becomes* who he is supposed to be; it is a revealing of the king's purpose. The introductory story involving the king and the sage deep in the forest is mythical in nature, set in archetypical images that are suggestive of personal exile, strangeness, aloneness, the magical, unexpected qualities of the forest – of a location distant from human habitation and work – and the figure of the hermit, sage, ascetic and man living in the wilderness who gains extraordinary abilities from this self-imposed remoteness in which aloneness and the lack of worldly authority, wealth and status become a source of power.

The story is not dissimilar to the German fairy tale of Eisenhans, or Iron John, in which a king's huntsmen enter a forest adjacent to the castle never to return. The huntsmen are pulled into a pond in the middle of the forest by a strong arm that emerges from the pond. It is only much later that a particular hunter with a dog approaches the lake into which his dog has disappeared and has the pond drained only to find a large, strong, bearded man with rust coloured skin lying at its bottom. The man is taken prisoner and held in a cage with strict orders from the king never to let him out of the cage. This lasts until the king's young son, who is eight years old, loses a ball that he is playing with as it rolls into the cage. The 'iron man' promises to return the ball on the condition that the young prince open the cage and let him free, stating that the key to the cage must be 'stolen' from underneath the pillow of the boy's mother, the queen. The boy extracts the key from under his mother's pillow and opens the cage, whereupon the 'iron man' carries off the prince back into the deep woods. A series of events follows including one which entails the second banishment, so to speak, of the young boy, this time from the woods for having broken strict rules laid down by the 'iron man' concerning dropping objects into the pond. The boy's 'banishment' from the woods involves him living in poverty in a distant land in which no one knows of his true identity. However, after many twists and turns the boy, having now turned into manhood through acts of bravery and courage, and after being wed with a princess, returns to his parental home together with Iron John who relinquishes his rough, iron or rust coloured exterior. As it turns out, this exterior was the result of a curse to become a great king with an entourage, which together with his kingdom he then bequeaths to the young prince.[97]

This story is closely replicated by a story concerning the existence of the alchemist's or philosopher's stone in the possession of the kingdom of Hammīra. The philosopher's stone – which turns ordinary metal into gold – is also cited as one of the main reasons for ʿAlāʾ al-Dīn's interest in occupying the fortress – a desire that is repeated by future rulers, including supposedly the former prime minister of India, Indira Gandhi.[98]

> In Hammeer's father, Raja Jaitra Singh's time, there were two bandits[99] called "Ivan" and "Bhuvan". One day, they decided to attack the fort of Ranthambore. On their way to the fort, they saw a crying pig. Ivan shot the pig with an arrow. The pig ran with the arrow in it, and Ivan followed it. At a distance from the original spot, he discovered the pig was dead. He lit some fire with firestones and began to skin the pig. After he was done, he put that bloody knife in a pond nearby (Padmala pond). Fortunately, that pond had the alchemist's stone, which turned the knife into gold. To test it again, Ivan immersed another knife into the pond, which turned gold as well. Then in the interest of the state, they gifted the stone to the king. The king ordered for 400 kg of iron to test the truth behind the stone. All the iron immediately turned into gold (Anver 2018, 79).

Similar stories are found in the rediscovery of the pilgrimage of Pushkar in Rajasthan and in the birth story of Goludev, the God of Justice in the Central Himalayan region of Kumaon. In the oral story relating the rediscovery of the pilgrimage site of Pushkar which had its origins in the *satya yuga* but was now in the *kali yuga* forgotten and had been overgrown by a dense forest, a king with a mighty entourage sets off on a hunt to chase down a spectacular boar. The boar enters the forest, drawing in the king into the dense woods. The king pursues the boar deeper and deeper into the woods, leaving behind his tired and lost entourage. Finally, the king himself seems to be lost when he sees the boar stop at a waterhole in the distance. The king follows the boar to waterhole but by this time the boar has run further and disappeared into the adjacent hills. The king who is tired, but also suffering from leprosy or a rare skin ailment alights form his horse to drink from the waterhole. As he drinks the water and washes his face and hands, he discovers that his has been healed of his disease. In that moment he realizes that the boar has been none other than Lord Viṣṇu himself and that the waterhole is the sacred water of Pushkar which in a bygone

97 See Grimm (1994, 230–231, 496–497) and Bly (2004).
98 See Appendix 2, Conversation 1.
99 The two bandits with rhyming names suggesting twins or brothers is a variant on the motif of the two brothers who are princes that are supposed to have discovered the hill upon which the fort is built.

age existed in the form of a beautiful, large lake. Transformed by this insight and out of deep gratitude for his own healing, the king orders that the forest be cleared, the waterhole dug out to the size of a lake again, and bathing steps and temples be built along its banks. The Pushkar forest or *āraṇya* is thereby transformed into the Pushkar region, settlement or *kṣetra*.[100] The king, not unlike the young prince who is kept by Iron John in the middle of forest at the edge of magical pond, also experiences being cut off and detached from his entourage while dwelling for a period of time in the wilderness of a dense forest in which there is a waterhole which unexpectedly contains miraculous healing properties. The king's point of entry into the wilderness is provided by the hunt for a wild animal with a somewhat rough, coarse but also fierce and strong appearance. The wild boar with its many layers of symbolic meaning connecting it to royalty, martial strength and fertility is, in this case, also a symbol of Lord Viṣṇu who incarnates himself in one instance to retrieve and save the Earth from destruction as a mighty boar (Sanskrit: *varāha*). The king is drawn into the forest by this symbol of strength but also divinity that leads to his own healing and ultimately to the re-establishment of the sacred centre in the current age of the *kali yuga*. The story is thus replete with images of abandonment, exile and forgetting,[101] and periodic contraction and expansion leading to regeneration and recreation for both the king and the pilgrimage place.[102] In the story of King Goludev, the God of Justice, Goludev's father, King Jhal Rai, enters a dense forest after leaving behind his train. Lost and thirsty he arrives at the hermitage of a sage who has adopted a young girl (now a young woman). The king requests the young woman to allow him to drink from a spring in the hermitage. He also witnesses how the young woman separates two oxen that have been locking horns with her own hands with great ease. Impressed by her strength and beauty, the king asks for her hand from the sage.[103] The king marries the young woman, whose name is Kalnar or Kalinga, and she becomes his eighth wife, and subsequently gives birth to the king's only progeny, Goludev. The following passages contain section from the oral narrative that is performed during a ritual called '*jāgar*' in which the deity is invoked and speaks through the body of a designated person:

100 See Sontheimer (1987, 117–164).

101 See Shulman's (1998) splendid essay on memory, forgetting and rediscovery in the great Sanskrit poet Kalidāsa's play, the *Abhijñaśākuntalā*.

102 See Malik (1994).

103 These details diverge slightly from the passage presented below, but are still very much part of the narrative that is told both orally and locally printed chapbooks concerning the birth, life and deeds of King Goludev.

> First there was King Kansrai, then King Hansrai, King Halrai, King Tilrai, then came King Jhalurai, who had a seraglio for his queens, and a kingdom that ran on magic (*chal-bal*). He had seven queens, but none bore even one child. Then King Jhalurai visited his Guru. Then his Guru began telling him how he was destined for an eighth marriage, only then would he have a child. The king was very old. Then the king departed and went into the jungle for a hunt. There were ministers and prime ministers with him. They kept going and going and reached Kunkhet. Then the king became distraught with thirst, he began saying: "I'll rest here, you go and find water, otherwise I'll die of thirst!" The ministers and prime ministers went looking for water. They reached Hariyayi Fortress where two streams of water ran. King Jalandhar's daughter sat in deep piety. The ministers and prime ministers who thought carefully looked over the place and quickly returned to the king. They took the king to the two streams. Then the young girl began asking: "Who are you? Drink some water!" Seeing the young woman, the king forgot about his thirst: "Give me your word first, then I'll drink water, otherwise you will receive the curse of my death!" The young woman said: "Ask whatever you want, you have my word!"
>
> The young woman gave her word to the king. Then the king began saying: "I have seven queens in my home, but I have no children. I am the king of Fortress Champavat. I will marry you!" Then the young woman began saying: "I gave you my word, you can marry me!" Then the king took the young woman, Kalnar, with him and arrived at Champavat. Preparations for the wedding were begun, invitations were sent out to everyone in the township, and the township was decorated. The seven queens heard the news. They began talking amongst themselves: "If the king marries, and if she has a child, he won't care for us anymore! He'll only love that queen!" Then they said: "Sisters, sisters, at the time of the wedding, let's bless her to remain barren!" Then the wedding began. The queens gave their blessings that she would have no children. Then the eight queens retired to the three-storied palace. The king sat on his throne. Slowly, over time, Queen Kalnar became pregnant.[104]

Again, the story of Goludev's origin and birth lies – like the other stories concerning Iron John, the re-establishment of Pushkar and, most importantly for this book, the establishment of the fortress of Ranthambore, the capital of Hammīra – in a king or royal figure loosing his way in the wilderness of a forest and encountering a magical body of water and/or the figure of a solitary, hermit-like man endowed with supernatural abilities.

4.4 Sacrificial Foundations

The story concerning the establishment of Ranthambore contains further details that are worthy of mention and analysis. The first detail involves the period when the fortress is being built. A wall of the portico falls down every time it is (re)

---

104 See Malik (2016/2018, 35–62).

built. The king is puzzled and anxious about this occurrence for which there seems to be no solution. In a final decision the king resolves to drastically intervene by sacrificing himself at the base of the wall in the belief that this radical act would bring an end to the inexplicable collapse of the wall. However, before he can undertake this self-sacrificial act, two members of the Bhīl community who live in the region, and who have presumably also occupied it before the establishment of Rajput lineages confront him. Prior to this encounter the text mentions that the Bhīl communities had acknowledged the Rajput king's authority and sovereignty.[105] The two individuals from the Bhīl community are named Ravana and Basava. The names are interesting in themselves. Ravana, who is usually considered the villain in the more universally read and recited tellings of the Ramayana in Sanskrit and Hindi, is in the Bhīl Ramayana a hero worthy of the name. Basava or Vasava could refer to a member of one of the subgroups of Bhīl called Vasava or Vasave. Ravana and Basava stop the king from slaying himself stating that:

> "Rao Jeyat, the fort is emphatically ours, although you have nominal title to it. You are but our guest. The fort is emphatically ours. It behoves you, therefore, to cut off our heads and raise the wall upon them." Ravana said, "Only look after my son Bhoj." The brave Bhils were beheaded, their heads placed as foundation-stones, and the wall built thereon became as firm and lasting as a rock.

The Bhīls claim that the fortress in truth belongs to them and their community and not to the Rajput king who is but their guest. The king's jurisdiction over the fortress is nominal being granted to him only by the Bhīls who have historically both occupied and held political control of this and other regions in Rajasthan, Gujarat and Maharashtra prior to the intrusions of both Rajput and Mongol/Turk rulers who pushed back the original inhabitants into the peripheral regions of forests and hills. The Bhīls demand that their and not the king's life be offered up in order to secure the foundation of the fortress. The foundation of the fortress therefore rests on the violent yet voluntary self-sacrificial deed of two Bhīl individuals who through this act also lay claim to the ownership and subsequent history of the fortification.

The above lines of narration suggesting that so-called tribal communities such as the Bhīls were instrumental in the foundation of the fortress emerges in different conversations conducted at the fortress in 2009 and 2018. The first conversation is with someone who currently works as a tour guide for the heri-

---

105 On the Bhīl community, and its relationship to Rajput clans, as well as for details on the Bhīl Ramayana, see Deliege (1985), Doshi (1978), Hardiman (1987), Harlan (1992), Mayaram (2003), Roche (2001) and Satchidanandan (2018).

tage site of the fortress. The story presented by the guide pushes back the establishment of the fortress to many centuries before the reign of Hammīra while at the same time bringing in an element of ambiguity and uncertainty about its origins. The second conversation, which took place with a resident of a nearby village who had also worked as a tour guide many years before, substantiates the view presented in the first conversation that no one knows when or by whom the fortress was built, thus leaving the historically decisive question of a chronologically certain or fixed 'origin' in abeyance. *No one knows who made it and when it was made.* This is a remarkable claim. The fortress knows no authorship. Perhaps it just appeared or manifested on the hillside through a series of quasi-magical, superhuman events that took place in a mythical time before the coming into the existence of a conspicuously concrete historical time. However, the uncertainty surrounding the origins of the fortress, rather than diminishing its worth, serves to raise – as a further conversation presented below shows – its special, sacred, auspicious character.

First conversation:

Guide 1: Sages used to meditate here ... right on this hill. Two princes came by here while they were playing and so they met the sages. After speaking to the sages they realized [that the hills were special]. Otherwise they never knew that hills like these existed. They had not travelled around much. So they did not know about these hills. So the sages told them that there are such hills and that there are no other hills anywhere else. They told them everything. Ever since then the princes started thinking about constructing the fort here. It began from there.

Questioner: Who were these princes of the past ... was it not Hammīra [who built the fortress]?

G1: No, no ... this was far, far earlier. This incident took place before the 5th century. The princes' names aren't mentioned. It just says two princes. It's from here that we believe – they didn't construct it – but that is from here where it all started. The princes spoke about this and later on discussions continued. Kings discussed it and later on the foundation of the fortress was laid. Its foundation is believed to have been laid by Maharaj Jayant. But it is also believed that in 944 CE Sabalak Chauhan laid the foundation, and in addition to these [kings], there were tribals and amongst them was King Hadda. [According to some] it was under his rule that this fort was constructed by tribals. This is mentioned in historical texts. According to the Archaeological Survey, it was constructed in 5th century by King Jayant, but before this even the Archaeological Survey put up a board here stating that Sabalak Chauhan laid the foundation of Ranthambore Fort in 944 CE. But three/four years ago they claimed that the fort was established in the 5th century.

Q: So it's much older? Who were these tribals? Were they people of the Bhīl community?

G1: Bhīl-Mina.[106] Bhīl ... it was the Bhīl tribe. So the king belonged to the Mina community. He was the king, so under his command, this was constructed. He was a Mina king, and under his supervision, the tribals constructed this fort. The people were tribals, this fort has been constructed by them. This is one of the explanations. The other one I told you is of Sabalak Chauhan who constructed it in 944 CE. Now since the past three years, the Archaeological Survey has attributed it to the 5th century. Just three years ago the same people used to attribute it to Sabalak Chauhan in 944 CE, that Sabalak Chauhan had laid the foundation of the Ranthambore fort in 944 CE. Later on when this was surveyed then they must have found something else so they now say this is to be associated with the King Jayant from the 5th century. So there are three views regarding [the construction of the fort]. It's not clear even today who constructed it and when it was constructed.[107]

Second conversation:

Guide 2: There is no history whatsoever of this fort as to which king made it or not.

Questioner: Really? There is no such history?

G2: There is no history of its construction. There is no history regarding who constructed it until this date.

Q: Is there no information on when and why the settlement was done here?

G2: This place was meant for getting ready for war and to attack. This was the place where the preparation for winning [wars] was made. Many [rulers] including Akbar, Humayun, Aurangzeb, King Hammīr, 'Alā' al-Dīn Khaljī, Babar came here. People used to construct many houses here. But when 'Alā' al-Dīn Khaljī ruled, he destroyed [instead of building]. Now there is not even a single house left. Everything has turned into ruins. Even today, though, there are trees and herbs on top of the fortress that are useful. For example, there is a tree called *athsote*[108] that is used to make gunpowder.[109]

4.5 The Sage's Body

In the *Hammīr Rāso* the Sage Padam is not only connected to the establishment of the fortress but significantly, as mentioned above, his death also results in the creation of four central characters of the historical narrative through different parts of his body. The Sage Padam remains steadfast for several consecutive seasons against the sensual temptation presented in the form of 'celestial nymphs,' particularly a nymph called Urvashi who has been sent by the king of the gods, Indra, in classic manner after perceiving the accumulation of tremendous ascetic

106 See Mayaram (2003).
107 See Appendix 2, Conversation 1 for a full transcript.
108 Unknown name of a plant.
109 See Appendix 2, Conversation 3 for a complete transcript.

heat (Sanskrit: *tap*) by the sage as a threat to his position and to the stability of the world, to seduce the sage and thereby destroy his meditative state. Urvashi manages after a lengthy period of time to draw out the sage's attention to her and seduce him. Once the sage realizes that he has destroyed his own inner resolve by being attracted to Urvashi, he relinquishes his physical body out of disappointment. The text goes on to state that: "The body of Ala-uddin was made of his head, that of Hamir of his breast, and those of Muhammad Shah and Mir Gabru of his hands." In other words, the principal characters of the narrative and of the historical account portrayed in this work and in other works such as the *Hammīra-Mahākāvya* are in fact intimately conjoined through the body of the sage out which they arise. The symbolism of both ʿAlāʾ al-Dīn and Hammīra as well as the rebel general Muhammed Shāh and his brother Mir Gabru[110] being born or having their origin in the same body is one that indicates profound belonging through the image of organic unity. The image is reminiscent of the idea of the cosmic man, Puruṣa, through whom various regions of space and social body emerge subsequent to him being sacrificed by the gods. The sage's body dies to its identity as the Sage Padam from which, however, the historical figures of Mongol/Turk and Rajput leaders and rulers emerge. The emergence of each individual from different parts of the sage's body – ʿAlāʾ al-Dīn from his head, Hammīra from his breast or torso, and the former's general Muhammed Shāh and his brother, Mir Gabru, from his hands or arms – may also indicate a hierarchy of importance and sovereign strength with the head representing the most significant part of the human body, while the torso and hands or arms represent physical strength, bravery and warrior-like qualities. The imagery is, however, deeply powerful in that it does not indicate separation or conflict, rather unity and a common source of origin – almost like referring to children of the same parent. This idea in itself emphatically counters the notion of an essentialized, historically 'true' 'Hindu–Muslim' enmity based on religious grounds, although a conflict does develop between ʿAlāʾ al-Dīn and Hammīra in a subsequent time, this clash can, on the basis of this 'origin story,' just as well be legitimately viewed as a confrontation between family members related through close kinship ties.

According to the *Hammīr Rāso* and following the embedding of the story of the sage's body and the emergence of the narratives main characters from parts of his body, ʿAlāʾ al-Dīn and Hammīra are born as contemporaries. While Hammīra's birth is marked by auspicious signs and rejoicing, the sultan's birth is overshadowed by dark, mythical circumstances – his mother abandons him

110 *Gabru* is a Punjabi and Hindi word for boy or youth.

at birth because of his "ugly" appearance while replacing him with another infant who is "handsome." The child, who is to become a mighty ruler, is brought up by humble parents, who also give him the name by which he will be later remembered. What is interesting is the fact that although the boy does not know of his true identity and destiny, he exhibits the characteristics of a king while at play. The child who had replaced him and lives in the royal palace, on the other hand, plays at being a person belonging to his father's profession:

> The great Ala-uddin was born a contemporary of Hamir. It is said that the princess, his mother, seeing the newly born very ugly and ill-shaped, commanded a nurse to carry it away and replace it by a child of handsome appearance. The nurse obeyed her orders, and thus was the boy, who was to be an emperor, brought up in the nursery of a carder. His foster father called him Ala-uddin. In the days of his boyhood he would sometimes play at king, making of his playmates, one the vizier, another the Bakshi, a third the attendant. He would dismiss some and appoint others. While in the king's palace, the son of the carder would play at his father's profession (Bandyapadhyaya 1879, 192).

ʿAlāʾ al-Dīn's true identity is revealed through a peculiar sequence of events that are set in motion by a supposedly "Buddhist sect" called Sharaoji whose temple is located ten miles north of Delhi. The translator of the *Hammīr Rāso* states that the name of the "principal *tīrthaṅkar*," is Parasnāth who "appeared" and blessed a widow who had been visiting the temple everyday with two sons who would be born "immaculately."[111] It is the two sons of the widow who once they are grown-up subsequently inform the child-to-be-emperor of his destiny. Some sections of this part of the story are presented here:

> Ten miles to the north of Dehli (*sic*) there was a temple of the Sharaoji sect of Buddhist. A widow, daughter of a merchant, used to visit it ever[y] day. Once, Parasnath, the principal tīrthaṅkar, appeared and in heavenly accents said – "Daughter, I am pleased with thy vows; blest be thou with the enjoyment of two sons."
>
> The woman replied – "Lord, I am but a poor widow, and therefore if I should be brought to bed of a child, it would bring a stain upon my name and that of my family."
>
> The heavens opened and the following words were heard. "None shall be able to perceive thy womb. Thou shalt be delivered of twins at the time thou dost please to appoint. They will be very rich, and their names will spread far and wide."
>
> [...]

111 It is actually the 24 Jaina saints who are called *tīrthaṅkaras*. Parasnāth or Parśvanāth is one of the main Jaina saints who immediately preceded Mahāvīra who is usually considered to be the founder of Jainism. The use of the word 'appeared' suggests that Parasnāth manifested in front of the widow (even though he does not have any physical existence) as deities in Hindu devotional narratives often do for particularly staunch devotees.

> The widow [...] fell on her knees and prayed to Parasnath, when lo! By the command of the god she gave birth to twins of very handsome appearance. One of them was named Basant Pal, and the other Tej Pal. Accidentally the mother found a very large pan of gold and diamonds buried under ground. Fortune smiled on her from that moment [...]
>
> When the twin brothers grew up to boyhood, they insisted upon their mother telling them, although she was very loth to do so, where their father was. As soon as they had the knowledge of their miraculous birth, they thought themselves to be the favourites of fortune and set about their business with redoubled energy. On attaining majority they, with all their treasure and establishment, removed to Delhi [...] at a meeting of that sect [Sharaojis] on Grinar [Girnar] [...] it was proposed to build two temples on that memorable spot.
>
> A few days after returning to Delhi, the merchants called a pandit to search for a lucky hour in which to lay the foundation-stones of the temples. The pandit replied, "I shall tell you the time, but it is no use your building the temples, because an emperor has been born who, it is predicted, will pull down all sacred edifices to the dust." "Where lives such an emperor?" "In a carder's house, playing in the dirt," [...] They filled two silver plates with mohars and, placing two diamonds on them, presented them to Ala-uddin at the playground. Thereupon the boy said – "See, Sirs I am but a poor carder. I need not such valuables. Pray, take these to the prince in the royal palace." The merchants replied: "You are our prince, the sole master of our lives and property." Ala-uddin looked pleased.
>
> [...]
>
> *Ala-uddin.* – "Merchants, what do you want done?"
>
> *Merchants.* – "We beseech your Royal Highness to give us permission to build two temples."
>
> *Ala-uddin.* – "Never can I grant such an unreasonable request. I have a made a point in my life to pull down all temples to the dust. The gods have unjustly cursed me by throwing me into such a miserable state, and I will drain the last drop of my blood in wreaking vengeance on them. But as you have done me an honour and made me aware of what I shall be, I feel bound to make an exception in your case [...] when I shall set out on a crusade against gods and their holy buildings."
>
> [...] On hearing this news the emperor had Ala-uddin brought to the palace, while the boy who had been brought up there was sent to the carder's hovel (Bandyapadhyaya 1879, 192–194).

These sections of the story, as mentioned earlier, are important and interesting in that they lay out the manner in which ʿAlāʾ al-Dīn's destiny is set to unfold. The connection with the twin brothers, born miraculously out of the blessing of a Buddhist or rather Jaina saint given to a widow, seems strange at this juncture. But together with ʿAlāʾ al-Dīn's 'emergence' from the sage's head and his abandonment at birth, the encounter with the immaculately born merchant twins accentuates the peculiar, mythical circumstances of ʿAlāʾ al-Dīn's birth and providence as an emperor. His childhood is fraught with injustice and poverty, but also pronouncements of thrift and asceticism, for example, when he rejects the offer of silver plates filled with gold coins and diamonds that he then goes on to distribute amongst his poor playmates. The passage also expresses an intimate link that he has, at least at this point, to merchants and traders belonging to the Jaina community. However, even more significant is his promise to destroy all temples.[112] It is crucial to note here that the reason for his vengeful feelings toward places of worship is not religiously driven in the sense of being directed at any particular community, such as Hindus, who may have wronged him, but stems out the injustice he has been subjected to by "the gods (who) have unjustly cursed me by throwing me into such a miserable state" His anger is directed at the non-human, divine 'agents,' so to speak, of his fate rather than at societal, human representatives of a religious or political ideology.

The text goes on to describe how ʿAlāʾ al-Dīn ascends the throne a year after he is married to a princess from Kandahar, and then besieges and captures eighty-four forts, presumably referring to his conquests of several kingdoms across the breadth of northern, central and southern India.[113] Following this brief reference to the emperor's marriage and military conquest are important passages that describe the events leading up to ʿAlāʾ al-Dīn's general, Muhammed Shāh, being exiled from the kingdom, triggering a sequence of events that culminates in the general being granted refuge in the fortress of Ranthambore by Hammīra, an act which ultimately results in the siege of the bastion by the emperor. The reason for Muhammed Shāh's exile is a romantic encounter[114] that he has with the emperor's queen during a royal hunt in which the emperor and his vast entourage are driven deeper and deeper into a dark, foreboding forest. Upon discovering their affair, the emperor chooses not to execute the general fearing that his queen would commit suicide out of sorrow. Instead he banishes the general with the threat of destroying anyone who dares to provide the general with protection. The general, rather than being fearful and submissive, is defiant stating that he will find refuge with someone who will challenge the emperor's might, and that he himself will never return to Delhi but will meet the emperor on the battlefield. After informing his brother Mir Gabru that he will be departing forever from his home in Delhi, Muhammed Shāh together with family, soldiers, servants, slaves, elephants and carriages set out to find a court that would offer him refuge. However, despite travelling great distances and visiting courts "of almost all the princes, both Hindu and Musalman," he

112 Since he does not specify any particular religion, by "temple" he presumably means all places of worship.

113 The sultan also lays siege of the famous Kākaṭīya fortress of Warangal in southern India.

114 This detail is also mentioned in one of the conversations I had during fieldwork at Ranthambore. See Appendix 2, Conversation 1.

was not granted asylum because of the reputation and might of ʿAlā᾽ al-Dīn. As a last resort he decided to visit the '*durbar*' of Hammīra who as it turned out offered him a warm welcome and refuge in the fortress:

> The heralds [of Muhammed Shāh] met with a warm reception. They informed the Rao of all things as they happened. The latter asked, "Is the Sheikh safe, is he well?" He was delighted and sent his son to call the exile to the fort.
>
> Muhammad Shah [...] took with him five horses, one elephant, one bow of Multan, made of nice pieces of buffalo horn, a sharp sword, a beautiful palanquin, two pieces of ruby, a necklace of pearls, two hawks and two hunting dogs [...] The Sheikh touched the Rao's feet with both his hands and stood up having joined them in submission. After having offered him the costly presents, he said, "Grant me shelter, generous Rao, shelter me in my distress. I have gone to the courts of the kings of Kandesh, Kabul, Multan, Kashmir, Guzerat, Gandwana and Bengal, but none has dared to receive me [...]"
>
> Hamir replied, smiling, "So powerful is Ala-uddin that none has ventured to shelter you from his anger. Live here safe, Sheikh, live here within the fort, under the shadow of my protection. I, Rao Hamir, will defend you, even if defending you should cost me my life. Need I tell you more?" (Bandyapadhyaya 1879, 197).

Chapter 5
The Poet's Dream

5.1 Simulated Worlds

> *I am most surprised by those moments when I have felt as if the sentences, dreams, and pages that have made me so ecstatically happy have not come from my own imagination – that another power has found them and generously presented them to me.*
>
> Orhan Pamuk (2006)

> Shri Nayendu[115] rules like a penetrating beam [of light] that shoots from the lotus-like crown [of his lord]; as the quintessence of all sciences; as a moon of the Sūri clan that exhilarates the swell of poets. It was in his dream that the king spoke of his longing for the composition of a memoir. Nayendu then wrote this beautiful piece of poetry that delights kings and adorns the limbs of heroes.[116]

Some may want to argue that the dream is symbolic, merely representing a form of legitimization. The poet does not claim that he is the source of his creative act; rather, it is the historical character of Hammīra who is 'dictating' the sequence of verse. In other words, perhaps the author is trying to say that the poem – precisely because the hero Hammīra has revealed it in a dream to him – is not a product of imagination but is true. The dream, in this case, states precisely the opposite of what 'we' as modern readers would understand it to be, an entity belonging to the larger realms of imagination, fiction, daydreaming, subtle disclosures of the unconscious, symbols of simulation. The dream legitimizes by belonging not to the realm of the imagination as a function of fickle thought but as being the presence of the concrete, of the real. The dream can only legitimize if it is not a representation or accumulation of fictitious scenarios. But in order for this latter argument – namely that the dream is being used by the author to legitimize – to carry weight, it must indeed coincide with the idea that the dream must belong to the realm of the imagination – or of perceiving and visualizing – that it is a portal, an opening to truths that are more real than those that appear to be

115 = Nayachandra Sūri, the poet. There is an alliteration in this verse with the words *bindu* (point, concentration, essence), *Nayendu* and *indu* (the moon).

116 tatpattāmbhojacañcattarakharakiraṇaḥ sarvaśāstraikabinduḥ
sūrīnduḥ śrīnayendurjayati kavikulodanvadullāsanenduḥ |
tene tenaiva rājñā svacaritatanane svapnanunnena kāmaṃ
cakrāṇaṃ kāvyametannṛpatitatimude cāru vīrāṅkaramyam || 26 ||
This verse belongs to the autobiographical note or rather "praise or eulogy of the poet" (*kāvyakartuḥ praśastiḥ)* by the author that appears after final chapter (*Sarga* 14).

https://doi.org/10.1515/9783110662795-008

real through our everyday experience of a reality that is presented to us through our five senses. The dream does not belong to the experience given to us through the senses. And, yet, while it is made of sensory elements it transports us or rather the poet into the past in a manner that is concrete and palpable – and in some ways indestructible: the narrative emerging out of the dream continues to exist through future centuries in a manner that is not available to actual events, which last only for the moment in which they come into existence, before disappearing or mutating into something else once the singular moment has gone by:

> The dream, or any of its analogues, offers a way back. It is a subtle and ambiguous state, often encoded. It is, however, an "earlier" form of consciousness than awakening, which is given to externalized and objectified fixations. In this sense, one does not actually "wake up" to enlightenment, or even to relatively less profound forms of truth; one is more likely to move toward insight by releasing oneself into dream. The dream, generally, acts like memory – a memory lost and restored. Its basic direction is backward, toward a beginning. It expands identity, on the one hand, by literally dis-closing its rupture with earlier lives and forgotten experience, but also loosening the tight grasping of present identity boundaries, on the other. It seems to fill up the porous and forgetful mind as food fills the hungry body or rain fills the fields (Shulman 1999, 59).

The poet's dream is thus a way of bringing into consciousness something that has been forgotten or perhaps only vaguely remembered; events whose contours are worn, dusty, like shapes of distant dilapidated huts on the edge of a sandy desert settlement. The dream resurfaces a buried knowledge that now demands attention by appearing in the central field of vision of the poet, but not only of the poet. The poet's consciousness of the past made present through the dream now becomes present to readers and listeners across great swathes of time and space, reaching outside the pinpoint of its beginning in a formidable fortress in Rajasthan. The poet's dream with its seeming interiority occupies ever-widening external realms of historical knowledge, poetry, literature, historiography and nationalism. The dream as an element of the imagination as a faculty that propels creation into physical, concrete shape becomes, to cite the title of David Shulman's (2012) deeply insightful work on the imagination, *More than Real.* The dream was never, and certainly is no longer, a subjective, individualized experience lacking 'objective' corroboration and validity, as 'personal' experience tends to be criticized for. The dream, in fact, protects the poet from claims of a subjective assessment of historical events. It retrieves the poem from the murky waters of fantasy and fiction, of diluted facts. The poem is real because it has been dreamt.[117]

The poem is presented to us in highly complex Sanskrit verse. The dream is translated, so to speak, into densely intricate images in twisting and turning alliteration, grammatical loops and knots that produce sound and meaning. The dream must be translated into a language that seems worthy of its content. The heroic, selfless, yet stubborn acts of the hero and his loyal associates must be placed in the language of beauty, in a language through which beauty becomes possible even if this involves violence, gore, bloodshed, treachery, greed and the desire for unrelenting power. The poetical images of such blood-drenched, gut-wrenching violence progress to the status of icons that index the values of sacrifice and valour that press the hero into forward-reaching memory, into the uninterrupted formation of identities of groups, individuals, communities and even nations over immense spans of time. The poetical images are icons of a both forward- and reverse-looking memory that collapses time into a flat horizontal plain, like rippled circles on the surface of a forest lake.

As mentioned above, the poet also asserts that it was not only the dream that motivated him to write the poem, but also a more exterior, common form of driven-ness produced by comparison and mockery. Members of the court of the Tomara king, Vīrama, reminded the poet and, presumably, also the king that no one had been able to compose poetry of the highest order.

> When those who were assembled at the court of the Tomara King Vīrama declared that it was impossible in the present time for someone to compose a poem comparable to the creations of earlier poets, the poet Nayendu's agile mind was persuaded and provoked by a playful impulse. He then set out to create a new poem on King Hammīra, which is permeated with [the *rasas*] of love, heroism, and amazement.[118]

Such poetry, written and composed almost a millennium ago, from the time of Nayachandra Suri by genius poets like Kalidāsa and Bilhana, represented a chapter in Sanskrit poetic composition that was now closed off – a caesura in creativity that was left in limbo. All that remained was a looking-back at glorious

---

117 The dream or dreamworld is also that through which our so-called immediate and certain grasp of an objective world is shaken and questioned. The dream and other states of hallucination and illusion intervene and impinge on the notion that the mind is connected to the 'real' world though our senses.

118 kāvyaṃ pūrvakarvena kāvyasadṛśaṃ kaścid vidhātā'dhune-
tyukte tomaravīramkṣitipateḥ sāmājikaiḥ saṃsadi |
tadbhūcāpalakelidolitamanāḥ śṛṇgāravīrādbhutaṃ
cakre kāvyamidaṃ hammīranṛpaternavyaṃ nayenduḥ kaviḥ || 43 ||

times, a memory and yearning of what was possible in a bygone era of greatness. The current age was no longer witness to exalted Sanskrit poetry, but to conquering forces of regional languages and their epic literature.[119] The 'second Millennium' in our epochal calculations (but not those of Nayachandra Sūri and other writers and historians) supposedly saw the dispersal of the "Sanskrit cosmopolis"[120] into the ever stronger and clearly present emergence of regions and their situated heroes and histories. The 10th and 11th centuries represent a watershed in political, social and cultural creativity and, perhaps, also crisis as old forms and configurations of behaviour and thinking are pushed into uncertain, shifting realms of state formation, social mobility and the accompanying literature that reflects these changes.[121] The challenge thrown by King Vīrama's courtiers to the poet represents a self-reflexive awareness of belonging to a particular literary lineage that has supposedly come to end, while at the same time prodding him to usher in a new one, or if not 'new,' at least one that bridges the past with the present through a form of intertextuality, or rather reflexiveness, that strives not at inversion, subversion or other forms of critical reflection, but at a kind of intelligent mimicry – a reflexiveness given by the qualities of resemblance, approximation and similarity. This is a reverse gaze that is guided by admiration, appreciation, perhaps even veneration. It is an attempt to forge, through self-aware effort, continuity with the past, and, in that sense, it is an attempt to inaugurate tradition.[122]

5.2 Future Traditions

The poet seeks to inaugurate a poetical and literary tradition by using the parameters of Sanskrit *kāvya* laid down by his literary ancestors. At the same time the subject matter of his poem does not reflect conditions or themes of the past, rather the concerns and vicissitudes of the age in which the poet lives. The poem while carrying forward poetical conventions is ensconced in a historical time given by the power plays of Rajput dynasties and the Delhi sultanate, both of which have begun, only a couple of centuries earlier, to take root as new social and political formations in northern and western India. While the po-

119 See Bronner, Shulman and Tubb (2014).
120 See Pollock (2006).
121 See Kolff (2002) for a later account of shifting allegiances and social histories reflected through wandering '*naukars*', soldiers and ascetic groups. Epic poems in different regions also represent these 'seismic' shifts in narrative form.
122 See Bronner, Shulman and Tubb (2014).

etical tradition that Nayachandra Sūri follows is 'ancient,' the social climate in which he composes the poem seems to be unique and 'new.' Different configurations of social and political 'traditions' are in the process of being formed together with the moral and ethical values of loyalty, bravery, friendship, keeping one's word and protection. While these are in themselves not newly invented modes of action and social behaviour, they take on new meaning in the emerging narratives of a Rajput ethos informed by the heroic lives and deaths of male and female warriors. The principal 'mood' or rather texture of the poem is thus one saturated by '*vīr rasa*' – the *rasa* of heroism and the actions of a warrior. According to Bharata, the author of the *Naṭyaśāstra* or treatise on performance that was composed between the 4th and 6th centuries CE, there are eight *rasas* or moods, or sentiments or 'essences' as the literal meaning of *rasa* indicates. These moods represent an abstract quality arising out of particular emotional responses.[123] The *rasas* themselves include:
1. Sṛṅgāra: romance or passion
2. Hāsya: comedy
3. Karuṇa: compassion
4. Raudra: fury
5. Vīra: heroism
6. Bhayānaka: horror
7. Bhībhatsa: revulsion
8. Adbhuta: amazement.

These moods that represent the 'cumulative aesthetic effect' of a dramatic performance are further connected to a series of emotions (*bhāva*) that an audience is meant to experience when the *rasas* are articulated through words and gestures on stage.[124] *Rasas* are in thus themselves not to be considered emotions; rather, they are the catalyst for emotions to arise in the minds and bodies of an audience. The series of emotions that the *rasas* are linked to comprise:
1. Sthāyibhāva(s): foundational emotions
2. Vyabhicāribhāva(s): transient emotions
3. Anubhāva(s): emotional reactions
4. Vibhāva(s): catalysts of emotions.

123 Compare Heidegger's notion of 'mood' (*Befindlichkeit, Stimmung*) that is a pre-objective and pre-subjective state in which human beings 'find themselves in' or are 'thrown into'.

124 There are other meanings of *bhāva*, for example, as in the Rajasthani phrase, *bhāv avṇo/ aṇo:* to be 'possessed' by a deity or spirit.

The first set of 'foundational,' 'constant,' or 'enduring' emotions – *sthāyibhāvas* – are eight in number, each intimately connected to the eight *rasas* as the source or origin of the latter. These 'foundational emotions' are:

1. Rati: 'love' to romance and passion
2. Hāsa: 'jest' to comedy
3. Śoka: 'sorrow' to compassion
4. Krodha: 'anger' to fury
5. Utsāha: 'willpower' to heroism
6. Bhaya: 'fear' to horror
7. Jugupsa: 'disgust' to revulsion
8. Vismaya: 'astonishment' to amazement.[125]

It is thus *utsāha* or willpower, effort, perseverance and power that give rise to heroism which is one of the principal qualities traced in the *Hammīra-Mahākāvya*. The poem represents a new evaluation, perhaps even interpretation, or at the very least an exploration of this particular quality through the events and actions – successes and failures alike – of its protagonists. It is a reflection and articulation of an age of heroes and heroism, of an age in which disenchantment has not set in[126] – in which aspirations and a faith in the kind of actions associated with the hero have not yet eroded. "Presence of mind, energy, agitation, joy, assurance, cruelty, indignation, intoxication, horripilation, change of voice, anger, envy, contentment, arrogance and deliberation, are the states applicable to the Heroic sentiment" (Ghosh 1950, 146).[127]

Nayachandra Sūri's dream represents

> a near-universal experience of dreaming as communication, a more or less enigmatic presentation of meaningful messages to the self (and *from* the self, or from some profound dimension of reality, or from God) [...] The basic pattern [...] is well represented in Indian literature. The dream is an objective "fact" that can be found or recovered in the outer world, and that makes itself present in consciousness through mechanisms, say, of karmic mem-

125 Buchta and Schweig (2010, 623–29).

126 In several oral epics in Rajasthan to be a hero means to die prematurely, tragically, to sacrifice oneself (Smith 1991; Malik 2005). See, for example, Taylor (2007) describing the situation of a 'post-heroic' age in which disenchantment with regard to the values of heroes and heroism has set in: "With the coming of a commercial society, it seemed that greatness, heroism, full-hearted dedication to a non-utilitarian cause, were in danger of atrophy, even of disappearing from the world" (185). "There seems to be no room for generous action, for heroism, for warrior virtues, a higher sensibility; or else for a real dedication to humanity, a more demanding ethic of sacrifice, or a sense of a greater whole, a relation to the universe; and the like" (545).

127 See also Vatsyayan (1996).

> ory or intersubjective sensitivity [...] In this sense [...] the dream speaks a powerful truth (Shulman and Stroumsa 1999, 7–8).

Why is the dream not so important in the prior analyses of the poem? Perhaps the dream is not so important because our modern sensibilities have relegated dreams into the world of the imagined, the fictitious and the non-real. Our response to the dream is also linked to our modern ideas of authorship, self and agency. As Mary Keller (2002) in her perceptive analysis of women, power and spirit possession shows, the idea of agency, and of authorship, is anchored in the post-Enlightenment notion of the autonomous individual who is capable of 'making their history' rather than being the subject of unconscious tradition. But as Asad's (1993) critique of universalist claims of modernity reveals to us, the idea of agency, was, prior to the Enlightenment construction of the 'autonomous individual,' rooted in the agency or will of God. Human subjects – bodies in fact – were receptacles for God's will or work to be performed. The availability of divine will in a human subject depended on the presence of power or *disciplina* that would direct the human subject toward religious truth or experience: "It was not the mind that moved spontaneously to religious truth, but power [*disciplina*] that created the conditions for experiencing that truth" (Keller 2002, 56). Human subjects were instruments rather than agents in the modern sense of the word. Drawing a link here, if we were to take the poet's dream seriously, just as we could take his comparison with Yuddhiṣṭhira and Rāma seriously, then it is in fact Hammīra who is compelling Sūri to write a history of past events that commemorates himself. Although this does not match perfectly with the pre-Enlightenment idea of the will or power of God, it does suggest an alternative view of agency, and of authorship. One could argue, that this is an example of a kind of embodiment or 'possession,' in which a disembodied, indeed dead, person seeks to retrieve his agency in the world by 'occupying' another person's memory, and having them act upon this in a distinctive manner. The poet is, we could thus assert, an instrument of the dead king's will. What sort of idea of history and of personhood do we need in order to understand what is going on without dismissing this point of inception as a quaint detail unworthy of the status of hard evidence? There is, I think, both a stretching of time and of person. A stretching and fragmentation of time brought about through repetition – through repeated but discreet visitations – each constituting something like a chapter or an episode that is then reconstituted in a seamless narrative beginning with Hammīra's ancestors and ending in his death. There is a quality of stubbornness in the repeated visitations, a stubbornness that qualifies Hammīra's actions in 'real' life too, for which he becomes famous as '*haṭṭa*' or staunch, stubborn, unbending Hammīra. A stretching of person is brought about by the insertion of Hammīra's remembrance into the memory of the poet. The remembrance of the warrior king put to writing through the memory of the poet then enters the memory of a region through other literary forms, scribing a spiralling conduit through time inside of which Hammīra himself is reinvented to suit the interpretative horizons of different literary genres and historical periods. Thus, Hammīra is simultaneously the poet's dream, the subject of his poetical challenge, the vanquished king of Persian chronicles, the hero of Rajasthani ballads, and the saviour of Hindu honour and independence.

5.3 Real Simulacrums

There is a powerful notion, found not only philosophical thought beginning with Plato in Greece and Upanisadic-Vedantic ideas in India, but also in recent quantum theoretical physics and in the literature of science fiction and feature films based on science fiction, that *the world around us might not be real.* The world, for all we know it, may be a simulation created by other more intelligent life forms or it may fundamentally be constituted by appearances or shadows that when penetrated by science or intellectual insight will be shown to be 'unreal.' The real then is located elsewhere – it occupies another metaphysical state – but perhaps there is also nothing real outside the unreal, illusion of appearances. Everything we experience is ultimately simulation. The unreal is the real.[128] The world is a perfect simulation that by virtue of its very perfection as a replica can no longer be distinguished from the real, that itself perhaps only began as a simulation of another reality and so on. In this simulated reality 'our' thoughts, actions, aspirations, dreams, feelings, moments of joy and sadness, of profundity and banality are but mirrors triggered by the images of another (someone else's?) set of thoughts, actions, feelings and everyday experience. What we consider to be 'ours' – belonging in some deeply intimate manner to who and what we believe to be 'ourselves,' our 'identities,' our 'lives' – is in fact only a seed planted as a potentiality by a prior existing mechanism that re-activates an experience that seems real but, as is shown in the film *The Matrix*, turns out to be a complex code running itself in the predictable format of a computer programme. The programme presumably was not created by itself. In other words, it was not created by the experiencers of the programme (human beings) – who as part of their programming think they are the creators of the programme – rather, it was created by programmers who have knowledge of the

128 See Baudrillard (1994).

rules, laws and complexities of computer programming. The world and our subjective experience of it as participants in and of the world – perhaps as that aspect of the world which begins to view, inspect, investigate, reflect upon and grow aware of its own location in the world – is a simulacrum of a reality that exists, at least theoretically, beyond the purview of concrete, everyday experience. The reality of the world as experienced is in its nature as a simulacrum flawed, somehow lesser, perhaps estranged, alienated from the reality from which it derives its own image that claims its own right to be real without flaws or incompleteness. But how does or can the simulacrum that is the both the source of our experience and its horizon know that there is something besides the replica or simulacrum? In other words, is it possible for the replica to know it is a replica? Where does this kind of knowledge arise? In dreams, sudden insights, in the unexpected breakdown of everyday assurances and patterns that abruptly reveal jagged edges, fuzzy borders, incomplete, fragmented shorelines drawn up by heaving lunar forces? The simulacrum must contain interstices, minute gaps, subtle porous surfaces that normally go unnoticed in the overlay and assurances of everyday knowledge and certainty. The programme upon which the simulacrum is based contains imperfections on a *nano*, almost invisible, level that eludes even the most thorough scrutiny. Where does or can the knowing arise that everyday thoughts, actions, notions of one's self and the world are framed by limitation, particularly if the programme that underlies the simulacrum itself produces a subjectivity which firmly believes that experience is the ultimate foundation of knowledge and that therefore the very possibility of something existing outside of that horizon – or indeed that experience itself could present us with a 'horizon' – becomes impossible. To break through or penetrate the 'matrix' so to speak is to enter into the realm of the im-possible, the ab-normal, the un-thinkable. And, yet we must at least consider the *possibility of the impossible* if we are to ever transcend a kind of inherent smugness that seems to accompany the condition of being human.

In the movie *Inception* (2010) the protagonists create the possibility of a shared dream in which intentionality and purposefulness continues – in contrast to the seemingly random concurrences of characters, situations and emotions in commonplace dreams – so as to plant an idea into a person's subconscious. The character in the movie – upon awaking from this shared dream – reinterprets certain critical events during his life, such as his father's relationship to him, in a new light leading to a different set of decisions and actions. The character is himself not aware of what brought about these changes in his thinking. He is only aware of the change in terms of a deep seated conviction, perhaps with the residual memory of a vague dream that motivates him to act, on a conscious level, in a different manner to how he was intending to before the idea was planted in his subconscious by the instrumentation of the shared dream, although he is unaware of the fact that he has participated in the dream. The dream then has a concrete impact upon the so-called waking reality of the character and his associates, but the agency involved in the actions that the character takes is the result of triggers planted in his subconscious by the protagonists of the story.[129]

In *Inception*, dream and waking reality merge in ways that make the boundaries of each imperceptible. There are actions that the protagonists undertake in the shared dream and in their waking lives. Each set of actions is embedded in a series of cause and effect, both within each state and crossing over from one state to the other. But even the protagonists, especially those who traverse the state of intentional and shared dreaming frequently, are unsure about which state they occupy: is it the dream state or the waking state? The dreamer's identity itself takes on a dream-like quality. It amounts to a fabrication, a mirage, an alleged, 'as if real' reality that even the dreamer acknowledges to be elusive. The protagonists require a 'sign' that enables them to distinguish between dream and reality. For example, one of the main characters has a simple hand twirled spinning top that in the dream state, once spun, continues to spin without toppling over, but in the waking state it wobbles and stops after a relatively brief twirling motion. But here too there is a measure of ambiguity and fuzziness; the final scene the movie does not provide a definitive answer to viewers or to the protagonist whether he is in a dream or waking state. Dream states and waking states both contain unanswered questions and their peculiar limbo-like quality. But despite the uncertainty with regard to the question of which state is 'real,' the dream state, while having its own rules of engagement and 'physical' laws, seems to have an advantage in terms of the potential to create and manifest worlds of imagination. The protagonists who are skilled at entering and inhabiting these dreamworlds are at the same time masters at creating worlds manifested in every minute detail through the effortless effort of imagination. These worlds are crowded with people sitting in cafes, shopping, walking to work, talking to each other; they have rivers, houses, seashores, tall buildings, blue skies, bridges, cobbled streets – the dreamworld is in fact a perfect simulacrum of the 'real' world! However, skilled 'dreamers' are able to manipulate these worlds in unexpected, fascinating and sometimes dangerous, threatening ways. The dreamworld is at once a world of careful, nurturing objects and people but also of captivity, destruction and death. Creation and manifestation of a person's intention in the 'real,' non-dream state is much more difficult, fraught with com-

129 See https://en.wikipedia.org/wiki/Inception for a synopsis of the plot of the movie.

promise and prone to failure, sometimes becoming utterly impossible. In the real world the intentions of one individual are pitted against the intentions and aspirations of other individuals and a convergence of partly hidden and partly explicit circumstances, causes, effects and influences.

The real world of human experience, though also profoundly grounded in intentionality and imagination as precursors to action and invention, does not have the same serene, vacuum-like space of the dreamworld in which universes come into existence by mere thought and free-flowing, unhindered inventiveness. The dreamworld thus presents human existence with a particular and peculiar form of freedom, the freedom to create and manifest freely and profoundly worlds held together by the scaffold of imagination. Grand edifices, intricate subterranean cities, emerald lakes, birds with shimmering wings, golden cupolas atop the domes of vast libraries – imagination itself is the commencement of creation and freedom. In Borges' short story, *The Circular Ruins*, the protagonist sets out to imagine another human being into reality:

> The purpose which guided him was not impossible, though it was supernatural. He wanted to dream a man: he wanted to dream him with minute integrity and insert him into reality. This magical project had exhausted the entire content of his soul; if someone had asked him his own name or any trait of his previous life, he would not have been able to answer. The uninhabited and broken temple suited him, for it was a minimum of visible world; the nearness of the peasants also suited him, for they would see that his frugal necessities were supplied. The rice and fruit of their tribute were sufficient sustenance for his body, consecrated to the sole task of sleeping and dreaming (Borges 1964, 54).

The act of dreaming up "a man [...] with minute integrity" was itself a tortuous, gargantuan task, exhausting 'the entire content of his soul' taking many years to master the ability to mould, sculpt and repetitively re-imagine a human physiology in his dreams. The region that he chose to occupy for this "magical project" was akin to a bleak, desolate though swampy landscape:

> The truth is that the obscure man kissed the mud, came up the bank without pushing aside (probably without feeling) the brambles which dilacerated his flesh, and dragged himself, nauseous and bloodstained, to the circular enclosure crowned by a stone tiger or horse, which once was the color of fire and now was that of ashes. This circle was a temple, long ago devoured by fire, which the malarial jungle had profaned and whose god no longer received the homage of men. The stranger stretched out beneath the pedestal. He was awakened by the sun high above [...] He knew that this temple was the place required by his invincible purpose; he knew that, downstream, the incessant trees had not managed to choke the ruins of another propitious temple, whose gods were also burned and dead; he knew that his immediate obligation was to sleep. Towards midnight he was awakened by the disconsolate cry of a bird (Borges 1964, 53).

The desolation of the landscape in which he begins his arduous task of creating another man is matched by the sheer impossibility of the project and the insurmountable effort required to build each portion of the human body in the imagination. This process proceeds step by step, not in a hurry. The entire person is not imagined in one thought; rather, each organ is meticulously assembled and put together until the whole human body stands erected:

> He comprehended that the effort to mold the incoherent and vertiginous matter dreams are made of was the most arduous task a man could undertake, though he might penetrate all the enigmas of the upper and lower orders: much more arduous than weaving a rope of sand or coining the faceless wind [...] To take up his task again, he waked [*sic*] until the moon's disk was perfect. Then, in the afternoon, he purified himself in the waters of the river, worshiped the planetary gods, uttered the lawful syllables of a powerful name and slept. Almost immediately, he dreamt of a beating heart.
>
> He dreamt it as active, warm, secret, the size of a closed fist, of garnet color in the penumbra of a human body as yet without face or sex; with minute love he dreamt it, for fourteen lucid nights. Each night he perceived it with greater clarity. He did not touch it, but limited himself to witnessing it, observing it, perhaps correcting it with his eyes. He perceived it, lived it, from many distances and many angles. On the fourteenth night he touched the pulmonary artery with his ringer [*sic*], and then the whole heart, inside and out. The examination satisfied him. Deliberately, he did not dream for a night; then he took the heart again, invoked the name of a planet and set about to envision another of the principal organs. Within a year he reached the skeleton, the eyelids. The innumerable hair was perhaps the most difficult task. He dreamt a complete man, a youth, but this youth could not rise nor did he speak nor could be open his eyes. Night after night, the man dreamt him as asleep (Borges 1964, 55).

Even though imagination and thought move at light speed, instantaneously, the making of a minutely, indeed infinitely complex human body proceeds gradually. Each detail must be refined, pondered over, re-formed. Observing, perceiving and witnessing – all practices that involve the non-action of standing back and 'letting be' – are crucial to this slow process of engendering, of biological gestation that takes place in the mind. Creation via imagination involves abstraction in thought, tactile, sensory touch like that of a sculptor working with wood, clay, stone, metal or other materials, along with observing and witnessing, which ultimately also requires the necessary though painful process of relinquishing control over the entity that has been created so that it can acquire its own, until then dormant, autonomy and sovereignty as a separate being. The protagonist who engenders this new being is called a magician.[130] Imagination and magic it

130 Indian deities are often referred to as 'magicians.' See for example, oral narratives concerning the Hindu folk-deities Khaṇḍobā (Sontheimer 1989) and Devnārāyaṇ (Malik 2005).

seems occupy the same realms of the impossible and the illusory that comes to occupy the real. The *imaginer* is a magician who through *sleight of thought* inserts the unreal, non-existent into the real and existent.

5.4 'Mind-Born' Worlds

As long as you think, there will be existence, person, place and thing, but when you stop thinking there is no existence...
Robert Adams

Thus while imagination – even though it demands great effort and perseverance – rules supreme in the world of dreams as described here, it appears as thwarted, stunted, incomplete in its pursuit of perfection in an unpredictable world of human and earthly tectonic processes and movements. In the story "Pūcalār of Ninravur" taken from the 12th-century *Periya Purāṇam* that expounds the deeds of sixty-three exemplary devotees of Śiva, the villager Pūcalār, who is a staunch devotee of Śiva, constructs a temple dedicated to his lord in his imagination. Moreover, it this imagined or 'mind-born' temple that Śiva feels compelled to visit and consecrate before he visits the grand edifice built of stone made by the powerful king of the region.

> Then he realized he would have to build the shrine in his mind [*ninaippu*]. He began to collect within his awareness [*cintaiyal*] all the resources he would need, from the tiniest bit on up. Mentally he sought out carpenters and masons together with their tools and materials. On an auspicious day, he lovingly, attentively [*atarittu*] laid the foundations according to Agamic rules. In his passion, he worked steadily, not even closing his eyes at night. From the upāna moulding above the plinth through the many layers and levels of the crowning śikhara tower, he gave it shape and precisely measured for in his mind; he worked thus for many days, until the whole edifice was complete as imagined [*niramp' ita ninaival ceytar*]. He put the finial in place and had everything plastered white; he dug a well and a tank, built the subsidiary shrines and the outer wall and, having to see to all the necessary details, set a day for the ritual consecration of the temple to Śiva.
>
> As the day came near, the king called Kāṭavar Komān was busy putting finishing touches on the great stone temple he had built in Kācci [= Kāñcipuram] for Śiva, at vast expenditure. On the night before the image of the god (who could not be seen even by Viṣṇu) was to be installed in the new stone shrine, Śiva, adorned with fresh konrai blossoms, appeared in the king's dream and said: "I'll be busy tomorrow. I have to enter into the magnificent temple that a certain Pucal from Ninravur, a man who loves me, has thoughtfully built over many days. You'll have to postpone your ceremony to some later date (Shulman 2012, 4–6).

The process of invention and construction in the imagination or mind of the devotee Pūcalār involves tremendous attentiveness and commitment: "he worked steadily not even closing his eyes at night." The temple that he is building must be, like in the case of the human that the protagonist in *The Circular Ruins* is creating, kept 'alive' through constant diligence and purpose. Both the temple and the human demand a single-pointed, steadfast imagination not a wavering one. The passage describing Pūcalār's 'work' is suffused with adjectives such as 'lovingly,' 'passionately' and 'attentively.' His work is not and cannot be mechanical. It is not about going 'through the motions;' rather, it is about dwelling deeper and deeper, like the wood-worker that Heidegger describes who enters the realm of shape and form through wood, in the possibility of building a temple through the imagination.[131] Pūcalār's work is one infused with caring and love, for this is the pursuit of perfection in the context of extraordinary devotion. Imagination and love arise together. To imagine then is to nurture and care. The king on the other hand choses a different path to express his devotion to Śiva. Here too a great edifice rises up, albeit, one that is supremely visible being built by 'real' masons, engineers, labourers and architects in hard, stony materials that stand up against decay and degeneration. The king chooses the 'real' over the imaginary. Yet, Śiva appears to him in a dream which the king knows to be 'real' indicating his preference for the imaginary temple over the real one of stone. Perhaps it is because the god knows that all that is real begins with and in the imagination. Imagination is prior to the real; they exist not in some relationship of interdependency to one another but in a vector that moves strictly in one direction from the imagined to the real. In this story, dream, imagination, truth and reality are interlocked; there is a seamless movement from one to the other.

Shulman (2012, 6) deepens our understanding of the imagination by outlining the process of creation of the 'mind' temple in terms of Tamil terms and categories:

> The temple comes into being in thought (*ninaippu*) or, possibly, in an act of projection or visualization or imagination (*ninaivu*) that is interior to the mind (*manam*). The process involves disciplined and highly detailed *cintai* – "mentation," some act of mental creativity, here somewhat meditative in quality; but also, perhaps, "awareness" in a subtler and deeper sense once removed from what we would call intellection. [...] Tamil contrasts the kind of knowing connected to *unarvu* – and intuitive, full, direct, sensed, whole knowledge – with that connected to *arivu*, that is external, object-oriented, discriminatory, discursive knowledge.

Imagination here is not an intellectual activity or an act of intellection, even though it does involve thought. It involves thought in a particular sense that is

131 See Heidegger (1954).

to be distinguished from thought or thinking that is required to know the external world and entertain discursive forms of knowing that are central to the analysis and description of objects and events. Thought as an act linked to 'mentation' is 'meditative' or 'contemplative,' and leads to a knowing that is intuitive and complete. This thought or thinking is similar to what Heidegger distinguishes as *Denken* or *das zu-Denkende* or a thinking that belongs and emerges out of Being. It is this thinking toward Being that holds within it creative possibility. It is also what Heidegger distinguishes from the imagination (*die Vorstellung; sich etwas vorstellen:* to imagine something) as an act of what is ordinarily considered to be thinking. The latter, however, is closer to the Tamil notion of *arivu* that results in a knowledge of things, objects and events in the world (Shulman 2012, 7).

Furthermore, the decisive priestly figure called *Brāhman* in Vedic ritual "sits silently *thinking* the entire ritual in his mind, also repairing – mentally – anything that might go wrong in it, while other priests are performing the visible, concrete tasks" (Shulman 2012, 7). This silent, interior act of creation and knowing is, in many ways, more critical to achieving the cosmogonic results of the ritual than are the exterior acts of pouring oblations and reciting mantras. Silence, non-visibility, interior thinking and imagination are prior to the external world of sense objects. This is the domain of the mind from which external world emanates and comes into being in a manner that paradoxically results in the forgetting of the source:

> In the beginning, all of this was, as it were, neither unreal nor real. It was in the beginning as if real, yet unreal. What there was, was mind. That is why the Vedic poet has said, "There was nothing unreal in the beginning and, at that time, nothing real" (Ṛgveda 20.129.1). For the mind [*manas*] is neither real nor unreal.
>
> Once this mind was generated, it wanted to become more visible – more articulated, more embodied. It sought a body-self [atman]. It heated itself; it embodied itself. It saw 36,000 Arka fires of its own body-self – made of mind, piled up by the mind. They were kindled by the mind and put in place by the mind. The cups [of offering] were drawn by the mind, they sang praises in the mind and recited in the mind (Shulman 2012, 8).

While the mind 'already exists' as neither real nor unreal, it also needs to be generated. What is it generated from? From itself? What is this process of looping, self-generation? The mind "is waiting, as it were, to be fashioned and formed, or perhaps discovered" (Shulman 2012, 8). The mind awaits as a potential or as possibility for its own self to manifest in a more concrete fashion. The mind generates itself through thought and speech which is as of yet enclosed in silence. Potential and possibility are enfolded within 'real and unreal,' within silence. Embodiment takes place by the piling up of the mind, like layers of imaginary bricks from which the mind temple and the ritual altar in the shape of a winged bird is constructed. Embodiment occurs with a layering of mind that creates substance, thickness, visibility. The visible world is nothing more than layers of invisible imagination and thought, and the desire for that thought to embody and manifest itself. The visible is a building up through interior thought and word as speech into an exteriority that begins to believe in its fabricated, *illusory thickness*, so to speak. Physicality, solidity, space and time become the new fad, so to speak, attempting to overturn and deny whence they arose. Yet our ordinary, everyday experience of the world of space and time, in which we walk, talk, eat, breathe, struggle, aspire and dwell, is only one of many possible worlds: "The mind is clearly capable of yielding worlds no less tangible and crisply contoured than the one we normally inhabit or the ones we are capable of putting together, in externality, by ourselves" (Shulman 2012, 10). The mind is the 'programmer,' 'constructor,' 'engineer' or 'source' of the different worlds each functioning on the basis of its own programme or laws. In other words, each world, as cosmologists, quantum physicists and experts of computer programming will tell us, is being thought up. Each world is a manifestation not of its inhabitants' thoughts but of *Thought* itself, of thought as dwelling in the receptacle of mind. Being born and dying are, however, very real even in these worlds of mind that arise 'merely' in thought and imagination.

The mind and the world are set on fire by imagination. It is inside of imagination that universes arise and subside, in which existence and non-existence, sky and non-sky, river and non-river, mortal and non-mortal, silence and non-silence, breath and non-breath coexist and do not coexist. The vacuousness of absence is full of emptiness. Emptiness is a vacuum that hides a myriad of cosmos each wildly singular. Each madly entangled with one another. Each echoing the other in slow moving yaw-like eddies of shrieking silence and song enveloping the crumbling outer ruins of dark inner palaces carved from unknown materials.

> There was a great forest, so large that in it millions of square miles were like the space within an atom. In it there was just one person who had a thousand arms and limbs. He was forever restless. He had a mace in his hand with which he beat himself and, afraid of the beating he ran away in panic. He fell into a blind well. He came out of it, again beat himself and ran away in panic, this time into a forest. He came out of it, again beat himself and ran away in panic, this time into a banana grove. Though there was no other being to fear, he wept and cried aloud in fear. He kept running as before, beating himself as before.
>
> I witnessed all this intuitively, and with the power of my will I restrained him for a moment. I asked him, "Who are you?" But, he was sorely distressed and called me his enemy and wept aloud and then laughed aloud. Then he began to abandon his body – limb by limb.
>
> Immediately after this I saw another person running like the first one beating himself, weeping and wailing. When I similarly restrained him, he began to abuse me and ran

away intent on his own way of life. Like this I came across several persons (Venkatesananda 1985, 96–97).

In this story of the "great forest," which is part of the *Yoga-Vāśiṣṭha* that is said to have been composed by Valmiki, the sage Vaśiṣṭha tells Rāma that there is a vast, immeasurable forest and within it a literally and figuratively vast and immeasurable single person with a thousand arms and legs. The person is alone in this vast almost galactic expanse. Being the only one inhabiting the endless wilderness of this space, the person cannot distinguish himself from himself. He seemingly creates another person from himself but this other who is himself inflicts and torments him. The thousand-limbed person runs away from himself but continues to be tormented because his tormentor is none other than himself. One or many of his limbs presumably beat his torso and other limbs creating the illusion of an external tyrant from which, alas, there is no escape. The person runs into a forest and then into a banana grove but the change in exteriority does not change his distressed condition. What is the forest? Who is the thousand-limbed person? Why does he have a thousand limbs? Why is he alone in this immense space? The immense space is the undefined, universal matrix or context of existence. The forest is the particular configuration of the person's existence. The thousand limbs are a thousand mirrors that are held up to the person creating the deception of multitude and difference where there is only organically, interconnected body. The person was, is and will be always alone, imagining the notion that there is another 'out there,' and inventing torment and suffering through its own actions while persisting in the belief that there is someone else who is the cause of pain (and joy) and also someplace else that will provide refuge and relief. *Is there an end to the endless mind?*[132]

> Why insist on the role of the mind? [...]
>
> [...] this universe, which looks so solid, is in reality entirely a tissue of mentation [*vikalpa-jalika*] and the stuff of reflections [*pratibhasatmika*]; like the story, it, too, is constructed from fierce, tough acts of imagination [*ugraih sankalpair dṛdha-kalpitah*]. Nothing whatsoever exists apart from the imagination. Whatever is there by force of the imagination is not really a "something," or it might be a "little something." Just like the boys, the rivers, and the city-to-be, the existence of the world is an imaginary production, tremulous, shimmering all around us (32–37) (Shulman 2012, 111).[133]

---

132 This is a line from a penetrating poem or *pādam* about the mind by the 15th-century Telegu poet Annamayya who was a devotee of Lord Venkateśvara, the presiding deity of Tirupati. See Narayana Rao and Shulman (2005, 6).

133 These lines are Shulman's translation of a passage from the *Yoga-Vāśiṣṭha Māhā-Rāmāyaṇa*. The story referred to in the passage is one of many stories accounted in the text. This story in particular deals with the question of existence, non-existence and imagination through the wander-

5.4.1 Invention and Manifestation

Invention and manifestation in the real world must bend to physical laws and the laws of economics, politics and culture. In this 'real' world, invention is an artefact produced as a consequence of such laws. But invention is also simultaneously the adversary of these laws as it attempts to simulate the liberty and ease of the dream state with its sovereign mental and physical constitutions. The transportation of a dream-like invention of social or physical worlds into the world of the 'waking state' is therefore considered to be remarkable, enormously impressive, an approximation of perfection, a utopia in the midst of dystopian conditions. The seed of manifestation which includes action and inter-action, making, and building, however, originates either in the dreamworld as in the movie *Inception* or in the world of imagination, which is the twin body of the dreamworld. The seed is itself the origin point, potential and intention all encapsulated in one densely compressed central space from which poetry, history, time, artefact and social existence burst forth.

The dreamworld may be a partial or complete simulacrum of partial or complete configurations found in the real world, but then, once created, the dreamworld becomes an impetus for an intervention in the real world. The real world begins to alter and shift its contours through the emergence of intentionality originating in the dreamworld. The dreamworld pressed upon the real world and vice versa. Dreamworld and real world are conjoined like a Möbius strip that has a single contiguous surface broken, if at all, for the sake of convenience, only by arbitrary points of commencement and departure. Inside and outside can become outside and inside at any given moment or through a change in perspective. The viewer determines whether he or she is in dream state or waking state, and that too remains – even with the 'sign' that signifies the 'real' – uncertain and ambivalent. But what is this sign? And how can the sign determine or distinguish which reality is which or which experience is 'real' and which is 'dream-like' or imaginary? The sign, in order for it to be able to determine whether a current reality is 'real' or 'unreal,' must itself embody a quality that is to be found neither in the real nor in the unreal. It must transcend both realities and be attuned at the same time in a special manner to both realms. The spinning top wobbles and stops in the waking reality but continues spinning indefinitely in the dream state. The spinning top adheres to the laws of the waking state just

ings of three boys, two of whom are non-existent and one of whom has not entered the womb. The boys bathe in rivers which have no water and settle in a city that has not been built, which has three palaces of which two have not have been built and one of which has no walls.

as these laws do not apply in the dream state that subverts the seemingly axiomatic laws of the former state. The dream state presents the viewer with different possibilities to those she or he encounters in the waking state. The dream state may therefore be a simulacrum of the waking state and yet it may deeply undermine its cherished processes and laws. As Deleuze (1994, 69) states:

> Everything has become simulacrum, for by simulacrum we should not understand a simple imitation but rather the act by which the very idea of a model or privileged position is challenged and overturned. The simulacrum is the instance which includes a difference within itself, such as (at least) two divergent series on which it plays, all resemblance abolished so that one can no longer point to the existence of an original and a copy. It is in this direction that we must look for the conditions, not of possible experience, but of real experience (selection, repetition, etc.).

The simulacrum contains within itself the sign(s) of difference that give the real its own signifier(s) of 'realness' and yet this sign(s) of difference creates a reality that consciously diverges and challenges that which it is modelled upon. While the model and its simulacrum resemble each other to the degree that one can only faintly and with great scrutiny be discerned from the other, the simulacrum presents us with a reality that is in foundationally different, pointing to what is claimed to be lacking in the original. The original and its simulacrum are known by virtue of difference and what is lacking not only in the original but also, from the perspective of the original, in the simulacrum as well. Difference is thus constituted by lack and the construction of a system that makes up for this lack. Does 'lack' then become the signifier of difference between the original and the copy?

The original and the simulacrum are signifiers in terms of the actual content and structures they contain. They become signified in the moment they are labelled as 'original' and 'simulacrum' since these terms represent conceptual worlds of meaning and social, philosophical, artistic and political significance. And, yet, as pointed above, there remains the question of the sign through which the original is distinguished from the simulacrum. In the case of the movie *Inception*, as I pointed out above, the sign is the spinning top that in one case continues to spin and in the other case wobbles to a stop after spinning for a reasonable amount of time.

In Borges' short story, *The Circular Ruins*, the sign is the protagonist's ability to walk through raging fire without being harmed:

> In a birdless dawn the magician saw the concentric blaze close round the walls. For a moment, he thought of taking refuge in the river, but then he knew that death was coming to crown his old age and absolve him of his labors. He walked into the shreds of flame. But

> they did not bite into his flesh, they caressed him and engulfed him without heat or combustion (Borges 1964, 57).

This superhuman-like ability is evidence of a world in which the usual laws of physics – in which organic substance is burnt by fire – do not apply. This is the world of a dream that is being dreamt by someone else. The protagonist partakes of the dream as an element of the dream himself not as a 'normal' physical entity. The realization of the fact that the protagonist occupies a dream – a simulacrum – is triggered by the sign contained in the ability to walk amidst the dreadful flames of fire that have engulfed a circular temple, soon to become the circular ruins. As in the example of *Inception* in which dreamworlds are intentionally created, the protagonist of *The Circular Ruins* spends arduous hours, days, months, indeed years imagining, and therefore creating, in his dreams a human youth, a son. The dream as the centre-stage of imagination becomes the platform from which to create a real, corporeal entity, first completely physical and then much more than that: infused with humanity, with *Being*. The dreamworld – or that which is considered to be the world of fantasy, unreliability, mirage-like illusion, in some ways the perfect simulacrum – becomes the firm ground from which to create the 'real.' The real springs forth from the imagined and dreamt up. The dreamworld is thus prior to corporeality, physicality and yet its very non-corporeality saturates the corporeal that emerges from it with authenticity, perhaps a level of authenticity and reverence that the corporeal that merely emerges from the mundane and corporeal cannot and does not ever attain. The dreamt-up human also suggests a level of control in terms of creation, and near or perhaps even absolute approximation to that which is imagined. The level of control is more so than the randomness of biological creation can ever achieve.

Imagination and its progeny are, simply by virtue of being imagined, 'perfect.' Even if the products of imagination contain flaws these too are perfect as they are imagined as such and therefore, in a sense, cease to be 'flaws.' Flaws can only arise in the corporeal world that is 'post-imagination' since they represent a gap between what is imagined and what is manifested in a particular physical reality. Flaws thus represent a 'lack' or 'what is missing' in a given manifestation in relation to what can be imagined or what is possible. To return to an earlier point, the simulacrum is born out of difference that refers to a lack in the original system thereby questioning, challenging, subverting the latter. In the case of *The Circular Ruins*, the dreamworld which would normally be considered the simulacrum becomes the realm from which the real (as in corporeal) is imagined, with the element of perfection available only in the imagination. The creation springing from the protagonist's imagination is in this respect 'perfect.' And, yet, as the protagonist discovers his dreaming up of the youth and his own everyday reality in his swamp, and jungle-like surroundings are but a dream in someone else's imagination. The dream as an instrument of creation and the dreamer turn out to be a simulacrum within another simulacrum and so on:

> *With relief, with humiliation, with terror, he understood that he too was a mere appearance, dreamt by another (Borges 1964, 57).*

Chapter 6
History as Simulacrum

The desire for the imaginary, the possible, must contest with the imperative of the real, the actual.
Hayden White[134]

6.1 Thinking about the Past

History can broadly and perhaps without much controversy be defined as the study of the past. But while History concerns itself with the past, it is also obvious that not all statements about the past are considered to be History. It is only when the past is presented to us – 'constructed' one could say – in a particular manner that it becomes 'History.' Not every statement or perspective of the past therefore qualifies as history. But how exactly does history get constructed? What indeed does it mean to state that History can be defined as a particular articulation of the past? To expand on this definition, one could say that History as a 'study' of the past involves thinking about the past in a particular manner. Before one can identify what this particular mode of thinking, of abstraction and articulation, involves, one must ask: What does it mean to *think* about the past? Where does thinking about the past arise? Where is this thinking about the past located? Where indeed is thinking located and what is thinking?

Before this can be examined adequately it seems that we need to make a distinction between thinking and having thoughts. Thinking is, as I am defining it here, is an active propulsion of (self-)reflection, awareness, persistent enquiry and critical investigation into the conditions of one's own perception and conclusions about the world, into the conditions for the possibility of something existing or coming into existence; but perhaps thinking also concerns something else which cannot be adequately grasped merely in conceptual terms as a quantity of rationality and reasoning. As I discuss below, following Heidegger, the way to understanding what *thinking is* is not through theorizing or *thinking about thinking.* It is by realizing first of all that *we do not yet think.*[135]

However, to continue with the distinction between thinking and thoughts (plural): the latter are articulations of the constant internal chatter of the stream of associative ideas, judgments, opinions, and fragmented and incomplete state-

134 White (1980).
135 Heidegger (1954, 2): "*Das Bedenklichste ist, daß wir noch nicht denken.*"

https://doi.org/10.1515/9783110662795-009

ments that move without one's own volition in an automatic mode as though working through the means of some pre-planned programme. Thoughts come and go in a seemingly random mixture, giving the impression of succession and linearity but actually appearing and disappearing in formless, succession-less, non-linear, even non-temporal waves. While thoughts appear to be triggered by psychological or physiological stimuli their causes cannot be fully ascertained. The causal structure of thoughts as with other events in the world remains only partially knowable. The story or narrative into which thought as a series of causes and effects is inserted is ultimately arbitrary, only giving a veneer of completeness to something that is perpetually in flux, thereby escaping all form of determination. Even though I am asserting that thought (as distinct from thinking), when carefully examined, occurs in a non-linear, simultaneous, non-temporal mode of, in a sense, only going round and round or going 'nowhere,' it seems that thoughts cannot occur without a notion of time that is, conventionally at least, segregated into future, present and past. Thinking is embedded in temporality, and simultaneously temporality arises when there are thoughts. This would seem to contradict what I have just stated before, namely that thoughts only seem to contain linearity, give the appearance of completeness and movement in some direction, and therefore are non-temporal just as the hard disk of a computer is non-temporal: coherent and perhaps sequential information surfaces from it on a screen when given the right triggers, but the information inscribed on it or in it isn't going anywhere other than awaiting to be triggered, activated or called up, or re-called, or invoked by an external mechanism.

6.1.1 Thought and Time

Can there be any thought without past, present and future? Put another way, can there be any thought without time? Put in yet another way, does time (past, present and future) come into existence when there is thought and *vice versa* does thought come into existence when there is time? In other words, can we say that thought and time arise together not as cause and effect but as co-dependent entities? In a sense thought engenders time and time engenders thought. It becomes impossible to conceive of the one without the other. In order for time to arise with thought the latter must be linked to memory which is composed of images, multi-sensory experiences and narratives that collectively could be said to constitute thought. These images, experiences, narratives and so on from the past (what has happened) are further distinguished from what is happening (the present) or what could happen (the future) by means of negation, resemblance, similarity and projection. Thought itself is thus made up of images, multi-sensory experiences and narratives. But it is more than that, or rather it occurs in something that encompasses it – not only encompasses it but actually represents the conditions for the possibility of thought. This is language. Thought with its apparatus of multi-sensory experience, which is made up not only of our memory of the past but also our recollection of the present and remembrance of the future, occurs in language that may have to do with words, but also sounds, images, and olfactory and kinaesthetic experience. To go one step further one can now state that thought, time and language all arise simultaneously. When there is language there is also the possibility of thought that gives rise to the possibility of time. Time, language, thought together allow for the possibility of *Being* to be known as being-in-the-world. Without time, language and thought, the possibility of *Being* as a being-in-the-world ceases. In other words, the possibility of *Being* as existence and non-existence occurs with the arising of language, thought and time.

6.1.2 Thinking about Not Thinking

Martin Heidegger in his essay on *Thinking* (*denken*) states that we are confronted today with many issues that are worthy of thinking or that are '*thought-provoking*.'[136] These issues are so acute that they would seem to demand immediate action and less talk at conferences, seminars and speeches. What is evidently required is a shift from 'talk' to 'action.' However, even though there are matters that would seem to demand our attention in terms of action rather than talk, Heidegger claims that the most thought-provoking matter that confronts us today is the fact that we have not yet learnt to think! And, looking back over centuries or even millennia of history, it seems humans have acted too much and not thought enough. We have not even begun to think:

> *Das Bedenklichste*[137] *ist, daß wir noch nicht denken*; immer noch nicht, obgleich der Weltzustand fortgesetzt bedenklicher wird. Dieser Vorgang scheint freilich eher zu fordern, daß

---

136 Heidegger (1954).

137 The adjective *bedenklich* also has the more common meaning of 'critical,' 'worrying,' 'alarming,' 'precarious,' and so on. In the translated words used here from the English translation (1976) of Heidegger's essay from 1954, the emphasis has been shifted to the inner core of the word which is occupied by the verb *denk(en)*, i. e. thought or thinking, thus offering a new meaning that suggests 'thought-full' or 'to involve in thought' rather than 'critical,' 'worrying,' 'precarious,' etc., although I would argue that Heidegger retains these meanings when he talks about the many issues in the current state of the world that are of critical and alarming nature. '*Be-*

> der Mensch handelt und zwar ohne Verzug, statt in Konferenzen und auf Kongressen zu reden [...] Somit fehlt es am Handeln und keineswegs am Denken.
>
> Und dennoch – vielleicht hat der bisherige Mensch seit Jahrhunderten bereits zu viel gehandelt und zu wenig gedacht (Heidegger 1954, 2).

But how is one to know that one is not thinking or that thinking has not even commenced despite the fact numerous individuals are professionally trained to think not only in the humanities, arts and social sciences but also natural sciences? If what such individuals claim is thinking is not thinking, then what is? How is one to know that thinking is not taking place without knowing what thinking is? Or if one does not know what thinking is, one must at least know what thinking isn't. Thinking or what is 'thought-provoking' is that which is worthy of thought:

> *Das Bedenklichste in unserer bedenklichen Zeit ist, daß wir noch nicht denken.*
>
> Wie der Name "das Bedenkliche" zu verstehen sei, wurde bereits angedeutet. Es ist das, was uns zu denken gibt (Heidegger 1954, 3).

But what is worthy of thinking of, rather that which is given by thinking, has already turned its back upon us. What is given by thinking or worthy of thinking has 'withdrawn' itself from us as human beings. In this sense 'it' is no longer 'with' us.

> [...] wir sind noch nicht vor das und noch nicht in den Bereich dessen gelangt, was von sich her in einem wesentlichen Sinne bedacht sein möchte.
>
> [...] daß wir noch nicht denken, liegt keineswegs nur daran, daß der Mensch sich noch nicht genügend dem zuwendet, was von Haus aus bedacht sein möchte [...]. Daß wir noch nicht denken, kommt vielmehr daher, daß dieses zu-Denkende selbst sich von Menschen abwendet, langher schon abgewendet hat.
>
> [...] das, was uns eigentlich zu denken gibt, hat sich nicht irgendwann zu einer historisch datierbaren Zeit vom Menschen abgewendet, sondern: das eigentlich zu-Denkende hält sich von einsther in solcher Abwendung (Heidegger, 1954, 4).

How does one know that 'it' has withdrawn itself from us? We know this because of the fact that we are drawn toward 'it.' We are drawn so to speak toward that which has withdrawn itself. This act of withdrawing is not anchored in any historical moment; it is in a sense not an event that took place in some distant or

---

denklichste' denotes the superlative form of '*bedenklich*,' thus suggesting the most 'thought-full' or the most 'to involve thought.' In other words, what Heidegger is referring to is that which demands the most thinking.

recent past. Rather, the withdrawing of that which is worthy of thinking, of that which we are drawn toward because it has withdrawn itself from us, is inherent to the condition we find ourselves in as human beings. To be human then is to experience being separate from that which we are being drawn toward.

> Das zu-Denkende wendet sich vom Menschen ab. Es entzieht sich ihm. Doch wie können wir von Solchem, das sich einsther entzieht, überhaupt das Geringste wissen oder es auch nur nennen? Was sich entzieht, versagt die Ankunft. Allein – das Sichentziehen ist nicht nichts. Entzug ist Ereignis (Heidegger 1954, 5).

Yet, that toward which we are drawn is not a 'thing,' it is not a 'something' that can be defined and pinned down, for to do that would be to end the question of what thinking is, and also of what thought is drawn toward, with an answer or conclusion that would limit and constrain. That toward which we are drawn (which is also that which is worthy of thought) can only be approached but never attained or owned. It can only be hinted or pointed at without ever being able to fully be circumscribed by a knowing informed by reasoning, logic or rationality.

6.2 The Empty Sign

A human being is a pointer or a *sign*. A human being is not first a human being and then a sign or pointer; rather, a human being is a sign inasmuch as a human being *is* that which points toward what has withdrawn itself from the inception, so to speak, of being human.

> Insofern der Mensch auf diesem Zug *ist*, *zeigt* er als der so Ziehende in das, was sich entzieht. *Als* der dahin zeigende *ist* der Mensch der Zeigende. Der Mensch ist hierbei jedoch nicht zunächst Mensch und dann noch außerdem und gelentlich ein Zeigender, sondern: gezogen in das Sichentziehende, auf dem Zug in dieses und somit zeigend in den Entzug, *ist* der Mensch allerst Mensch. Sein Wesen beruht darin, ein solcher Zeigender zu sein. Was in sich, seinem Wesen nach, ein Zeigendes ist, nennen wir ein Zeichen. Auf dem Zug in das Sichentziehende ist der Mensch ein Zeichen. Weil dieses Zeichen jedoch in das Sichentziehende zeigt, deutet es nicht so sehr auf das, was sich da ent-zieht, als vielmehr in das Sichentziehen. Das Zeichen bleibt ohne Deutung.
>
> Hölderlin sagt in einem Entwurf zu einer Hymne:
>
> "Ein Zeichen sind wir, deutungslos" (Heidegger 1954, 6).

The sign is not grounded in what has withdrawn – it does not reveal what it is that has withdrawn – rather, it is grounded in that which is withdrawing from itself, and thus is a sign for that which is withdrawing from itself. The sign therefore shows itself in the 'withdrawing from itself,' and not in what is being withdrawn. Heidegger continues to point out, while quoting a verse from the draft of a poem composed by Hölderlin which says that "We are a meaning-less sign," that the sign is without meaning.[138] In other words, human being as a sign of that which is withdrawing from itself, remains without meaning. What does it 'mean' to be a sign without meaning? If there is no meaning, can this question be asked at all? Perhaps to be a sign without meaning 'means' that the sign and also that to which it is pointing to is *empty*. Here again the question of the sign appears as it does in the case of the movie *Inception* and Borges' story *The Circular Ruins*. In both cases the sign lies at the centre of the question of what is real and what is imagined or whether one can actually distinguish between what is real and what is imaginary. The sign in the example of the feature film and story is something that is observable by the protagonists. While being intrinsic to their assessment of reality, these signs (the spinning top and the ability to be unharmed by flames) seem to be external to the protagonists. The observer and the sign that he or she is observing are distinct from each other, although the presence of each sign alters the metaphysical status of the observer. Each sign is self-referential in the sense of referring back to the self of the observer or protagonist. The sign that Heidegger refers to is, however, intrinsic to the entity, namely a human being, that has the capacity to create, observe and think about signs. The sign and its 'observer' are not two; they are one and the same. The *Being* of human being *is Sign*. Human being and sign are not distinct entities. A human being is a sign that is meaning-less and empty, referring to that aspect of being human that has withdrawn itself from its human being-ness. But it is this withdrawn-ness that draws us in, that beckons us.

> My eyes already touch the sunny hill.
> going far ahead of the road I have begun.
> So we are grasped by what we cannot grasp;
> it has inner light, even from a distance–
>
> and charges us, even if we do not reach it,
> into something else, which, hardly sensing it,

---

138 *Deutungslos* can also mean lacking interpretation, in which case the sentence could be translated as "We are a sign without interpretation (*Deutung*)." But what is a sign without interpretation? Is it the same thing to say that the sign is empty as it is to say it is without interpretation? For something to be empty does it need to be without interpretation or is something without interpretation automatically empty? Does being without or lacking in interpretation mean that an entity (or sign in this case) is waiting to be filled with interpretation (and therefore meaning)? Or is the sign in some fundamental, essential manner empty, i.e. it cannot be filled with interpretation and remains 'meaning-less'?

> we already are; a gesture waves us on
> answering our own wave ...
> but what we feel is the wind in our faces (Rilke, 2004).

That the sign is empty and bereft of meaning that does not, however, 'mean' that it is point-less. The sign is empty; it is an empty sign that points to the 'no-thingness' of that which is withdrawing from itself. What is withdrawing from itself can only be pointed toward. As mentioned earlier, it cannot be defined, and therefore we cannot categorically state what thinking as a thinking toward that which is withdrawing from itself is. This thinking is also not 'mere' reflection or a thinking about thinking made up of critical self-reflection, for this too would be to bind it in a process that is already known, entailing perhaps results or answers that are already expected. It cannot be 'learnt' through a process of self-reflection. What thinking is or means can only be learnt by entering the 'tide' so to speak of thinking, just as one cannot learn what swimming is or means by discussing or theorizing about it. The meaning of swimming can only be learnt by the participatory act of swimming itself, by jumping into the current of water.

> Was, z. B. Schwimmen "heißt", lernen wir nie durch eine Abhandlung über das Schwimmen kennen. Was Schwimmen heißt, sagt uns nur der Sprung in den Strom. Die Frage "Was heißt denken?" läßt sich niemals dadurch beantworten, daß wir eine Begriffsbestimmung über das Denken, eine Definition, vorlegen und deren Inhalt fleißig ausbreiten. Wir denken im folgenden nicht *über* das Denken. Wir bleiben außerhalb der bloßen Reflexion, die das Denken zu ihrem Gegenstand macht. [...]
>
> Gleichwohl fällt auf unserem Weg ständig ein Licht in das Denken. Allein dieses Licht wird nicht durch die Laterne der Reflexion erst herzugebracht. Das Licht kommt aus dem Denken selbst und nur aus ihm (Heidegger 1954, 9–10).

When we remain, through effort, outside of mere reflection on the way to understanding thinking, then a light is shed on thinking. But this light does not come into existence because of the "lantern of reflection." The light that illuminates thinking comes out of thinking itself and only out of thinking. In other words, the question 'What is thinking?' begins to reveal itself only by embarking on thinking but not on reflection and theorizing. Illumination begins with praxis. Just as a carpenter's apprentice who has a true calling to being a carpenter will go beyond the learning of the trade or skill of making things out of wood by entering or at least considering the world of what is possible in the material form of wood and the imaginative world of carpentry. This world of texture, form, senses, instruments, wood, focus and attention, physical labour and learning is revealed only through practice to be a world that is continuously unfolding. Similarly, one cannot arrive at the end of what it is to think. *One can, however, be brought into the presence of the possibility of what it means to think.*

6.2.1 The Presence of Thinking

But what does it mean to be brought into the presence something, of thinking? What does presence mean? Is presence connected to *being present?* The question of what it means to be present must bring us automatically to the question of time and its temporalities, and to the question of history that has, in a fundamental sense, to do with time, and with memory. The question of what it means to be present must also, to begin with, concern the present, or rather the *now.* The now, by virtue of being neither past nor future nor anything else but 'this' which cannot be grasped as it speeds away, is not a temporal category. The now is neither time nor not-time. It is not a something that can be defined and completely or even incompletely understood in the moment of its occurring, and yet it is the location for our entire human experience which takes place only and ever in the 'here and now.' Both past and future spring from the presence of the now as what is no longer present and what is about to be present (but will then retreat almost instantaneously into being what is no longer present). Past and future both represent forms of the imagination.

> Wie verhält sich die Sache der Zeit? Was ist an der Zeit seiend? [...] "Seiend" heißt: anwesend. Seiendes ist um so seiender, je anwesender es ist. [...] Was ist an der Zeit anwesend und damit gegenwärtig? Gegenwärtig ist an der Zeit je nur das "jetzt" (νῦν, nunc). Das Künftigte *ist* das "noch nicht jetzt"; das Vergangene *ist* das "nicht mehr jetzt". Das Künftigte ist das noch Abwesende, das Vergangene ist das bereits Abwesende. Seiend: anwesend an der Zeit ist je nur der schmale Grat des jeweiligen flüchtigen "jetzt", das aus dem "noch nicht jetzt" herankommend in das "nicht mehr jetzt" weg geht. [...]
>
> Was ist an der Zeit seiend, anwesend? Das jeweilige "jetzt". Aber das je jetztige "jetzt" west an, in dem es vergeht. Zukünftiges und Vergangenes sind *Nicht*-Anwesendes, solches, von dem man nie einfach sagen darf, es wese an (Heidegger 1954, 40–41).

Thinking about History

History as a study of the past, is particularly, as mentioned before, concerned with the imagination. But what does thinking about the past, following from the foregoing discussion mean? If thinking is about realizing or acknowledging that we have not begun to think and that that which is most worthy of thinking or 'thought-provoking' is, in the very constitution of being human, withdrawing from us as those who think, then where does this leave us with regard to the past, the past as that which has ceased to be present in the now? As that which is no longer present, the past has retreated from us much like what is 'thought-provoking' has withdrawn from us. Yet this withdrawal or retreating does not seem to be the same. We are not present to what is the most 'thought-provoking.' The past, however, exists as that which is no longer present. What is most 'thought-provoking' exists in front of us, giving us, in a sense our being-ness as entities who are drawn toward 'it.' Yet we may not be present to the presence of what is in front of us even though it acts upon us as much as the future that we live into acts upon us. The past, on the other hand, as a condition of time, is not present in the now. It reveals itself as a presence in the imagination. However, the imagination too, as with all our experience, must be present in the now. In fact, we can only have an epistemic connection to what presents itself to us in the now. Both past and future as situated and arising in the imagination can only present themselves to us in the now. Time (and its primary conditions of past, present and future) and, therefore, also history exist only now. The past and future, as loci of knowledge, must be imagined in order to become something known. Does that which the most 'thought-provoking' also require the imagination for us to become present to it? Where do imagination and thinking stand in relation to one another? This question is critical to our understanding of history as a *thinking about the past* that profoundly concerns the imagination.

> Wir gelangten in die Frage: was ist dies überhaupt – das Vorstellen? [...] Auf dem Weg der Frage: was heißt Denken? gelangen wir in die Frage: was ist dies – das Vorstellen?
>
> Die Vermutung regt sich, Denken und Vorstellen könnten wohl das Selbe sein. Die Aussicht auf eine Möglichkeit öffnet sich; daß nämlich das bisherige Wesen des Denkens vom Vorstellen her und als eine Art des Vorstellens geprägt sei. So ist es in Wahrheit. Allein es bleibt zugleich dunkel, auf welche Weise sich diese Wesensprägung des bisherigen Denkens ereignet. Dunkel bleibt, woher dieses Ereignis kommt. [...] Zwar verstehen wir und nehmen es als die klarste Sache von der Welt, wenn einer sagt: ich denke mir die Sache so und so, und dabei meint: ich stelle mir die Sache so und so vor. Woraus sich klar ergibt: Denken ist ein Vorstellen (Heidegger 1954, 60).

The German reflexive verb '*sich (etwas) vorstellen*' or the noun '*die Vorstellung*' which are often translated as 'to imagine' or 'imagination' literally mean to put or place something forward or in front (of oneself).[139] The English words 'to imagine' and 'imagination,' on the other hand, contain the word 'image' which suggests a representation of something else. 'Image' in its root meaning also denotes 'a likeness.' To imagine then is to produce an image – that is invariably understood to be constructed in the mind – that in turn has a likeness or

139 *vor:* in front; *stellen:* to place or put.

similarity to something else, usually some concrete object or event. Because of this similarity to something that may be concrete, the imagined object is considered to be a representation. However, the object that is imagined may not have any similarity to some concrete object or event that has a prior or current existence that the person who is doing the imagining is aware of. The object that is imagined may thus be detached from 'reality' and participate in the creation of a world that is distinct from a world that is known through empirical evidence or through the avenue of the senses. This imagined world that is no longer a derivative of the 'real' world can be sometimes labelled as 'fantasy' or 'fiction.' Imagination thus lies at the core of the creation of a simulacrum. Baudrillard (1994, 6) distinguishes between four forms of the kind of representation or 'imaging' via the imagination that we are talking about in the following manner:

> These would be the successive phases of the image:
> 1. It is the reflection of a basic reality.
> 2. It masks and perverts a basic reality.
> 3. It masks the absence of a basic reality.
> 4. It bears no relation to any reality whatever: it is its own pure simulacrum.

In the first 'phase' or kind of representation, the image reflects what Baudrillard calls 'basic reality,' i.e. the image is recognizable to the extent that it resembles or attempts to 'map' sensory and 'evidence-based,' empirical reality. In the second form of representation via the imagination, the image seeks to move beyond being a mere faithful 'copy' of reality to becoming a commentary on this 'basic reality.' Basic reality is masked, perverted or perhaps one could say 'subverted.' But more so than in the third case – the image is created in such a way as to suggest a faithful representation of reality that is, in fact, absent or has no existence. In the final phase the image has detached itself from reality and is pure creation not based on any prior empirical knowledge. The image is no longer a copy or representation of anything, neither in terms of being faithful nor concealing or subverting the presence or absence of something: "it is its own pure simulacrum." Baudrillard summarizes a story by Borges in which cartographers draw up a perfect map of a territory, which in order to be perfect and flawless as a representation, i.e. as a map, takes on the exact size and features of the territory which is to be mapped. But this ultimate representation that is literally mapped onto the reality that it seeks to become an image of is no longer the endeavour or marker of modernity. This fourth or final phase of the imagination is what he calls the "hyperreal." Abstraction and simulation have become the 'real' taking precedence over other forms of sensory, empirical reality.

> Abstraction today is no longer that of the map, the double, the mirror or the concept. Simulation is no longer that of a territory, a referential being or a substance. It is the generation by models of a real without origin or reality: a hyperreal. The territory no longer precedes the map, nor survives it. Henceforth, it is the map that precedes the territory – precession of simulacra – it is the map that engenders the territory and if we were to revive the fable today, it would be the territory whose shreds are slowly rotting across the map. It is the real, and not the map, whose vestiges subsist here and there, in the deserts which are no longer those of the Empire, but our own. The desert of the real itself (Baudrillard 1994, 1).[140]

6.3 Mnemosyne and the Desert of the Real

The real has become a "desert." It has become a location of spiritual dryness, a place that lacks the oozing dampness of sensory experience, a region of undulating fragmentation and alienation, strewn with illusions and mirages masquerading as the real, as something that they are not. The desert's borders are shifting constantly, eating into greenery, suggesting finitude while becoming infinitely jagged and worn. The desert calls forth an imagination that imagines itself in circular eddies of fatigue and desperation. The traveller in the desert shields herself from too much light while peering into the sandy, shrub speckled distance looking for a companion. The desert is bare, stark, harsh. Companions are shadows that shrink and disappear in spirals and wisps of funnelling dust. Although the desert is unrelenting it is also the place for aloneness, inner cleansing. A place for introspection. Yet in the hyperreal world that Baudrillard speaks of, the desert is a metaphor for degeneration and decay. Heidegger refers to Nietzsche when he talks of "The desert" ("*die Wüste*"). The desert grows ("*die Wüste wächst*") bringing with it devastation, desolation, deprivation and annihilation ("*Verwüstung*"). These words carry more dread than mere destruction:

> "Die Wüste wächst". Das will sagen: Die Verwüstung breitet sich aus. Verwüstung ist mehr als Zerstörung. Verwüstung ist unheimlicher als Vernichtung. Die Zerstörung beseitig nur das bisher Gewachsene und Gebaute; die Verwüstung aber unterbindet künftiges Wachstum und verwehrt jedes Bauen. Die Verwüstung ist unheimlicher als die bloße Vernichtung. [...] während die Verwüstung das Unterbindende und Verwehrende gerade bestellt und ausbreitet. Die Sahara in Afrika ist nur eine Art der Wüste. Die Verwüstung der Erde

140 "*Welcome to the desert of the real*" – one the of main characters in the movie *The Matrix*, Morpheus, uses this line which is borrowed from Baudrillard's work on simulacra when he speaks to the main character of the movie, Neo, after his first experience of being hooked into a computer generated reality. It is also the title of a book by the philosopher Slavoj Žižek (2002).

> kann mit der Erzielung eines höchsten Lebensstandards des Menschen ebenso zusammengehen wie mit der Organisation eines gleichförmigen Glückszustandes aller Menschen. Die Verwüstung kann mit beiden das Selbe sein und auf die unheimlichste Weise überall umgehen, nämlich dadurch, daß sie sich verbirgt. Die Verwüstung ist kein bloßes versanden. Die Verwüstung ist auf hohen Touren laufende Vertreibung der Mnemosyne (Heidegger 1954, 11).

Heidegger emphatically points out that this devastation is no mere "desertification" (literally: "*die Verwüstung*") or filling up with sand, getting bogged down, stagnating and fizzling out. The deprivation that accompanies the 'growth of the desert' in Nietzsche's sense is one that is more subtle and sinister than plain destruction which does away with structures, buildings and whatever has been built so far. The desert stands for the erasure and stunting of a future of growth and creativity. A 'real' desert such as the Sahara is only a particular kind of desert. The desert that is being spoken of here points to the desolation of the earth. Paradoxically this annihilation escorts the pursuit for the establishment of the highest quality of life and uniform happiness for humanity across the globe. But above all the desert signifies the banishment and ultimate expulsion of Mnemosyne, the Goddess of Memory and Remembrance. Mnemosyne is not merely memory in its commonplace meaning of a capacity or skill to recall or think about something that has happened in the past. Mnemosyne is the assembly or congregation of all that is worthy of remembering. Memory in this sense does not concern any object that can be thought about. Here it is the source of poetry that returns one to the fountain of creativity and thought. It is the collection of all that already desires to be thought about and is commendable of thinking:

> Mnemosyne, die Tochter von Himmel und Erde, wird als Braut des Zeus in neun Nächten die Mutter der Musen. Spiel und Musik, Tanz und Dichtung gehören dem Schoß der Mnemosyne, der Gedächtnis. Offenkundig meint dieses Wort anderes als nur die von der Psychologie feststellbare Fähigkeit, Vergangenes in der Vorstellung zu behalten. Gedächtnis denkt an das Gedachte. [...] Gedächtnis ist die Versammlung des Denkens auf das, was überall im voraus schon bedacht sein möchte. Gedächtnis ist die Versammlung des Andenkens. [...] Gedächtnis, die Mutter der Musen: das Andenken an das zu-Denkende ist der Quellgrund des Dichtens. Das Dichten ist darum das Gewässer, das bisweilen rückwärts fließt der Quelle zu, zum Denken als Andenken (Heidegger 1954, 7).

To restate what has been mentioned earlier, Heidegger distinguishes between memory as what he calls the psychological ability to imagine what is past with Memory who is the mother of the muses of dance, poetry, play and music. Mnemosyne – or Memory, the mother of the muses – refers to or thinks of what has *already been thought* ("*das Gedachte*"). Further Memory, in this sense, is the coming together, assembly, or gathering together of all that already desires to be considered, thought upon ("*bedacht sein möchte*"). Memory is the gathering together of remembrance ("*das Andenken*") of what is to be thought upon ("*zu-Denkende*"). As Heidegger ardently points out we do not think because what is worthy of thought has withdrawn itself from us. Then what is it that is to be thought upon? It is *Being* ("*das Sein*").[141] But thinking about Being is not to be reduced to a banal subject–object pairing in which Being becomes the object of thought and rational or philosophical enquiry. Rather thinking is an occurrence ("*ein Ereignis*") of Being. In this sense thinking *belongs* to Being, but thinking is also that which *listens* to Being.

> Das Denken ist des Seins, insofern das Denken, vom Sein ereignet, dem Sein gehört. Das Denken ist zugleich Denken des Seins, insofern das Denken, dem Sein gehörend, auf das Sein hört[142] (GA 9, 316).[143]

Memory as a gathering together of what already desires to be thought upon, is a gathering together or remembrance of Being. Memory as the remembrance of Being is the font of poetry or the returning to the source. But Memory is not imagining (*sich etwas vorstellen*) Being or thinking *about* Being. It is that aspect of Being enclosed in thinking as a movement toward that which is worthy of thinking that begins to reveal, lay bare or return to Being as 'something' that has withdrawn and therefore concealed or hidden itself from thought. Memory, and in this context thinking, is about re-turning, re-membering, re-participating in that which already comprises being human. To be human then is to both forget and remember Being that qualifies and gives rise, so to speak, to human Being.

Heidegger states that while imagination and thinking are linked, and that imagination is thinking in the commonplace understanding of the latter, it is still not thinking in the sense he is referring to. One can nevertheless enquire into what the German word '*sich etwas vorstellen*' (to place or put something in front of oneself) means since it seems to denote something different to the English word 'imagination' which, as previously mentioned, contains 'image.' One could begin by asking what does placing something in front of oneself

---

141 Lee (2001, 179). "Das wesentliche Denken heißt dagegen für Heidegger das Denken des Seins, d. h., das *Denken an Sein.* Wie Heidegger schon früher gesagt hat, ist das 'zu-Denkende' nichts anderes als das Sein. ... Im Gegensatz dazu ist das Sein nach Heidegger nicht als Gegenstand des Denkens oder Element des Denkens zu verstehen. So heißt es: '*Das Sein ist kein Erzeugnis des Denkens.* Wohl das wesentliche Denken ein Ereignis des Seins.' (GA 9 308, Herv. von Verf.) Das Denken ist das Denken *des* Seins."

142 'Listen to' (*auf etwas/jemanden hören*) can have a double meaning. It can mean 'to obey,' to carry out, follow what someone is saying. Or it can mean to pay attention, dwell, seek out.

143 Heidegger cited in Lee (2001, 179).

mean? Where is this 'in front' located? Is it a physical location in the present moment? Or is it a temporal location as in placing something in the future? If it is a placing something in the present moment – whether physically or in the mind – then this would suggest an engagement with what is placed in front of oneself (by oneself). What could this engagement be? It could involve observing or analyzing what is placed in front or changing and altering the object that is being observed. If the object is placed in front of oneself physically or even in one's mind, both locations require thought – and language as arising together with thought – to identify, label and describe the particular object. Even if the object is placed in front of oneself in the present moment, it is still an object that is remembered, i.e. our knowledge of it is inescapably linked to what we already know from the past. The present moment, and not only the past, is therefore also being remembered. The present resembles and replicates the past. To place something in front of oneself in the location of the present is to re-cognize an object through a process of comparison with prior experience and knowledge. To place in front of oneself also involves the act of placing. To place in front is an active act in which something that was presumably located elsewhere is placed by oneself in front of oneself. Something that could be located behind us or on the side or out of view is placed in front. We would also say that something that was out of our field of attention is now placed in our field of attention. Placing in front then is a matter of placing into our field of attention, or of paying attention to something that has been brought to our attention by placing it in front of us. 'In front,' while suggesting a location that is physical, is simultaneously a metaphor for a location within one's field of attention. To place or have something in front of one's field of attention could mean many things. It could mean *being present* to something. Or being in the presence of something. *Sich vorstellen* could therefore also mean *anwesend sein* – to be present to the presence of something or someone or to the presence of Being. To place in front of and therefore also be in front of something or someone suggests a form of engagement which in its most effortless and fundamental form could be to simply *be*. To be without the addition of judgment, comparison, measurement, bias, indeed without the addition of thought in the sense of automatic chatter as outlined earlier.

However, there is another sense of placing something in front of oneself. While this also involves bringing something into one's field of attention, the meaning of 'in front' is a temporal one. To place in front then requires placing something, an idea, an expectation, aspiration or a possibility, in the forward directed temporality of the future. The future here is not the future that will become the present once it comes to pass through the present moment. It is not the future as that which is not yet present (*noch nicht anwesend*), rather it is the future that exists now as a future that is being lived into. The future that is being lived into as a forward leaning of human being exists as the future that is giving the present lived moment its being-ness. Rather than turn around and look to the past to explain and understand the condition of the present moment, this view shifts the perspective to the future as a creation of thinking that in turn is a direct correlation of the state of being now. This created future is causally correlated to how we experience the present moment. It provides the context, so to speak, for our actions and ways of being in the present. In other words, our experience of the world is an occurrence shaped by the context or framework given by the future not as it will come to pass, but as *a future that is being lived into*. Being-ness in the present is therefore a product of a future that exists as a possibility. The possibility of peace, for example, leads to ways of being and of acting that are deeply shaped by that possibility. Possibility is not something concrete although it may result in concrete achievements or in the planning of concrete events. Possibility exists in the realm of creation. It arises from the source of creativity which is Being or that which is to be thought upon (*das zu-Denkende*). Possibility arises out of the no-thing-ness of Being while pulling the tangible being-ness of the present moment forward into existence. Possibility exists in the temporality of the future which gives description and shape to the embodied form of material existence, consisting of actions, thoughts, feelings, attitudes, speaking and listening in the now. The latter are formed by possibility, which does not exist as something concrete or tangible. Perhaps one could say that possibility is an idea. But it is not an idea emerging through the commonplace process of thinking about something or as a reaction to something that already exists. It is closer to Plato's *Idea* that exists as a proto-type or form, of which concrete objects are a reflection or even manifestation. Possibility as it is being used here gets created in the space of nothingness. Nothingness is the *possibility of possibility* from which particular possibilities arise. Possibility thus comes into existence out of nothing and occupies the temporal realm of the future which simultaneously informs our present moment. Possibility is not probability or options or choices and so on. It is not tangible and yet it profoundly gives rise to that which is tangible and embodied.

> Bei der Uneinigkeit der Philosophie darüber, was das Vorstellen im Wesen sei, gibt es offenbar nur einen Ausweg ins Freie. Man verläßt das Feld der philosophischen Spekulationen und untersucht erstmal sorgfältig und wissenschaftlich, wie es mit den Vorstellungen, die bei den Lebewesen, vor allem bei den Menschen und Tieren, vorkommen, überhaupt steht. Mit solchen Untersuchungen beschäftigt sich neben anderem die Psychologie. [...] (auch) wenn innerhalb der Psychologie in keiner Weise zur Klarheit kommt, was das ist, wohin die Vorstellungen eingeordnet werden: nämlich der Organismus des Lebendigen, das Bewußtsein, die Seele, das Unbewußte und all die Tiefen und Schichten, in die der Bereich der Psychologie gegliedert wird. Hier bleibt alles fragwürdig; dennoch sind die wissenschaftlichen Ergebnisse richtig. [...]

> Wir stehen außerhalb der Wissenschaft. Wir stehen stattdessen z. B. vor einem blühenden Baum – und der Baum steht vor uns. Er stellt sich uns vor. Der Baum und wir stellen uns einander vor, indem der Baum dasteht und wir ihm gegenüber stehen. In die Beziehung zueinander – voreinander gestellt, *sind* der Baum und wir. Bei diesem Vorstellen handelt es sich also nicht um "Vorstellungen", die in unserem Kopf herumschwirren. Halten wir hier einen Augenblick inne, so wie wenn wir Atem holen vor und nach einem Sprung. Wir *sind* nämlich jetzt gesprungen, heraus aus dem geläufigen Bezirk der Wissenschaften und sogar, wie sich zeigen wird, der Philosophie. Und wohin sind wir gesprungen? Vielleicht in einen Abgrund? Nein! Eher auf einen Boden; auf einen? Nein! Eher auf einen Boden; auf einen? Nein! Sondern auf den Boden, auf dem wir leben und sterben, wenn wir uns nichts vormachen (Heidegger 1954, 16–17).

To be in front of something is to be present to whatever is in front of us, to be present to the presence of what is in front of us. Whatever is in front of us also leads to our being present to ourselves. The presence of oneself arises, so to speak, in the presence of whatever is in front of us. It is through the 'being present in front of us' of something that we become present to ourselves, becoming aware that we are being present as something that is present. To be present is to exist. To exist outside of the ground provided by thoughts as reactions and concepts is to exist as a being that is present. To be present requires something to exist in front of us but also to realize that we are not present to what is in front of us and therefore not present to ourselves as a *presence*. But this realization of not being present, where does it come from? It cannot come from an act of will because that would presuppose a prior knowledge of not being present. The realization comes without warning, without explanation and indeed without being caused by something else. It is there and, in the moment of being there as a realization of not being present, it is immediately an ushering in of being present to presence. What is presence? Presence, it would seem, is not the sheer physicality of a material, embodied object existing in time and space. It is not a *thing* just as beings are not things. Presence like possibility cannot be grasped in the same manner as we think we grasp the existence of a table, or a chair, or a faint aroma, or sunlight on one's skin, or the chill of ice water, or the purring of a cat, or the sound of a conversation. Yet presence *is* there...or here. It is here when one is present to *it*. Is presence prior, concomitant or subsequent to the subject? Is this question of causal and temporal sequence relevant? Perhaps one could say that presence is prior just as context is prior to content: although both arise and exist simultaneously, context provides the framework for the occurrence of content in terms of shape, form and meaning. Presence is space. Space is the emptiness that surrounds objects and beings; it is that from which objects and beings are brought forth into existence. Space is clearing, is emptiness and clearing; emptiness is space which allows the embodied subject and everything that is experienced by the embodied subject to occur. The embodied subject as a coming into existence or as an occurrence from the space or clearing of *being nothing* arises as a particular perspective of that space. In other words, the embodied subject comes into existence from a clearing as the possibility of knowing the clearing both directly through experience and indirectly through reflection. It is the clearing that engenders or allows 'this' to come into existence. 'This' exists in successive moments of now.

> And yet – beyond what is, not away from it but before it, there is still something else that happens. In the midst of beings as a whole an open place occurs. There is a clearing, a lighting. Thought of in reference to what is, to beings, this clearing is in a greater degree than are beings. This open center is therefore not surrounded by what is; rather, the lighting center itself encircles all that is, like the Nothing which we scarcely know. That which is can only be, as a being, if it stands within and stands out within what is lighted in this clearing. Only this clearing grants and guarantees to us humans a passage to those beings that we ourselves are not, and access to the being that we ourselves are. Thanks to this clearing, beings are unconcealed in certain changing degrees. And yet a being can be concealed, too, only within the sphere of what is lighted. Each being we encounter and which encounters us keeps to this curious opposition of presence in that it always withholds itself at the same time in a concealedness. The clearing in which beings stand is in itself at the same time concealment (Heidegger 2001, 51–52).

6.4 History as Possibility?

The seemingly simple and straightforward temporalities of past, present and future with which we are all familiar are entangled with one another. Past, present and future are imbroglios of one another. We cannot talk about the past without invoking the present and the future. This insight requires no great effort of intelligence. Yet, as historians and social scientists we must ask in what manner these temporalities are entangled. What are the ramifications of these imbroglios? If past, present and future all exist in the now, what are the implications for a study of the past? Not only the past but also the present and future are steeped in memory and imagination. Not only is the past as a present that is longer present a function of re-imagining what took place, but the present too as it presents itself or unfolds itself before us is re-cognized based on our imagining of the past. The future too as the present that is yet to become present is inhabited by our imagination that almost completely originates in our knowledge of the past. The future as the present that has not yet come to be present does not occur to us as the empty space of potential or as a clearing for possibility, but as a room that is occupied with aspirations, fears, anxieties and dreams somehow curbed by good sense and reasonableness – it occurs to us as the location not for unlimited expansion, opening and creativity but for limited action and movement forward. Yet all this has to be imagined. *Time is otherwise empty.* It takes on form and meaning only when anchored by our imagination of events that have arisen and disappeared into and from our view or events that lie beyond the horizon of our view, that are about to occur and show themselves to us such that they become part of who we are, through which our own being acquires a shape and form. Past and future are thus empty spaces that require imagination in order to come into existence. The present too is imagined inasmuch that we re-cognize it and treat it as something that we know, that we somehow remember as resembling what we have already experienced. Yet the present is the location for '*this*' '*now*.' It too is empty as a signifier for *what is* – for what cannot be thought of, for what cannot and need not be imagined. The present *is*. In order for it to become something, it too must be imagined.

The Plain Sense of Things

After the leaves have fallen, we return
To a plain sense of things. It is as if
We had come to the end of the imagination,
Inanimate in an inert savior.

It is difficult even to choose the adjective
For this blank cold, this sadness without a cause.
The great structure has become a minor house.
No turban walks across the lessened floors.

The greenhouse never so badly needed paint.
The chimney is fifty years old and slants to one side.
A fantastic effort has failed, a repetition
In a repetitiousness of men and flies.

Yet the absence of the imagination had
Itself to be imagined. The great pond,
The plain sense of it, without reflections, leaves,
Mud, water like dirty glass expressing silence

Of a sort, silence of a rat come out to see,
The great pond and its waste of the lilies, all this
Had to be imagined as an inevitable knowledge,
Required, as necessity requires (Stevens 1972, 382–3).

As Wallace Stevens's poem says, even the absence of imagination had to be imagined. The absence of imagination leaves us not with despair and ruin, rather it catapults us into the suchness of the present moment, stripped of pretention, fame, effort and meaning: *to a plain sense of things as they are and as they are not.* It is above and inside this plain sense of things that time hovers, spiralling out like a swarm of bees or locusts that clouds this plain sense, bringing moments of presence and non-presence, concealment and unconcealment. Imagination is the source of the swarm that adopts an ever twisting and turning phantasmagoria of events, people, feelings, actions, memories, dreams, stories and more in an unending mixture. If imagination is the swarm of images without which there is no past or future, without which there is no history, then what does it mean to think about the past that is the purpose of history, if thinking is thought of as a turning toward that which has already withdrawn itself from human being? Can there be an engagement with the past that involves thinking in the sense we have been discussing it? Or must history as a study of the past that is deeply anchored in imagination be relegated to a second level of thinking that endorses and valorizes the phantasmagoria of the dream, of the simulacrum that is detached from the real, that has become the desert, racing away from what is worthy of thinking, speeding away from the question of *Being?* Does history promote alienation – alienation and detachment from what is, from a plain sense of things?

6.4.1 History, Language, Thought

History like thought and time arises when there is language. Without thought there is no time; there is no becoming aware of what is no longer present and what is about to become present. All there is is the present moment or now. When thought ceases so does the existence of time and its occurrence as a pulling in and releasing out of objects and events. However, apart from the present moment, our experience of past and future is conceptual, embedded in narratives, stories, a putting and piecing together of what has happened or will happen in some sequence that purportedly makes sense to us and to the people we join hands with in agreement or even disagreement. This making sense is contingent. It is not absolute. It is contingent on many things: community, Zeitgeist, prejudices and judgments that do not show up as prejudices and judgments but rather as 'facts' and the 'truth,' on culture, on language itself as the compass that we use to describe and orient ourselves in the world. But while language represents a set of distinctions through which we not only know the world but also 'create' as something we have albeit limited access to it is also a constraint. It limits our access to world in its expression as a conceptual apparatus that labels, defines and contains experience and possibility, although the latter emerges in language. Language in its deepest senses involves both creation or *bringing forth* but also interpreting and narrating. While it seems that History clearly lives in and is skilled at producing interpretation and narration, it is not clear to what extent History can or does participate in the act of bringing forth or creating new possibilities. As an act of interpretation and a discipline that is committed to fostering narratives that sustain interpretation, History must always be one step removed from experience:

> as ultimate codified 'truth' (History) [...] must always present itself as story. Since History exists in language, its strange task becomes the giving of an unavoidably spectral half-life to events which no longer exist in experience, only in words (White 1984).

Although History sometimes deals almost exclusively with written texts (as though all reality and experience is encoded in writing) – i.e. with language or words in a particular configuration or order that is intended to make sense – the meaning behind that language and words and the context (author, society, political and religious milieus, patronage, cultural and temporal regional – language as it used in a particular province of the past and so on) must all be (re-) imagined. In other words, our access to texts that are often considered to be prime bearers of language, truth and meaning is again through the language and words we use now and their situational significance. There seems to be no escape from the covering and layers of language, words and concepts not only to perceive and understand events of the past but also texts that describe events or ideas that have their origin in the past. Still, those events and texts come into existence within and from the intentionality of the present moment that hauls back that which is no longer present into being present through memory, language and narrative. The past as event(s) and as text(s) and non-event(s) and non-text(s) exists solely in the present moment together with scholarly or other texts that function as commentaries that also exist in the present moment. In other words, everything that exists or does not exist outside the present moment cannot be experienced, but known only in a second order as concept, interpretation and story. In short it can be known only as a model, likeness, image, representation, i.e. as a simulacrum.

History is, as Collingwood points out, a way of knowing the past.[144] Upon reflection, History is not simply about stating that such and such sequence of events took place in the past, rather it is about establishing a system of knowledge concerning the past. How does one, or can one, know the past? How does one know something that no longer exists in material form?

> Historical thought has an object with peculiarities of its own. The past, consisting of particular events in space and time which are no longer happening, cannot be apprehended by mathematical thinking, because mathematical thinking apprehends objects that have

144 See Collingwood (1994, 3).

> no special location in space or time, and it is just that lack of peculiar spatio-temporal location that makes them knowable. Nor can the past be apprehended by theological thinking [...] nor by scientific thinking, because the truths which science discovers are known to be true by being found through observation and experiment exemplified in what we actually perceive, whereas the past has vanished [...] mathematical, theological and scientific knowledge [...] if they offer themselves as complete accounts of knowledge they actually imply that historical knowledge is impossible (Collingwood 1994, 5).

As Collingwood persuasively shows, historical knowledge, if compared to the content and manner through which other forms of knowledge, even scientific knowledge, are arrived at, becomes unachievable or void since the object of historical knowledge, namely the temporal category we call the past has disappeared. History, then deals with what has vanished, disappeared, with what does not exist any longer – at least not in any empirical sense of the word 'existence.' The content of historical knowledge is no longer in front of us in manner that can be directly observed or experienced. Neither is it in front of us in the same form of abstraction as mathematical axioms, theorems, equations or truths that also do not strictly occupy an empirical realm of observation and experience. Historical knowledge does, however, seem to involve a level of abstraction in the sense that we are dealing with objects in the mind, thought or imagination. These objects of our imagination do not exist in the same manner as mathematical objects of imagination that claim to have relinquished any attachment to particular anchors of time, space, culture and language. The objects of historical imagination are, on the contrary, anchored in the specific location of culture, language and communities of thought that agree or disagree on the content of that particular imagination and how it is being presented through narrative or other material expression. What then is historical knowledge? Is such a thing as historical knowledge at all possible? Thus, Collingwood (1994, 282) asks:

> How, or on what conditions, can the historian know the past? In considering this question, the first point to notice is that the past is never a given fact which can apprehended empirically by perception [the] possible knowledge of the past is mediate or inferential or indirect [and] this mediation cannot be effected by testimony [...] If then the historian has no direct or empirical knowledge of his facts, and no transmitted or testimoniary knowledge of them, what kind of knowledge has he: in other words, what must the historian do in order that he may know them?

6.5 History as 'Andenken'[145]

Collingwood continues to answer these questions by stating that History involves *a re-enactment of the past.* What does this mean? How does a historian go about the activity of re-enactment? On the surface, to re-enact, implies repeating an action or doing something again – to act out again something that had previously been acted out. But where and how does, in the case of the historian, this acting out again of something that has already been acted take place. What does this re-enactment look like? First, it should be stated that re-enactment, while clearly containing the root form of action in the verb 'act' which can often denote a physical or quantifiable movement, must in the case of the past also include actions that involves ideas, thoughts, laws, rules, narratives and abstract forms of knowledge found in philosophy, mathematics, architectural design, political systems, religious ideology and so on. To re-enact is thus not only to retrace a movement, for example, of a community migrating from one town to another, or of an army marching toward a battlefield, or labourers constructing an architectural edifice such as a temple or memorial to a king or political leader. In order to re-enact even the above examples, the historian must be able to know by way of re-imagining the conditions that give rise to such actions. What, for example, were the reasons and motivations of the communities who were migrating? Which members of the community actually participated and in what capacity in the move from one place to another? What happened along the way? What sort of reception did the community encounter by other communities along the way and once they arrived at their destination? The historian must therefore re-enact not only the seemingly empirical or physical dimension of the migration through particular locales or landscapes but also the situation that gave rise to the community's desire to shift its home from one place to another. Not everything that the historian re-enacts is quantifiable. In other words, the historian may or may not have access to documentation from the period when the migration took place to support his or her perspective on what, how and why the migration took place and so on. The situational context must therefore be primarily imagined. It must be brought into existence through thought. Again, we must ask what kind of thought is this? Surely, this is not the kind of automatic thought or 'chatter' that I distinguished earlier.[146] Is it thought or rather thinking as distinguished by Heidegger? Or is it closer to the kind of thinking or imagining we en-

145 *Andenken* can mean memory, remembrance, souvenir or memento. But it also explicitly means *'to think on'* (an + denken).
146 See section 6.1 *Thinking about the Past.*

counter in Indian literary and philosophical theory – a thinking that is at once tactile, sensory, charged with potential to create the concrete and the real as in the story of the Śiva's devotee Pūcalār or Borges' unnamed protagonist in *The Circular Ruins?* The re-enactment that the historian undertakes must be alive; it must have the ability and power to create the past that is no longer visible or palpable into something that is profoundly, intensely and brilliantly substantial, tangible – a shimmering object that enters the realm of experience.

6.5.1 Re-enactment and Imagination

What else is this re-enactment but the intentional galvanization of the imagination? This imagination, that is at the same time a re-enactment, requires the same kind of thinking or thought that Pūcalār's mind temple requires. A kind of thinking that visualizes each detail of the temple, not just each brick, but also each craftsman and architect. The mind temple is brought into existence by imagining not only the object that is being created but also what went into building it and who needed to be involved in its creation. The mind temple arises conjoined to its immediate surroundings of materiality and agency. It is built in thought with care and passion. It is not a random, fleeting fantasy of thought, but a construction that requires tremendous perseverance night and day. Each detail is imagined and kept in place by the effort of exact and exacting moments of re-imagining. The mind temple will vanish otherwise, just as random thoughts and feelings come and go. The 'mind-born' artefact becomes real through layers of imagination: imagined bricks, mortar, plinth, arches, paint, sculpture, minute architectural design, niches, spatial depth, inner sanctum – all resting on ground that had to be imagined, with a pinnacle that sways in a sky that had to be imagined. This act of imagining reality into existence is not an act of remembering. Or is it? Does it involve memory? Perhaps not memory in the sense of simply recalling a past event.[147] The mind temple is not a recreation of a past event. It is a creation in the present, but it resembles and replicates, if not other temples, then, at least the ideal design of a great temple. Perhaps, however, the mind temple involves memory as Mnemosyne, the daughter of Heaven and Earth, the mother of the muses, the source of poetry that returns

147 Collingwood (1994, 293) distinguishes between memory and history. Whereas for him the past in memory is 'mere spectacle,' in history the past "is re-enacted in present thought. So far as this thought is mere thought, the past is merely re-enacted; so far as it is thought about thought, the past is thought of as being re-enacted, and my knowledge of myself is historical knowledge."

one to that which has been forgotten or lost. Mnemosyne returns one to that which is worthy of thinking, namely Being. The mind temple is not a mere artefact; it is an *Andenken* on Pūcalār's Lord. The mind temple commemorates Śiva. It assembles together through the material form of the imagination everything that is worthy of being remembered. It is a remembrance of God, a tireless demonstration of dedication and devotion. It makes present the memory of God who is the eternal source of the present that is being remembered. God, imagination, Being, existence, remembrance follow and refer to each other in no particular order. Each traces the other's trail. The re-enactment that historians absorb themselves in is similar to the mind temple that Pūcalār creates. The historian re-creates via the imagination each miniscule detail not only of a social or political event, edifice, text, or artwork that he or she examines but ideally also the situation or context which provided the conditions for its existence. This is also a form of commemoration or memorialization, of bringing something that no longer exists into being in the present moment. Thus, historical knowledge too is a kind of *Andenken* in that it employs imagination to create a sensory, tactile world – a world that can be both envisioned in the mind and understood through the intellect via discursive forms of language. But is it an assembly of all that is worthy of thinking? Does it invoke the quality and memory of Mnemosyne in remembering the source of thinking, time and Being?

Chapter 7
Interiors of the Past

7.1 Remembering Ranthambore

This chapter is concerned with a presentation and analysis of excerpts of conversations that took place during a brief period of fieldwork at the fortress of Ranthambore. The full content of these exchanges with different people who are connected in one way or the other to the fortress is reported in Appendix 2. The interactions tend to be relatively long, sometimes running into several pages of transcribed text. Their content focuses – through the prism of the speakers' interests and connection to the bastion – on varied descriptions of the same object, thereby providing a shimmering, vibrant, imaginative set of verbal narratives that interlock in unique ways with the written historical record gleaned from various textual sources. The ideas that come to the fore in this quasi-historical contemporary narrative concerning the citadel are saturated with an almost mythical and magical quality that is at times braided together with deeper historical and philosophical ideas involving kingship, ascetic and ritual practice as well as warriorhood, war, death and sacrifice. The narrators – unlike modern historians acting under the persuasion of empiricism – do not attempt to sift through their narrative in order to present 'pure' historical fact. In fact, 'historical fact' in these exchanges is deemed to be an interpenetration of different interpretative possibilities encompassing the material past along with philosophical, ritual, mythical, religious-sacred knowledge and narrative.

7.1.1 Objects of the Present-Past

The conversations at the fortress of Ranthambore thus serve as a way of imagining the terrain or landscape of the 'past' that lives as an experience of people and events tethered to objects such as monuments, buildings, lakes, hillsides, trees, rocks, animals, temples and shrines. This 'tethering' or 'anchoring' reveals the interiors and contours of the past and of memory in the shape of rooms, chambers, archways, water wells; in the texture of stone, iron, and wood; and in the stories of the shrines of deities and the resting places of saints. In this 'tethering,' however, what also gets revealed is the interweaving, so to speak, of past and present into a continuous narrative in which ordinary people and those people who more recently hold positions of social and political importance participate and indeed 'create' an ongoing history of Hammīra and of the fortress

https://doi.org/10.1515/9783110662795-010

of Ranthambore as a site of sacred and political power. The fortress is, therefore, not the location of actions and negotiations sealed off or completed in the past but continues to engender meaning in the present in the form of journeys of tourists, in the ritual worship and stories of devotees and priests, in the significant interest of organizations concerned with national heritage and its preservation, and in the visits of important domestic and international political figures. The fortress then becomes the cause for its own re-imagining, evoking visible and invisible structures that collapse time in a continuum of past and present. Memory is not only anchored in these locations and the objects associated with these locations, in fact, they *are* memory. The objects when viewed, touched and spoken of become an *Andenken* or memento along with the narratives embedded in the fortress of Hammīra.[148]

7.2 Jogi and Pīr

The Jogi Mahal or Jogi (Yogi) Palace is situated at the foot of the hill upon which the fortress stands. It is an isolated building located on the bank of the Padam Lake which runs parallel to the Tiger Sanctuary, that surrounds the hill upon which the fortress is built. The Jogi or Yogi is supposed to have assisted Hammīra in his victorious battles by performing an elaborate Vedic ritual (*yajña*).[149] Similarly, in the next conversation there is a *pīr* (Sufi saint, holy man, mentor) in the camp of ʿAlāʾ al-Dīn who assists the sultan in being victorious after many failed attempts over Hammīra. Thus both Hammīra and ʿAlāʾ al-Dīn take recourse to using the 'superhuman' abilities of individuals practising forms of asceticism – a yogi and a *pīr* – in order to gain military and political victories. This connection between worldly/political and 'spiritual' power is borne out in several other instances both textual as well as historical.[150] There is a kind of Hindu–Muslim mirroring or layering in the stories of the yogi and *pīr* who both assist their re-

148 See Chapter 6.3 use of the term *Andenken* in Heidegger's work, and its meaning for an understanding of History.

149 The *yajña* which was the pre-eminent sacrificial ritual arena during the Ṛgvedic period often used to gain material prosperity but also to secure a place in the afterworld, is used here by the king to gain further worldly power through sacrificial acts arising out of the violence of war.

150 See Bayly (1990), Gonda (1969), Heesterman (1985), Olivelle (2013) and others for notions of kingship, and the association of yogis and *pīrs* with royal courts and the rivalries between yogis and saints that get played out through rivalries between kings (for example, between Hammīra and ʿAlāʾ al-Dīn).

spective rulers in victory as well as in the case of Gajānand Pīr, who becomes known as Ganeśa. Ganeśa, however, remains in a hidden manner – beneath the visible idol – as Gajānand Pīr residing in a subterranean *dargāh*. The fortress is, therefore, a layered and 'contested' site which derives historical meaning not simply through the visible markers of religious communities provided through Hindu temple and shrines, Jaina temples and the *dargāhs* of Sufi saints, but through the layering of sacred power stemming from its being a tantric field and a battlefield and concurrence of Hindu and Sufi shrines along with narratives concerning yogis and *pīrs*. The imagery of Hammīra and ʿAlāʾ al-Dīn arising so to speak from one body and the juxtaposition of one the main shrines within the fortress, namely that of Lord Ganeśa, with the *dargāh* of the Sufi saint Gajānand Pīr, suggest a powerful entwining of what in the context of modern social and political configurations are considered to be discreet religious identities and communities. Once can speak here of a kind of stratification of the manner in which the history of the fortress is imagined. However, the stratification or layering is one that is dynamic, looping and Möbius-like rather than rigid, fixed and discreet.

The Jogi Mahal, as a representation or rather site of political and spiritual power, interestingly continues to be visited by representatives of power in India and elsewhere including in the past by the Mughal emperor Jahangir, and more recently the former President of America, Bill Clinton, the late Prime Minister of India, Rajiv Gandhi, his children Priyanka and Rahul Gandhi, as well as Bollywood stars such as Amitabh Bacchan and Sanjay Dutt, amongst others.

> **Guide 1:** Someone told me that according to the *Akbarnāmā*,[151] Jahangir visited once and he told the Prime Minister of this place that accommodation was not comfortable, [so] he should build another place. So, the Rajbagh Palace, which is about one hundred metres away from the Jogi Mahal, within the ambit [of the fortress] was built later on. But [Jahangir] unfortunately, never returned.
> As far as I know about the Jogi Mahal, there was a Jogi, just like there are *Fakirs* who care about this world.
>
> **Questioner:** Yes, yes, *Fakirs*.
>
> **G1:** Yes, like a *Fakir*. So, he [the Jogi] performed a *yajña* here. He performed a *yajña* for Hammīr so that he could successfully defeat 32 kingdoms[152] and win all his battles. He prayed a lot [for the king's success]. Indeed, Hammīr emerged victorious, and therefore he constructed the Jogi Mahal in memory of the Jogi. It can be seen from up there ... the most beautiful place. Not just the building, but the whole environment, it's lovely. It

151 Fazl (2015/2016).
152 See Chapter 1 for a reference to Hammīra's *digvijaya* ("conquest of directions").

used to be a hunting reserve and hunting lodge later on and also a tourist lodge when this became a sanctuary for tigers. There were not many places around here, not many hotels, before 1970. Maybe after 1973 [hotels were built], and I am telling you about much earlier than that ... Tourists would stay there. It contains only four rooms, four suites. All of them used to stay there, but later when they realized [probably] for conservation purposes [they stopped staying here]. Even Rajiv Gandhi stayed there in 1986. He stayed there with Priyanka and Rahul Gandhi. Yes, they were kids. There are many photographs of them as well. And Amitabh [Bacchan] also came here to join them. They stayed here for seven days. Rajiv Gandhi spent seven days at this place and it's only subsequently that Ranthambore became famous. And an even bigger [tourist] boom was seen after Clinton visited here.

Q: Clinton also came here?

G1: Yes, Clinton [came here] in 2002, [when] he was the President. After that there was a boom [in visitors]. They came by helicopter, visited [this place] for couple of hours and the forest for tigers and flew back to Jaipur.
There is a huge banyan tree in front of it. From up here, you can see its crown. That is the second biggest banyan tree in Asia. The largest one is in Kolkata, in the National Botanical Garden. Once its crown was measured, it was found to be about 377 sq. metres with thousands of aerial roots. It is the second largest. This is the other reason why it is famous, [because it has] one of the oldest banyan trees.
A Bollywood film was also shot there. Sanjay Dutt starred in *Daud*. An entire song for that film was shot there, under the banyan tree. It's a huge tree.

Q: There is a Jain temple and a *dargāh* as well?

G1: Sadruddin Aulia's *dargāh.*

Q: Was he a *Pīr?*

G1: Yes, he was a *Pīr*; a very famous one. There is also a story related to him. 'Alā' al-Dīn Khaljī was not able to seize Ranthambore fort, then Sadruddin Aulia ...

Q: Was he from Delhi or from here?

G1: No, he was not from Delhi. Though he came with 'Alā' al-Dīn Khaljī – he was a holy man – but he belonged to a nearby place called Bundi. 'Alā' al-Dīn had heard that he [the *Pīr*] did not care about the world and that God would grant him anything he would request. 'Alā' al-Dīn was told to go to [and meet] this holy man. When 'Alā' al-Dīn failed to [capture the fort] in two attempts, he went to Bundi. He requested the holy man to tell him a way to win this fort. The holy man said [it's good] that you've come to me, but there is a man in your army who is even more well-connected to God! Then 'Alā' al-Dīn asked "How will I be able to identify him?" The holy man told him that on such and such date there will be very bad weather and storm, and during that storm you will discover that in one of the tents [in your camp] a lamp is still burning despite the forceful storm and then you will know that it is him. 'Alā' al-Dīn waited for the day and when the foretold storm started, he searched for that tent and found the tent where lamp was burning despite of the storm. 'Alā' al-Dīn bowed down touching the feet of the saint. The saint asked the king to explain how he got to know about him. 'Alā' al-Dīn told him whole story. The saint then cursed that (other) holy man and said that after the holy man dies, donkeys will wander on his grave till eternity. And, even today when people visit the grave of that holy man, they see donkeys wandering on his grave.

Q: When I was there, I saw four donkeys as well!

G1: Yes, that's because of the curse.

Q: Yes, they were either donkeys or mules.

G1: Yes, he cursed him (saying) that donkeys will wander on his grave. Even now, whenever you will visit his grave, you will see donkeys there – standing or rolling on his grave. The saint then prayed for 'Alā' al-Dīn and finally in the third attempt, he won the fort.[153]

7.3 Battlefields and Tantric Fields

A second detail from *the Hammīr Rāso*[154] that is equally if not more important in its singular imagery and symbolism than the role played by tribal communities is the role of the Sage Padam (*Padam Ṛṣi*) who directs the king to where he should establish the fortress. This detail concerning the origin of the fortress and the perhaps hidden 'real' essence of the region occupied by the fortress is also echoed in a conversation with a *Sadhu* (holy man) residing at a Śākta temple inside the fortress. Here again the Sage Padam is named as the person who establishes the temple and fortress. But equally, if not more interestingly, the Sadhu explains how the area or field (Sanskrit/Hindi: *kṣetra*) is one imbued with tremendously potent tantric power. The distribution of tantric deities including Śiva, Bhairo (*bhairava*) and several tantric goddesses within the perimeter of the fortress establishes the claim that this a special, indeed sacred, region whose power emanates from the tantric *sādhanā* (discipline) that has been practiced here. The fortress and its confines are, following the fact that their sacredness arises due to the *sādhanā* that has been performed here in the past, also a location in which the goals of *sādhanā* – whether these be emancipation from the world or material success – can swiftly be achieved in the current age. The fortress contains within itself multiple layers of imagination that persist into the current time. On the surface it is something material – a massive, imposing and impregnable structure made of stone and mortar on top of a steep hill – but this seemingly impenetrable matter is overlain or perhaps imbued with an invisible almost magical, supernatural power that derives from ritual practice and the often self-produced, divine emergence of deities and the human construction of temples and shrines. This supernatural power is further enhanced by the power that is un-

153 See Appendix 2, Conversation 4 for a complete transcript.
154 See Chapter 4.

leashed by the visceral sacrifice of warriors and soldiers slain in successive wars. The intensity released through the ritual practice of Tantra intermingles with the potency released through the ritual of battle.[155]

The fortress predates, so to speak, temples and shrines. The fortress was established in the *dvāpara yuga*, in an age prior to the current age of Kali. The fortress is thus founded on the sacrificial deeds of members of so-called tribal communities and its chief actors on the division of the body of Sage Padam. It is through this powerful sacrificial imagery – that in the latter instance is reminiscent of the Ṛgvedic verse involving the emergence of the physical and social cosmos out portions of Puruṣa – that both the fortress as an apparently material object (whose origins once again are obscure) and the main protagonists of the narrative that surrounds it, namely Hammīra and ʿAlāʾ al-Dīn, emerge or are literally created.

Questioner: When was the temple established?

Sadhu: This was established by Padma [Padam] Ṛṣi ... There was king called Rashidev. The idols were installed during his time. They were all here. The temple was once a fort. In the *dvāpar* era, it was a fort then it became a temple. When this fort was made then these *maṭhs* (temples) came into existence, as the kings ruled, they built *maṭhs*. The *maṭhs* which were inside ... so this is a tantric region. This entire area is blessed. All the gods and goddesses of Tantra are here; all the idols which are installed here have all been done so according to tantric [rules] ... All the prayers that are done to the deities are done according to tantric [rules]. This means that all rituals conducted for the deities are conducted according to tantric [rules]. So the tantric mothers are the *solhā mā* (16 Mothers); these are symbolized by sixteen Śivaliṅga. Lord Śiva is worshipped to acquire knowledge ... to free oneself from fear and to acquire knowledge; that is why Lord Śiva is worshipped ... Lord Śiva has different forms ... He has manifold forms so different things are offered to him ... So considering [all] these things and keeping these [things] in mind, the sages have dedicated years [reflecting and meditating] on these matters ... There is a gold idol of Lord Ganeśa there ... it is self-generated ... In tantric rituals, it is supreme ... in the tantric ritual system, Ganeśa is termed as Guru ... and the Guru is supreme ... Therefore, it is the self-proclaimed and self-emerged idol of Lord Ganeśa ... In tantric rituals, he is considered as supreme. Considering this, the sages established him at various places. Now there are all ten Mahāvidyas, all three Mahādevis, sixteen Śivlingas. These belong to the old era established by the sages ... they offered the prayers ... and established all these [deities], the temples and the mosques were established later ... The one where we are standing was constructed later. So this fort was constructed after that, it is written on the fort ... As the kings started coming here, they kept establishing new temples. There are many temples here. In addition to those, there are many more small temples in the entire region.
[...]
... There were kings [back then]. They had their priests and sages who used to provide them

155 See Hiltebeitel (1990) and Lincoln (1991).

> with special powers. They used to bestow them with special powers. They used to chant *bhajans*, offer prayers, and by doing this, they used to make them capable so that by practising the 'power' meditation and prayers, they could move ahead. To get into the 'power' meditation, it is important for one to be powerful. Only then you can do 'power' meditation. ... If you make the gods happy through *sādhanā* – if you make them happy – then everyone around you will be happy. You automatically become auspicious for everyone. You will receive respect wherever you go. You will get everything [you want]. So it is the same as [performing] *vaśīkaran*. [Once you do *sādhanā*] then there will be no requirement of *vaśīkaran* at all. It is the misuse of such things. So whatever is happening these days, it is the misuse of it, whatever people are doing today ... and all the knowledge today is knowledge acquired through cramming. Knowledge is being used for business. The priests have knowledge and they are all business oriented. That is how they earn [their living]. But the *sādhanās* that existed there earlier, they used to be successful because they were done without any bias. There was no ill-intention brewing in people's minds. There was no greed, no lust, no consumption and there was no desire for anything at that time. Even if today you practice this, and if you are working to get your desires fulfilled, even then do it without greed. Then you will achieve it in this life. If you are doing it out of greed, attachment or fear then you will not be able to get its benefits in this life and you will only get [the benefits] in your next birth. Therefore, the *sādhanā* and rituals become unsuccessful. *Havan* and *yajña* venues catch fire today. It is because rituals are not being followed as they should be. People get things done on the basis of their income. You can take any example or take your own *sādhanā*, whatever the thing is, you collected all your money through your hard work, etc. So then bring it to good use; if you do this, you will never be destroyed. You will get [what you want], and you will get twice [what you want]. But if you use if for satisfying your lust, or for materialistic consumption, then you will be destroyed one day. So whatever name you have earned, whatever money you have earned, that will be destroyed one day. So therefore after [singing] *bhajans* you are either sent as a king or as a hermit [into the world]. So if you do *tapasya* (ascetic practice) in any era then you end up either as a king or as a hermit. The hermit will move ahead in life but the king will fail at last in his life. So if the head of the clan (king) is not *dikṣit*, (consecrated, anointed) then he will fail. And, as a king, he will be arrogant and out of arrogance he will trouble his people, will misuse his money and enjoy everything and will run away.[156]

This passage is both a discourse on the sources of power such as *bhajans*, meditation, and *sādhanā* in general (spiritual practice; perhaps implying tantric practices) and an expose on good and bad kingship as well as the relationship between the hermit or renunciant and the king.

The power and sacredness of the fortress is further strengthened by the fact that it is a *raṇbhūmi* (battlefield) which is drenched so to speak with the sacrificial acts of soldiers, ordinary people and members of the royal family dying in or as a consequence of defending themselves in war. The origin of the fortress

---

156 See Heesterman (1985) on ancient Indian ritual and kingship. See Appendix 2, Conversation 2 for a complete transcript.

which also has many names (see below) in this and another, prior, age is thus submersed so to speak in the violence of sacrifice that continues into historical times. The fortress is a battleground which not unlike Kurukṣetra where the final, devastating battle of the Mahabharata takes place is also a sacred-ground. It is therefore both a 'tantric field' and a battlefield:

Guide 1: This place is called Ranthambore, because as you can see the hills in the front of here, that is the battlefield ... and battlefield means *Raṇbhūmi* in Hindi ... the fort is called *thaṃb*, because it has been made on a single hill ... there is no other hill adjoining it ... it is standing straight like a pillar ... pillar is known as *thaṃb* in Hindi ... *Raṇ* means *Raṇbhūmi* (battlefield) plus *thaṃb* (pillar). Between the outer wall and here there is a 500–700-ft-deep drain. This is called *Bhanwar* [or *bhor*] ... hence *Raṇ* plus *thaṃb* plus *bhor* ... joining these three words together gave birth to the name of this place, i.e. Ranthambore. In 1972, this place was declared as the site for the Tiger Project. In 1982, it was given the status of the National Park, before that it was also known as *Ranat-bhanwar-gad.*

Questioner: *Ran* ...?

G1: *Ranat-bhanwar-gad.* It was believed that Ranat and Bhanwar were brothers and princes, so *Ranat-bhanwar-gad* was also named after both of them. Later on when it was declared to be the site for the Tiger Project, it was named as Ranthambore Fort. It was done because they extracted the meaning: battlefield means *Raṇbhūmi* or *Raṇ* in Hindi, which is a battle place, and *thaṃb* or pillar because the fort was made on a single hill and the hill is standing straight like a pillar, as you have already seen ... Therefore, it is called a *thaṃb* in Hindi plus *Bhanwar,* as there is a drain passing between these two. So *Raṇ* plus *thaṃb* plus *Bhanwar* ... adding all three of them, gave this place a name, i.e. Ranthambore. I was talking about this drain – this hole that you can see, it is *Padmāvatī Tālāb.* The hole was opened to fill the drain and when the pond filled, then it was opened again. It was cleaned then. Now it is again full and deep.

Q: What were the names of the brothers again?

G1: Ranat Bhanwar, Ranat and Bhanwar were two brothers. You can find all this written in history. It's from their names the fortress gained its name, i.e. *Raṇthaṃban.* It is also known as *Ranat-bhanwar-gad.* There was also a king, named Raṇthaṃban Dev. Ranthambore is also known by his name, Raṇthaṃban Dev. So there are three to four such reasons it seems [for naming the fortress].

Q: Oh, I see!

G1: Yes, it has different names from the beginning. This is known as Ranthamban Dev, Ranat-bhanwar-gad, and then Ranthamboregad. This has been changing [again and again].[157]

157 See Appendix 2, Conversation 5 for a complete transcript.

7.4 The Mythical Fortress

In the following conversation the person interviewed takes the listener into a narration that describes the fortress as a sequence of signposts that unfolds gradually, beginning with the forest that surrounds the fortress at ground level and leading upward and inside into the fortress. The description of the forest, its caretakers and animal inhabitants, and the several successive gateways that fortify the bastion along with the numerous deities installed in temples and shrines, mosques, the *dargāhs* of Sufi saints, as well as windows, archways, walls, palace rooms, water bodies and other materials features that make up the entire structure are imbued with a sometimes mundane but oftentimes magical and fairy-tale-like if not mythical quality. For example, the forest with its many creatures, many of whom could be life-threatening towards humans, is guarded by a '*Harijan*' named Maliya Baghel who protects, feeds and looks after the animals, who in turn listen to him and guard and love him. Hammīra himself possessed the *pāras*-stone (philosopher's stone) which turned ordinary iron into gold. The stone was lost when his daughter committed suicide by jumping into the Padam Lake. Then there is the famous temple of Lord Ganeśa that is visited by hundreds of thousands of devotees each year. Beneath the shrine of Lord Ganeśa, however, is original sacred site of Gajānand Pīr, a Sufi saint, who was there and is still there – though hidden from the view of most devotees – underneath the visible image of Lord Ganeśa. Here again we have an example of twinning as in the case of Hammīra and 'Alā' al-Dīn Khaljī who are both born from the body the Ṛṣi Padam. The Sufi saint is named Gajānand Pīr – 'Gajanand' being another name for Ganeśa coupled here with the Sufi honorific 'Pīr' denoting an 'elder,' mentor, guide or master (often translated into 'saint'). The Sufi 'elder' or saint with the name Gajānand is transformed so to speak into Ganeśa. But this a kind of esoteric knowledge that is known only to a select few, including the senior and now aged priests of the temple of Lord Ganeśa. How did Gajānand Pīr appear? He appeared or manifested himself or was self-generated so to speak. This idea is similar to the creation stories of many Hindu deities who manifest on their own without human impulse. This act of self-generation is pristine and causeless excepting for an inner motion. But later, according to the narrator who is Muslim, "people of Hindu faith" began believing in him (i.e. Gajānand Pīr) and they installed an image of Trinetra ('the one with three eyes'). This image was worshipped as Gajanand or Ganeśa for whom a huge *melā* (fair) with hundreds of thousands of devotees is celebrated in the month of September. The fortress transforms into the potent site of a pilgrimage reinforcing the idea that its compounds and ramparts are an auspicious location whose sacredness is engendered not only through the presence of shrines, temples and *dargāhs* but also through the fact that it is a battlefield (*raṇbhūmi*) and tantric field (*kṣetra*). According to this account and others retold at the fortress, after losing the battle to ʿAlāʾ al-Dīn Khaljī through acts of treachery on the part of his own generals and the overseer of the royal granaries, Hammīra severs his own head in an offering to Lord Śiva. But because he is such a staunch devotee of Lord Śiva his head is re-joined to his torso again and again until at the seventh and final attempt it falls away from his body and lands next to the *Śivaliṅgam* that he has continuously worshipped. Thereafter this image is called Hammīr Śiva.[158] The narrative journeys through different gates and important locations of the fortress before finally turning into a biographical account in which the narrator interweaves his own experience as a guide and as someone who has worked for the Archaeological Survey of India into the remnants of the historical narrative he has been recounting.[159] These personal details give us an insight into the more recent history of the fortress and the gradual development of the forest into a tiger sanctuary and important tourist attraction. The account also moves from more 'legendary,' 'mythical' tropes to concrete transactional descriptions involving payments for services in rupees and the transportation of goods such as sugar, wheat and so on in the present time. Thus, the narrative re-telling of historical memory is based on a 'composite' construction or amalgam of different and differently recognizable registers of historical meaning derived from a temporal palette of events and actions reaching back several centuries until a few decades ago, each with variable degrees of substance.[160]

158 See Appendix 2, Conversation 3 for the complete transcript.

159 The narrator also states how he has – even though he is a Muslim – benefited from Lord Ganeśa (or Gajānand Pīr) by bringing devotees to the deity's shrine in the fortress. This again represents, in a sense, an 'inter-' or 'co-mingling' of religious identities at a heritage site that, as we have seen, historically encouraged the bonds of friendship, loyalty and mutual respect across religious and ethnic boundaries.

160 See Narayana Rao, Shulman and Subrahmanyam (2001). See the final sections of Conversation 3 in Appendix 2.

Fig. 4: Ruins of an inner courtyard

Fig. 5: Outlook post on the rampart

Fig. 6: Ruins of a balcony

Guide 2: I am from Sawai Madhopur. In the Ranthambore [area], Sawai Manpur was named after King Sawai Man Singh. He was the king of Jaipur. So possibly, it was named after him. Ranthambore is 13 km from the railway station. In between, you will see Amaresar, Misaldara, Keshdhar. From then on, the forest entry gate starts. When enter you into the forest, you will find yourself in Misaldara. Misaldara was earlier known as Gomukh and there you will see the statue of a cow with water flowing through its mouth. Gomukh means where water comes from the mouth of cow. Beyond that there is the forest. And that's the area from where our Ranthambore national park starts. Ahead of that the area is known as Bahadurpur. So, there was a guard named Bahadur. The area was named after him. At that time, all the animals, be it tigers, bears and so on knew him by the smell of his body. He used to call out to them once, and they would come to him immediately. He was a *Harijan*, and was known as *Maliya Baghel.*[161]

Questioner: Around when was this?

G2: I am talking about 1982.

Q: It's fairly recent, then?

G2: So, he was a guard and he used to roam around to check security [in the forest]. He was the only guard in the jungle and no one else was there with him. Animals loved him so much that they would always accompany him. There were trees everywhere and he used to prepare his cot near some trees. The animals used to guard him. He used to feed them and if any of them got injured, he used to take care of that animal. For example, if a thorn pierced an animal's paw, he used to pluck it out and take care of it. He loved them like his own pets just as we love our pets and cattle and the animals loved him as well. So, [that location] was named Bahadurpur. After it, comes Singdvar. It is called so because *sambhar, cheetal* and other deer used to shed their horns here. Then comes gate number 1, from there four/five paths branch off ... after that comes the uphill route ... the Mor-

161 It is not clear whether Baghel actually refers to a '*Harijan*' group as the speaker claims or to a subgroup of the Rajput community,

kund (peacock basin) comes before that ... Sorry, I forgot Adavaleji. That's the name of a temple. The uphill route starts from there and it goes down and then comes Bahadurpur. Singdvar comes after that. There comes an uphill route from Singdvar and then comes the *dargāh*. The *dargāh* comes only after the uphill route from Morkund. The *dargāh* is named after the Sufi Saint Fateh Sahab. There was another *dargāh* after the name of Kalushāh behind that ... then Amrahi. That area is known as Amrahi.

Q: Okay, which is up there?

G2: When we move uphill from Singdvar, after the second upwards slope from Morkund there is a small sewer. The *dargāh* is located after that. Its name is Fateh Sahab. There is another *dargāh* behind Fateh Sahab called Kalushāh. He too was a Sufi saint. After that comes the region of Amrahi. The area is full of mango trees. Therefore, it's known as Amrahi. As we move ahead from there, there comes the last uphill path ... the last uphill path ... after that as you go inside and there appears the Jogi Mahal near the police department. It is right ahead. There is a pond in front of the Jogi Mahal Gate where kings used to fight battles.

Q: The Jogi Mahal which is down there?

G2: Yes ... It goes toward the town ... Ranthambore ends here and over there Jogi Mahal Gate which was a battlefield ... Battles were fought there ... If we start from there, the first gate that comes is called Naulakha Gate.

Q: Is the *dargāh* down there? The one that you were talking about?

G2: It has been left behind down there ... The *dargāh* of Kalushāh has been left behind down there ... You have walked uphill now ... You have come above Amrāhi ... Jogi Mahal Gate has come ... and then comes the temple of Lord Ganeśa. There is a big *Pipal* tree there and also a well in front of it. And as we go around, there is also an office of the Archaeological Department. It is known as the Foreman Department, Archaeological Survey Department of India, Ranthambore. After that we climb the twenty-two steps and take a turn. They make those turns because the elephants used to break the gates using their backs, so very fine nails were installed on the gate. So these gates were constructed in such a way that they didn't get damaged, and no attack could take place from Delhi. The gates used to be very heavy and 12–14 feet tall. Someone could try and ram them but the gate couldn't be broken. If they were able to break it, then the army had to be ready for war. As we go ahead, there are two rooms where the watchmen used to stay. Then further up, there is a temple of Lord Hanuman. There is an idol of Lord Hanuman, Lord Ganeśa and Goddess Parvati installed there. There used to be a mosque on that path earlier where people used to live.

Fig. 7: One of the many, massive gates

Q: There was a mosque?

G2: Just a few moments ago, the place where we were visiting, there is a mosque by its side ... it is at a distance of around ten feet from the temple ... there is a minaret ... a pole, then as you move from there, we find the temple of Lord Hanuman. After that there is another place.

Q: Is the mosque presently there?

G2: Yes, the mosque is still there and it is a very old mosque. After that we shall enter the second gate. Its name is Hathipur. There is a skull there belonging to a person called Mingangdu. He used to go to the battlefield frequently. ʿAlāʾ al-Dīn Khaljī's son Jalāl al-Dīn Khaljī had claimed that he was go to an absconder from Delhi. So he had asked for refuge. He was kept in the mosque. He was an absconder from Delhi. The king recruited him in his army. And he was put on duty at the gate. What Mingangdu did after that ... we will move on to that story later. Now we arrive at the third gate called Ganeśpur. There too the gate is in the opposite direction. If we go from the top, there comes the Andheri Gate and Tar Gate. This part of the fort has been constructed in such a way that it resembles the betel leaf. It is known as Supari Mahal (Betel Palace). An officer of the Archaeological Department stays there only along with a watchman and an office staff. Now if we climb the twelve steps, we come to the Raghunāth Temple. If we go on that side, there we will come to Mina Mahal and Rani Mahal that are just next to it. There is a temple of Lord Hanuman right in front of the Rani Mahal. Then there is a garden and as we take a turn from the garden, we arrive at the temple of Lord Hanuman. It is known as the Raj Mandir and near that is Jatuyan. This the location of 'an unfulfilled dream.' Rani Handi, the wife of Rana Sanga, had a desire to construct it, but it could not be constructed, and it remained 'an unfulfilled dream.' After that comes the umbrella (*chattrī*) of 32 pillars. There is a Śivalinga inside it. It is huge. The queens used to worship it by circumambulating it. All the pillars have been constructed in the memory of the ones who were martyred in the war. So, whenever somebody got martyred, a pillar was constructed in his name. So, that umbrella got the name "32 pillars". The women used to worship it by circumambulating it. There is a huge Śivalinga when you go inside. If we leave the route below the steps, and if we go straight, there comes Rani Mahal. After that comes Hammīr Mahal. The entire route from Hammīr Mahal to Rani Mahal is in ruins. This happened because the second gate of Hathipur had a watchman. As King Hammīr went to fight the battle, he showed the black flags which indicated that King Hammīr had lost the war. The queen was sitting in the Supari Mahal, she saw it and believed that they had lost [the battle] and that the King had died. She went to her Mahal and committed suicide. Hence it all turned into ruins. And all the queens who were sitting in the Padmavati Mahal came to know about it and they all died. There were many conflicts due to the *pāras* [stone],[162] as its touch could convert iron into gold. So majority of the wars were fought because of the stone.

Q: Okay. They had it?

G2: Yes, King Hammīr had it. King Hammīr's daughter, Queen Padmāvatī, took the *pāras* stone and jumped into the pond. Hence it is known as the Padam Lake. Moving further, we come to the Annapurna temple. All the people who used to live nearby the Annapurna temple used to worship there during hard times. There is also a *dargāh* nearby in the name of those who have been martyred ... there are four-five *dargāhs*. Going further, there are plenty of Gumtis (small domed tomb or shrine). That is the uppermost *morcha* (fortification), so if anyone attacked from the front, this wall used to stop them. It is a very thick wall on the side. The temple comes only after that and there is a shop alongside it. The people who now live there, only their grandfathers were allowed to live here earlier. There were four houses only for them. There are four/five quarters constructed in the front [of the houses] where the staff members of the Archaeological Survey of India reside. There is a Ganeśa temple and it is believed that Lord Ganeśa had appeared here.

162 Hindi: *Pāras*; Sanskrit: *Pārasmani* – or the philosopher's stone that turns base metals into gold.

Fig. 8: The shrine of Trinetri Ganeśa

Q: Oh ... on his own?

G2: Yes, on his own ... so the public started believing in him. Now the real idol is beneath and is known by the name Gajānand Pīr.

Q: Oh, Gajānand Pīr!

G2: Yes, Gajānand Pīr. The Madohi priests [residing there], Shuklājī and Madhubanijī, can tell you what it really is. Today there has been a proliferation of many smaller priests, the new youngsters have turned into priests. However, the ones who were there earlier are still here. There is a small temple where they sit. They are both very aged now. This is famous by the name Gajānand Pīr. It is beneath the temple; they know it is a *dargāh.*

Q: Oh, it is below.

G2: Yes, it is below ... There is a vault in which there is a *dargāh.*

Q: It is a *dargāh?*

G2: Yes, it is known as Gajānand Pīr. People having Hindu faith started believing in him so they established an idol and they began worshipping him as the Trinetra. And this region came to be called as Ranbhom due to the battles that took place here.

Q: So when did he ... How did Gajānand Pīr come here?

G2: He appeared on his own. So he is known as Gajānand Pīr. A fair is organized in the month of September and people in their hundreds of thousands pay a visit to this temple. A fair is organized and food is offered to the people. People are served and the place is equipped with police and doctors and other things. Beyond that walls (*parkoṭā*) have been constructed. Thereafter is Gupt Gaṅgā. People living here used to claim that there was a great sage who used to meditate here at the Gupt Gaṅgā. As the army used to get ready for battle here, he used to release the water from Gupt Gaṅgā from above. Even today there is round the clock availability of water in the Gupt Gaṅgā. The city is established there, so he would make the water exit from there. They had an arrangement of bringing the excreta of donkeys and other animals and mud to the top, so the soldiers used to get washed away by the flow of the water. That water would exit from the Satpol gate. The Satpol gate is the gate just behind the temple. There are three gates named Satpol gate.

Q: Below the Ganeśa temple?

G2: There is a Śiva temple of King Hammīr just below the Ganeśa temple, so it is known as the Satpol gate. The water flow would flow from there and all the soldiers used to get washed away. It happened during the battles. There were furnaces built inside the fort where *ghee* was made. The people used to throw the canisters filled with *ghee* on the soldiers which used to make walking uphill difficult for them. There were plenty of furnaces and all the arrangements of weapons and gunpowder inside the fort. All their clothes were also kept inside the fort. Also there were many different idols belonging to them kept inside the fort. All the equipment of the ironsmiths to make weapons too was kept inside the fort. The places of gods and goddesses are there as well. There are two places, one of Dhumejī and other of Mātājī. The water used to flow from the Gupt Gaṅgā and it used to be an advantage for the king as the flow of the water used to wash away the enemy soldiers, bringing their morale down. As the black flag was waved at the Hathipol, the queens saw it. Seeing the black flag, they believed that they had lost. They went inside the fort and committed suicide. The daughter jumped in the pond. There is the *dargāh* of Sadruddin here. The King came here leaving Gupt Gaṅgā behind towards Raniodh. He is known as Sadruddin Baba and was believed to have magical powers. When the king came here, he saw the flag in the market. So he thought that, we have not lost, we are all alive and the queen must have betrayed us. She has done something mischievous. The king took his soldiers and horses and proceeded so as to go and kill the betrayer. The skull idol has been installed in the memory of the killing of the watchman who was an absconder.[163] The king then went ahead and the gate of Ganeśpol was shut. Everyone had asked, including the queen, to lock all the gates. Hence the horses had climbed from Ganeśpol. Their marks are prevalent till date explaining that the horses had climbed. As the kings reached the palace, he saw all the queens dead. The daughter had jumped into the pond. King Hammīr was a devotee of Lord Śiva who used to serve Lord Śiva continuously. Hence, in order to take his own life, he went to the Satpol gate to that spot and cut off his head seven times using his sword.

Q: Seven times?

G2: Seven times! But his head would join back on to his torso every time. On the eighth attempt, his body fell on the floor. Hence an idol of the king was established. It is made up of seven metals and is placed inside the palace. It is known by the name of Hammīr Śiva temple.[164]

163 The sequence of events is not clear here.
164 See Appendix 2, Conversation 3 for a complete transcript.

Epilogue

The Dream Again

> I have caught life. I have come down with life. I was a wisp of undifferentiated nothingness, and then a little peephole opened quite suddenly. Light and sound poured in. Voices began to describe me and my surroundings. Nothing they said could be appealed. They said I was a boy named Rudolph Waltz, and that was that. They said the year was 1932, and that was that [...] Year after year they piled detail upon detail (Kurt Vonnegut, '*Deadeye Dick*').

We seem to occupy an age in which the 'otherness' of the other is becoming an unbearably oppressive, violent burden, a location of discontent and discomfort, an unbridgeable chasm for the self that is seldom itself considered to be 'other' to the other who is demonized and exiled through harsh judgment, biased opinion or sheer physical abuse. What is this condition that humanity finds itself in? What does this say about the human condition? What does this say about human being and about being human? Political scenarios across vast geographical and national spaces of the world are increasingly committed to the creation of fixed, unshifting boundaries of ethnic, religious, national and racial symbols and realities. The solutions offered to economic inequality, environmental degradation, distribution of natural resources, population control, issues of social justice, etc., revel in the partial or complete eradication or exclusion of communities based on religion, race, ethnicity and political affiliation.

The purpose of looking back into the past is to bring the conditions that were different, though perhaps not less violent, into the awareness of the present moment which itself 'contains' both future and past. The present moment alone is also the bearer of all possibilities that in turn arise in language, at the source of which lies imagination as that from which self and therefore world begin to emanate. The withdrawing of imagination into itself, which is also a state of silence, is also the cessation of world. Self and world are both arising and subsiding from and into the substratum of imagination.

> It is only a thought that apparently divides the seamless totality of experience into an experiencer and an experienced. There are no personal entities or independent objects anywhere to be found in actual experience. 'Me' and 'the world' are co-created in imagination. They always appear together and disappear together in that which never appears or disappears [...] This division of experience into a perceiver and a perceived, a knower and a known, a lover and a loved, is like a mirage (Spira 2016).

What is really at stake it seems is the very manner in which the relationship between self, other and world is imagined. Underlying this there seems to be a

https://doi.org/10.1515/9783110662795-011

deep misapprehension. A misconception so arcane regarding the nature of being human that compares to the pre-Copernican geocentric view of the earth, sun and stars wherein a complex system was erected and protected that ultimately had no substance – a hollow grand edifice that was swept away, albeit with great courage and steadfastness, by a heliocentric model in which the movement and position of celestial bodies fell into their natural order.

Could it be that so-called modern human societies and individuals are beleaguered and diseased with a mistaken sense of identity? A misguided quest for certainty and dense substance where, in fact, there is none – like the emperor's new clothes? The very belligerent assertion and defence of identities seems to hint at a much more profound vulnerability: the futile exertion of hiding the simple emptiness of one's being. An emptiness which is the substratum of imagination from which form, shape, colour, perception, touch and the persuasion of a 'real' world begins and ends. An instantaneous movement that is forgotten once one 'finds' oneself in a world that *appears* both separate and concrete. This immediate forgetting of the simultaneous arising of self and world in language, thought and imagination leads to an apparent chasm between self and world, and self and other.

This is the solidification and sedimentation of something that began as pure possibility, as a mere "wisp of undifferentiated nothingness" – the incessant repetition of a story that masquerades as unbending, eternal truth. To be human is then to forget that one is sheer possibility from which the apparent limitation of name, form, body, circumstances, history, coming into existence (birth) and going out of it (death) emerges and returns.

There is no better way to expresses the possibility of being human as in Helen Keller's (2016, 6–7) poignant words which show how thought, language and world are primordially interconnected, arising together:

> We walked down the path to the well-house, attracted by the fragrance of the honeysuckle with which it was covered. Someone was drawing water and my teacher placed my hand under the spout. As the cool stream gushed over one hand she spelled into the other the word water, first slowly, then rapidly. I stood still, my whole attention fixed upon the motions of her fingers. *Suddenly I felt a misty consciousness as of something forgotten – a thrill of returning thought; and somehow the mystery of language was revealed to me.*
>
> I knew then that "w-a-t-e-r" meant the wonderful cool something that was flowing over my hand. That living word awakened my soul, gave it light, hope, joy, set it free! There were barriers still, it is true, but barriers that could in time be swept away. I left the well-house eager to learn. Everything had a name, and each name gave birth to a new thought. As we returned to the house every object which I touched seemed to quiver with life. That was because I saw everything with the strange, new sight that had come to me.

Miss Sullivan touched my forehead and spelled with decided emphasis, “Think.” In a flash I knew that the word was the name of the process that was going on in my head. This was my first conscious perception of an abstract idea. For a long time I was still [...] trying to find a meaning for “love” in the light of this new idea. The sun had been under a cloud all day, and there had been brief showers; but suddenly the sun broke forth in all its southern splendour. Again I asked my teacher, “Is this not love?”

“Love is something like the clouds that were in the sky before the sun came out,” she replied. Then in simpler words than these, which at that time I could not have understood, she explained: “You cannot touch the clouds, you know; but you feel the rain and know how glad the flowers and the thirsty earth are to have it after a hot day. You cannot touch love either; but you feel the sweetness that it pours into everything. Without love you would not be happy or want to play.”

The beautiful truth burst upon my mind – I felt that there were invisible lines stretched between my spirit and the spirits of others.[165]

165 Emphasis added.

Appendix 1

1 Synopsis of the Hammīra-Mahākāvya

The following synopsis is based on the longer summary given by Kirtane in his introduction to the edited text of the *Hammīra-Mahākāvya* (Kirtane 1879).

The *Hammīra-Mahākāvya* consists of 1500 verses divided into 14 *Sargas*. The initial *Sargas* deal with the origin of the Chauhans and with reigns and deeds of early Chauhan rulers, including Pṛthvīrāj Chauhan III. The *Sargas* 5, 6 and 7 contain descriptions of the seasons [*vasanta* and *varṣā*] as well as *sṛṅgāra rasa*. The latter half of the poem is dedicated to Hammīra, his birth, his *digvijaya* and *koṭi yajña*, various deeds of his generals, his brother, allies and his battles against ʻAlāʾ al-Dīn Khaljī. The poet has used a variety of metres, twenty-four in fact, and a number of sometimes rare and occasionally difficult grammatical forms (for example, *red. aorist*). The predominant *rasas* are *sṛṅgāra* and *vīra*. Figures of speech such as *rūpaka*, *upamā*, *virodha*, *atiśayokti*, *parisaṃkhyā*; a variety of *alaṃkāras: utprekṣa*, *arthānataranyāsa*, *aprastutapraśaṃsā*. *Virodha* seems to be the chief *alaṃkāras*.

In *Sarga* 4.131–160, Hammīra's birth is described. He is born to the Chauhan ruler Jaitra Simha and his queen Hīrā Devī. During her pregnancy Hīrā Devī has many forms of cravings.

Hammīra is an expert in the arts of war. As soon as he grows up, he ascends the throne and embarks on a *digvijaya* raiding and conquering different cities and kingdoms mentioned above. While performing a *koṭi yajña* subsequently his fortress is attacked by Malik Muizzu'd din Ulugh Khan, the younger brother of ʻAlāʾ al-Dīn Khaljī. Since he has not completed the *koṭi yajña*, he dispatches two generals Bhīma Siṃha and Dharma Siṃha to defend Ranthambore. Although Bhīma Siṃha drives back the Muslim general he is unintentionally abandoned by Dharma Siṃha and his soldiers, is then surrounded and killed by Ulugh Khan's soldiers. Hammīra upon learning of Bhīma Siṃha's death castigates Dharma Siṃha calling him blind and impotent, having him then blinded and castrated. Dharma Siṃha manages to escape after this and befriends Rādhā Devī (the Sanskrit text mentions Dhārādevī) a courtesan in Hammīra's court; Rādhā Devī keeps Dharma Siṃha acquainted with the daily events of the court. Later on, he is reinstated by Hammīra.

Subsequent to this, the next undiplomatic move that Hammīra makes is to estrange his younger brother Bhoja. After being relieved of certain responsibilities and being at the receiving end of covert and overt taunts and insults, Bhoja decides to go on a pilgrimage to Benares. But this is only a ruse, because he fi-

https://doi.org/10.1515/9783110662795-012

nally seeks refuge at the court of ʿAlāʾ al-Dīn Khaljī whom he ultimately befriends and informs of various details of the fortress of Ranthambore and how to capture it.

Prior to this, however, ʿAlāʾ al-Dīn's generals Ulugh Khan and Nusrat Khan, while returning to Delhi after a raid and plunder of Gujarat, cause a mutiny amongst their soldiers. The mutiny is led by Muhammed Shāh, a 'neo-Muslim' leader, along with his brother and other followers. Muhammed Shāh and his band of men subsequently ask for refuge at Ranthambore, which is granted to them by Hammīra.

Fuelled by Bhoja's anger, the information he has provided and the fact that the rebels have been granted asylum by Hammīra, ʿAlāʾ al-Dīn sends two generals together with an army of 100,000 cavalry consisting of soldiers from the kingdoms of Anga, Telanga, Magadha, Maisur, Kalinga, Banga, Bhot, Medapat, Panchal, Bangal, Thamins, Bhilla, Nepal, Dahal and some Himalayan kingdoms. This huge army is, however, badly defeated by Hammīra's brother Vīrama, the generals Ratipāla, Jayadeva and Raṇamalla as well as Muhammed Shāh and his brother Gaubharukha.

Once again ʿAlāʾ al-Dīn's generals launch an assault on Ranthambore, again with the armies of Anga, Telanga, Magadha, Maisura, etc. They lay siege to the fortress at which point they are joined by ʿAlāʾ al-Dīn personally.

ʿAlāʾ al-Dīn makes an offer of peace and Hammīra sends his general Ratipāla to ʿAlāʾ al-Dīn's camp to negotiate. Once there, Ratipāla is treated lavishly and convinced by ʿAlāʾ al-Dīn that if he were to capture the fortress, Ratipāla would be made chief. Ratipāla divulges various secrets regarding the fortress and returns as a traitor to Hammīra. Ratipāla manages to turn another general Raṇamalla against Hammīra. Both of them abandon Hammīra by leaving the fortress and joining forces with ʿAlāʾ al-Dīn. To add to all of this Hammīra is informed by the keeper of granary that the store is empty whereas in fact it is in reality full. Apparently, the fortress now faces starvation. Hearing this, Hammīra believes that there is no chance for victory. Muhammed Shāh, his close friend, then slays his own family. Hammīra's wife Āraṇgidevī and his daughter Devalldevī prepare to commit *jauhar* together with the other women of the fortress. After his wife and beloved daughter commit *jauhar*, Hammīra, his brother Vīrama and Muhammed Shāh (aka Mahimā Sāhi) ride out of the fortress to face ʿAlāʾ al-Dīn's army. Vīrama is killed and Hammīra beheads himself after being pierced by a hundred arrows. Muhammed Shāh or Mahimā Sāhi, who is wounded and taken captive, is crushed by an elephant on ʿAlāʾ al-Dīn's orders. Instead of being made chief of the fortress, Ratipāla is flayed alive by ʿAlāʾ al-Dīn for being a traitor. Similarly, Raṇamalla and his followers are put to death for being disloyal to their king (i.e. Hammīra).

Fig. 9: Head of the traitor Raṇmalla at the entrance of the fortress

2 Passages in Translation

The passages translated here begin with *Sarga* 8 in which King Jaitra Siṃha decides to bestow the kingdom on Hammīra even though he is not the eldest son. The proceeding chapters draw out, in particular, a poetic illustration of the life, deeds and heroic death of Hammīra along with his band of loyal warriors headed by Mahimā Sāhi.[166]

Sarga 8

[Jaitra Siṃha, Hammīra's father, decides, after Lord Viṣṇu appears to him in dream, to bestow the kingdom on the latter even though he is not the eldest of his three sons.]

53: "When there is an elder son, the wealth of the kingdom doesn't belong to the middle son. Even though you know this and tread the path of regal testament, why do you want to give me the wealth of the kingdom?"

54: "O Son! While I slept in the palace, Viṣṇu Bhagavān [appeared] in the morning hours [and] said to me: 'Bestow the kingdom on Hammīrdev and place yourself in my service!' Now, what am I to do?"

---

166 Certain sections within the chapters have not been included here. These sections invariably contain longer, highly embellished descriptions of war and combat or the fortress or other features such as the instructions the new king receives from his father.

55: Then in Samvat 1339 on the auspicious conjunction that astrologers had determined on the day of the full moon falling in the light half of the month of Māgh as the sign of Scorpio ascended,[167] the king anointed Hammīra [as his successor].

67: Have not the fame of King Karṇa, the just rule of Rāma and the bravery of Dhananjaya[168] become examples for the assembly of Pandits in the *kali yuga?*

69: When Hammīra ruled no one had to endure becoming the beloved of the time-devouring Agni, nor suffering like Rāma, nor penance like Bharata or renunciation like King Janaka.

[71–104 *Jaitra Siṃha instructs Hammīra in how to be a good king.*]

84: The combination of bravery and intelligence bring about the upliftment of the kingdom. [It does] not [happen] through one object alone. After all the entire world has arisen through conjunction![169]

86: A king who follows the law gives honour even to an enemy who has sought refuge [in the king]. Even as Venus becomes exalted when it is in proximity of the sign of Pisces![170]

103: Do not battle against the cunning and mighty Śaka king! Even the powerful [King] Bali was defeated by a cunning Viṣṇu!

[*After instructing Hammīra, Jaitra Siṃha withdrew to a town called Śrī Āśrama for the upliftment of his ātma (mind, soul, inner being). There was another auspicious town nearby that was free of merchants called Ambupanth in which the self-generated (svayaṃbhū) Śiva was present. ... The Chambal river meandered nearby like the braid of the auspicious [Goddess] Lakṣmī.*]

129: Even Rāma, who bearing his bow slew Rāvaṇa, and drove thousands of demons into the mouth of Yama [...] even that Śrī Rāma who was the icon of fortune was swallowed by time which wore a terrifying countenance.

Sarga 9

[Bhim Singh's encounter with Ullugh Khan]

142: Some vile Śaka [warriors] picked up dry grass between their teeth and took refuge, some fell to [their] feet, and others, while pleading for their lives said: "I am your cow!"

---

167 "*vṛścika lagna*". This is the sign of a powerful ruler.

168 Epithet for Arjuna.

169 "*dvand*": pairing, the state of being 'two', duality.

170 This instruction is critical to Hammīra's later actions when he provides refuge to Mahimā Sāhi, the enemy general.

143: After destroying the Śakas in this manner, Bhīm Singh returned [to the fortress]. After a while Ullu Khan too left quietly [for home].

144: Then innumerable *kṣatriyas* donned golden crowns and carried the spoils of war. [They] followed Bhīm Singh in glorious victory and entered the city.

145: When he entered the [narrow] valley between the hills with great contentment, Bhīm Singh seized the musical instruments of the Śakas and shouted aloud:

146: "Wherever the sound of these instruments spreads [the Śakas] should acknowledge their defeat and retreat from there!"

147: Tricked by this warning the Yavanas thought that they were defeated. And so it happened that they all started assembling together.

148: Seeing that his forces had assembled, the Śaka Ullu Khan proceeded into battle [again] and so did Bhīm Singh! Although how could such cowardly people like the Śakas withstand him?

149: Then after a tremendous battle in which hundreds of Śakas were killed, Bhīm Singh fell dead having been struck by arrows on his entire body.

150: The victorious Śaka chieftain immediately retreated to his encampment. Fearing the *kṣatriyas* he made his way back towards his home town.

151: Then the king who [always] fulfils his word – on the advice of the minister Dharam Singh – crossed the [narrow] valley of the hills and thinking that it was Bhīm Singh approaching, called out to him.

152: He was blinded because he didn't notice the Śaka chieftain, and you who remained behind him do not have any virility.

153: In rage the king castrated and blinded him in front of all the courtiers.

154: Like [King] Pandu this king too had a younger brother named Bhojdev who displayed the intensity of Śri Vijaya and was called *khadga-grahi*.[171]

155: With confidence the king gave him [Bhojdev] Dharam Singh's position while exiling the latter. And through Bhojdev he issued a sanction [against Dharam Singh].

156: In the meantime, [Dharam Singh] began harbouring an enmity in his mind because of the insult. At home he began giving Bhārata Nāṭyam lessons to the [dancer] Dhārādevī.

157: And even though he stayed at home, it was through Dhārādevī that he learnt each and everything about what was going on with the king.

---

171 In literal terms this means 'receiver or holder of the sword.' It may also refer to a designation indicating an officer or leader of swordsmen.

158: Then one day after returning from the king's assembly, Dhārādevī revealed the thing that was tearing her heart apart upon his enquiring to the blind Dharam Singh.

159: "O Father! After learning about the disease called '*vedha*' that has killed the king's horses, I do not have [any] desire for dance, music, etc. I am extremely troubled [by this]."

160: Dharam Singh told her not to worry about meaningless things. However, at the next opportunity to go and request the following of the king.

161: "O Lord! If you give back Dharam Singh his position he will bring you twice the amount of horses as those that have died!"

162: Dhārādevī said: "Alright!" and went and told the king exactly this. Out of greed [for acquiring twice the number of new horses], King Hammīra agreed to reinstate [Dharam Singh].

166: The enraged [and] the blind Dharam Singh began to think of various means of avenging himself on King Hammīra and destroying his kingdom.

167: He strengthened the king's greed [by suggesting that he] extract money or taxes [from the populace]. He tormented the subjects by inflicting huge penalties.

168: From the horse traders he took horses and from the wealthy [he took] money. With these cruel actions he brought the subjects to their ruin.

169: As the vaults filled with wealth, [he] became the immense favourite of the king because prostitutes and kings adore only those individuals who ply them with wealth.

170: Not only did the money in the vaults grow from penalizing the subjects, his own person [i.e. well-being and wealth] grew as well.

171: On account of the immense desire for revenge in his heart, he asked for an entire year's wages [as a security] from Bhoj in order to remain on his position.

172: Observing the inconsistency of the blind minister, the angered Bhojrāj went immediately with bowed head and folded hands to the king and said:

173: "O King! If the lord wishes to take my life then so be it, but I cannot allow myself to be humiliated by the word of the blind minister."

174: Then the king said: "The person whose devotion to me can never diminish – Dharam Singh – his command cannot be overturned!"

176: After hearing this talk and observing his anger filled eyes, the pure minded Bhojdev realized that the king was a rogue. He shrugged off everything just as a person with a disinterested mind does. What can a strong man do if the roots of desire have been wrecked?

179: The next day the king undertook a pilgrimage to Baijnāth. Then when he saw Bhojdev standing behind him, he spoke [in the form of] an allegory.[172]

180: "There are innumerable birds over here, but nowhere are there any unfortunate, lowly birds that out of anger settle down in a gathering of clever owls and after having received hundreds of wounds [that even] break their wings continue to be unconscionable and do not leave the tree on which they dwell!"

185: After consulting with his brother, he went to the king and said: "If the king permits, then I would like to set off on a pilgrimage to Kāśi."

186: The king replied: "Why don't you go far way? This city was glorious before you were here and it will remain glorious after you leave!"

188: After Bhojdev departed, the king was contented. He nominated the warrior Ratipāla to the position of judge. Then in the practice of *dharma*, *artha* and *kāma*, the king passed his days in a wholesome manner.

Sarga 10

[Bhojdev forms an alliance with 'Alā'al-Din]

1: Because he had been disgraced by King Hammīra, Bhojdev left for Shirohi.[173] Again and again he pondered over his hopeless situation. Then in his heart he contemplated the following:

2: "If I don't avenge the hollow contempt shown to me by the king, then what will be the condition of cultured men?"

8: Then after speaking to his brother Pitham who agreed with him, Bhojdev [decided to] leave quickly for Yoginipura[174] to meet the Lord of the Yavanas.

9: Upon his arrival, the overjoyed 'Alā' al-Dīn gifted him the village called Jagra. [And] he gifted him a full length garment. This town belonged to the Mudgal king.

10: After leaving his fearless brother [Pitham] in the wondrous city of Jagra, Bhojdev hastened to return to Dilli[175] in order to be in the service of the Śaka king.

14: After some days in which the Yavana king began trusting [Bhojdev], he asked: "O Bhoj! Tell me! How does can I quickly defeat this Hammīra in battle?"

---

172 "*anyokti*": This is an *alaṃkāra* which suggests a form of speech that conveys something hidden, an innuendo or insinuation.

173 A town in southern Rajasthan that is near the famous Jain pilgrimage of Mount Abu.

174 This was one of the so-called 'pre-Muslim' names for Delhi.

175 = Delhi. The capital of 'Alā' al-Dīn.

15: "O respected, honourable Lord! If you really want the answer to this question, then do not be enraged at me!" Saying this, the fearless Bhoj said: [*extolls the unconquerable and mighty stature of King Hammīra.*]

30: "O King! Once your armies kill him, his subjects who have been tormented by the blind Dharam Singh will become despondent and leave!"

31: After listening to everything that [Bhojdev] had said, the Lord of the Śakas quickly summoned Ullu Khan. He gave him [command] over 100,000 cavalry which proceeded toward the Chahamana kingdom.

33: In the meantime the jewel in the crown of kings, Hammīra, received word through labourers (?) that the enemy was approaching. He summoned his cheerful warriors to his court and glanced quickly at them.

34: Then the cheerful Vīrama and eight other chief warriors understood very well the meaning of the king's gesture. And, with lotus-like smiling faces, those warriors quickly took up the chase with the Mleccha army.

38–40: Śrī Viramendra went from the east; Mahimā Sāhi from the west; Śrī Jājdev from the south and Gharbharuk from the north. The warrior named Ratipāla from the southeast; the Śaka lord Tichir from the left corner. The warrior called Raṇmalla from the northeast and Śrī Vaichar from the southwest. [They] surrounded the encampment of the mighty Śaka king's brother Ullu Khan from all directions and began attacking it. They had taken a pledge and [they] personified a passion for war.

50: Under the frenzied torrent of arrows fired by the warriors, the Yavana army began trembling on the battlefield like the wind blowing at the end of time.

56: Seeing his own army emasculated and besieged by rods and arrows by the tremendously brave *kṣatriyas*, Ullu Khan was fortunate to survive and escape.

57: Some groups of Mlecchas grew weak, some fainted, others grew fearful and many Mlecchas ran away. Some Yavanas were in a tumult, and others hid in secret places to save their lives.

61: The raging warrior called Ratipāla blindfolded the doe like eyes of Yavana warriors and made them sell buttermilk in each village. He wanted to spread King Hammīra's fame.

63: Upon hearing about the bravery of Ratipāla that would surmount [even the boldness of] an elephant, the exuberant King Hammīra placed golden chains around his feet saying: "This is my drunk elephant!"

64: Even after gifting many individuals with beautiful garments and bidding them farewell respectfully, the Yavana warriors[176] did not move. The king asked them for a reason and they replied saying:

65: "If we are alive even though the traitor Bhojdev continues to rule over the town called Jagra, then what use is our pledge? O King, do not fear!"

66: "Whatever we have borne for so long it is because of our bond with you, O Lord! What sort of bond does Bhojdev have who has brought so many enemy soldiers into your country?"

67: "O King, therefore give us permission to embark on a battle excursion!" Listening to these words of the Yavana warriors, King Hammīra grew pleased. He said: "O noble men! Begin this task quickly, hurry!"

68: As though the command of the king were like the sweet words of the Goddess of Victory, all the Yavana warriors ransacked Jagra city and captured Bhoj's brother Pitham together with his family, and returned.

69: And, somehow this vile Khan named Ullu who had run away from the battlefield reached Dilli. [There he] laid out the entire details of the battle to King 'Alā' al-Dīn.

70: Then king said: "Why did you run away like a coward?" Ullu Khan replied: "O King! If I hadn't run away how would I meet you?"

71: When Ullu Khan fell silent after telling his brother the Śaka king what had transpired, Bhojdev entered [the court] lamenting [and] in front of the astonished courtiers he fell to the ground [writhing] like a person possessed by a ghost. He threw off his clothes and began yelling loudly!

72: "Hey, hey what has happened?" asked the king of the Śakas. [Bhojdev replied:] "O Lord whatever transpired today, I will not forget this even after death!"

73: "On the command of King Hammīra the celebrated warrior Mahimā Sāhi ransacked Nagara city and took my brother along with his family captive!"

77: Then 'Alā' al-Dīn enquired: "Why are you stretched out [on the floor] on your outer clothes?" To this Bhoj replied: "Don't you understand that the Chahamana king has triumphed over the entire earth!"

78: Saddened after listening to Bhoj's word and the lament of his brother who had run away from the battle, the anger in King 'Alā' al-Dīn's swelled just like flames into which *ghee* is offered.

85: "Even if Hammīra enters the underworld, I will dig him out of the earth! Even if he enters heaven, I will bring him down together with Indra! If he doesn't

176 These are the 'neo-Muslim' warriors under the command of Mahimā Sāhi who have taken refuge with Hammīra.

see the might in my arms with his own eyes, will he hear [of them] anywhere with his ears?"

Sarga 11

['Alā' al-Din prepares to attack Hammīra together with his armies]

1–2: The Śaka kings of Aṅga, Tilaṅga, Magadh, Masūr, Kaliṅga, Vaṅga, Bhaṭa, Medpaṭa, Pāṇcāla, Baṅgāl, Thamim, Bhill, Nepāl, Dāhāl, Himādri, Madhya and so on arrived together with their experienced, magnificent armies in the city of the Yavana Lord ʿAlāʾ al-Dīn.

7: Then placing the brothers Ullu Khan and Nusrat Khan at the head of the mighty army, the Śaka king proceeded to conquer Hammīra.

8: "The Lord of the Śaka is following behind today!" In this manner [he] created fear amongst the *kṣatriya* clans, but himself remained on his own. The tactical knowledge of the Śakas was extraordinary.

9: With Nusrat Khan as his ally, Ullu Khan burned with a rage that desired to completely crush his enemies in the same way that fire incinerates bamboo with the help of the wind.

10: Wherever this army went even Śeṣ Nāg would move [himself] here and there, fearing that the earth would be destroyed. And due to the Śaka king's command his steadiness began to diminish.

22: Then after explaining carefully they instructed [the messenger] Śrī Molhan. They wanted [to send someone] cunning to become familiar with King Hammīra.

25: With the instructions of the king, the messenger named Molhan somehow entered [the fortress]. He was amazed when he beheld Ranasthambapura!

[*A description of the bedazzling city of Ranthambore from the perspective of the messenger follows*]

60: "O Hammīra! If you desire to continue enjoying your kingdom, then give us one hundred thousand gold coins, four mighty elephants, three hundred horses and sheep, and also your daughter [in marriage]. Listen to our demand carefully!"

61: "If you don't want to fulfil this demand then return the four Mughal Pathans who have violated our commands. After that [you can] amuse [yourself] with the Goddess of Victory who sits in your lap!"

99: Three months passed with the Yavana king's Śaka warriors demonstrating their prowess in trying all kinds of means of moving forward [penetrating the fortress].

100: On the second day a cannon ball fired from a canon of the Śakas collided with another cannon ball fired by them. It exploded and a fragment struck Nusrat Khan in the head from which died.

101: The middle, unmarried Śaka chieftain [Ullu Khan] began wailing after the seeing [his brother] die suddenly.

102: After somehow restraining his hurt, the middle Śaka, Ullu Khan, prepared a beautiful, jewel studded basket in which he placed a gift and with great forbearance [he wrote] a letter describing what had happened during the entire battle [and sent it] to Dilli to the Emperor. In it he also placed the corpse of Nusrat Khan.

103: Steeped in sorrow and trembling with anger upon learning of all the dishonour heaped upon them by their enemies, the chief of the Śakas, ʿAlāʾ al-Dīn performed all the last rites for Nusrat Khan, and departed toward Ranthambore! Brave people can never tolerate the dishonour done to them by their enemies.

Sarga 12

[The battle between Hammīra and ’Alā’ al-Din]

1: When Hammīra, the [one endowed with] noble intelligence and [the one who was] like the embodiment of [rain] clouds for the forest, heard that ʿAlāʾ al-Dīn had arrived [at Ranthambore], he had thatched awnings attached to the [ramparts] of the fortress.

2: Watching with amazement and surprise with a smile on his face, the Śaka leader gestured to people near the ramparts and asked [them what this was].

3: Upon hearing this King Hammīra was pleased and with a joyful expression he spoke to the Śaka king:

4: “O King of the Mlecchas! By coming here you have done something auspicious! When a house is completed by collecting so many objects, what burden can arise through the accumulation of winnowing fans?”[177]

5: Listening to the [Chahamana] king’s words the Śaka king replied: “O King Hammīra! I am very pleased with you! O Brave Warrior, ask for whatever you desire!”

6: Then the chief amongst *kṣatriyas* said: “If that is the case, then fight us for two days! What else do these mighty warriors desire but to fight?”

7: The Śaka king kept praising the pledge of the *kṣatriyas*. “So be it! [We will fight] tomorrow morning!” he said and retreated into his tent.

177 *bhārāya kiṃ bhavati śūrpasaṃcayaḥ. Śūrpa* = Winnowing fan.

11: Then the king prepared a sacrifice, made himself ready for the entertainment of war and took his soldiers into battle.

[*A long, elaborate description of the battles follow.*]

27: The wives of the soldiers placed jars of cool water filled with cardamom and cloves on their heads and readied themselves to lovingly follow their brave, beloved husbands.

66: It appeared as though some warriors whose entrails had spilled after their torsos had been rent apart by swords were being carried up in chains by Apsaras to heaven.

85: "A thousand warriors have perished here!" Thinking this, a warrior started doing a dance with the fingers of both hands, [a dance] that had been begun by a headless warrior whose head had been severed by his enemies.

86: A battle comparable to the Mahābhārata went on for two days such that it seemed that the sun had travelled to the far mountain [behind which the sun sets] in the west in order to speak to the horizon.

88: In this battle 85,000 great, radiant Yavana warriors arrived in Yama-Loka.

89: Then, after much time had passed, the lords of the Mleccha warriors, Ullu Khan and ʿAlāʾ al-Dīn, refrained from fighting and pulled back the warriors from the battle. They quickly left for their military camps.

Sarga 13

[The slaying of the dancer Dhārādevi]

1: On the second day [of the battle], heavy with ornaments, the capable king Hammīra embellished the hall named 'Four Adornments' [by his presence].

11: The magnificent Vīrama stood adorning the southern side of the king while Ratipāla entertained the gathering by prompting laughter.

12: In similar manner, Mahimā Sāhi who embodied the qualities of perfection stood there like a divine being in the midst of his three younger brothers.

17: Right then the dancer named Dhārādevī began dancing. She had covered herself with a bodice and a saree. She was paying attention to her breasts and bottom that seemed to be competing with each other in largeness. Her body which seemed to be made for pleasure like a slender vine was intoxicating [...] With endearing sideways glances which seemed revive the lord of love she penetrated the minds of the courtiers and made them exultant.

26: The courtiers kept eyeing her up and down like a monkey climbing up and down a vine.

27: "She is dancing exuberantly!" The instant this news reached the encampment, the Śaka king saw her [dancing] with her back turned on him.[178]

28: The Śaka king was troubled by this. He spoke to the assembly of chiefs surrounding him: "Is there an archer who can shoot this dancer down?"

29: His younger brother replied: "O King! We should tell Uddan Singh whom we had imprisoned to kill her. There is no [archer] like him!"

30: Then the Śaka king called Uddan Singh quickly and had his handcuffs unlocked. He tempted him with all kinds of endearing [gestures], wealth and so on. [Then] he prepared him with a bow and arrows.

31: Then that criminal took up the extraordinary bow and immediately shot down that dancer just like a lion kills a deer.

32: [When] she was struck by the arrow, she went into a deep faint and fell directly into the gorge just like lightning separates from the sky [and falls to the earth].

33: For a moment the king [and chiefs] felt fearful and shook their heads in praise of the archer's skill.

34: Still pained by that hurtful incident, the next day Mahimā Sāhi took aim on the Śaka king, 'Alā' al-Dīn, and spoke to King Hammīra:

35: "If the king permits, then I will slay the enemy with my arrow just like the great archer Arjuna took aim and shot a moving image."

36: The king replied: "If he is killed then with whom will I find pleasure in battle? Therefore, O Mahimā Sāhi, let him be and instead kill the archer Uddan Singh!"

37: When he did not get permission to slay the Śaka King, the troubled Mahimā Sāhi reproachfully [threw down his] bow after he had killed [Uddan Singh].

38: The astonished Śaka king immediately withdrew his encampment from the front of the lake to its far side.

39: After the aggrieved Śaka king had given away various gifts, he began tunnelling in the nearby hillside.

40: Ullu Khan filled the ditch [moat] with stones, mud, and grass.

41: After it had taken months to complete both measures, the Śaka king commanded the Śaka soldiers to go to war.

42: When the Chahamana Rajputs learnt of this, they burnt the ditches with cannon ball fire and poured oil and lacquer into the tunnels.

178 Presumably he is insulted by the fact that she has her back turned to him in a sign of disrespect.

43: When the oil filled the tunnels, the enemy soldiers began jumping [up and down] just like fish leap out of a burning lake.

47: The soldiers of the Śaka warriors of the Lord of Śakas, ʿAlāʾ al-Dīn who had dug the tunnel, those very soldiers' bodies [now] blocked the tunnel.

48: Hammīra thwarted each effort that the Śaka king made to capture the fortress.

49: The Śaka king could neither leave the fortress nor conquer it. He became despondent just like a snake that can neither swallow nor eject a shrew.

50: He abandoned all pleasures like a *yogi* and would look [up] at the fortress or [down] at the earth [again and again].

61: The clouds that appeared after the summer months created an immense roar as though trumpeters were arriving.

67: Horses turned pale and elephants became emaciated; chariots sank into the water and boils appeared on men.

69: Then the Śaka king summoned one of Hammīra's warriors called Ratipāla. The king thought: "Let's see what the Śaka king has to say," and gave him permission [to meet ʿAlāʾ al-Dīn].

70: When Ratipāla left to [meet the Śaka king], the *kṣatriya* warrior called Raṇmalla grew annoyed thinking "My heroism has no value now!"

71–72: Now when Ratipāla went to meet him, the clever Śaka king rose up from his seat and asked [Ratipāla] to be [seated] on it and gave him many gifts as diplomacy demanded because a [good] diplomat never commits an error.

73: ʿAlāʾ al-Dīn asked his courtiers to leave and only with his brother Ullu Khan by his side he pleaded with Ratipāla:

74: "I am ʿAlāʾ al-Dīn, Emperor of Śakas, and with great difficulty I have conquered many renowned fortresses. If I depart without bringing this fortress under my command, my fame will shrivel up just like a tender branch thrown into a fire."

75: "Even Indra is incapable of conquering this fortress, but fortunately you have come here and now my wish will be fulfilled. Therefore, you should do whatever will make me victorious in battle. This kingdom will be yours! I am only desirous of victory!"

80: The mighty Ratipāla took command in his imagination over the fortress. He became the embodiment of Śakuni for the Śaka king who desired to bring the '*kali yuga*' fortress of Ranthambore under his command.

81: Thereafter, [ʿAlāʾ al-Dīn] took [Ratipāla] to Anantapur where he fed him and in order to gain his confidence; then he served him with alcohol in the company of his sister.

82: Then that evil minded Ratipāla took an oath to say the things the Śaka king intended and told the king [Hammīra] everything that had been said against him.

83: "O Sir! Proud like Rāvaṇa, the Śaka king exclaimed: 'Is Hammīra [so] foolish that he won't give me his daughter?'

84: 'Alright, don't give me your daughter but if I, ʿAlāʾ al-Dīn, won't possess your daughter, then I will capture all your wives!'

85: 'So what if some of my men die? Does a centipede become handicapped if it loses one or two legs?'

88: "I am suspicious that Raṇmalla has become angry because of some reason. For certain he knows about this situation. He has become arrogant!"

89: "Therefore, go to him with 5–6 men in the evening and quickly satisfy him. [Tell him] what sort of creature this Śaka king is!"

90: After saying that the king should please Raṇmalla, Ratipāla exited [the courtroom] while passing nearby Vīrama.

91: When Ratipāla passed by Vīrama, he reeked of alcohol just like the trace of perfume follows an embrace with a strange woman.

92: Then Vīrama took the king aside and said "It would appear as though the cunning [Ratipāla] has joined hands with the enemy king!"

93: "O King! When he was exiting, he smelt of alcohol. I think this sinner has certainly joined hands with the enemy!"

97: "O Lord! If I strike him down with my sword just like killing a sheep, then the Śaka king ʿAlāʾ al-Dīn will fail and will [then] leave!"

100: "If [we] slay Ratipāla and he is no longer part of the fortress who will stop the rumours that will spread?"

101: 'Certainly our lord Hammīra and his family are evil minded that they should have killed Ratipāla without thinking!'

102: "Can these Śaka folk[179] remain in the fortress while I am alive? Can there be any fooling around in a lion's den when he is there?"

103: "Just as there will be a time (celebration) similar to [when] Hanuman [destroyed Laṇkā] if we win, Ratipāla's time on earth will end if we die!"

105: After saying this the Rāṇā[180] grew quiet. [In the meantime] word got around in the city that the Śaka king was asking for Hammīra's daughter.

106: Then after the queens had tried to reassure her, Hammīra's daughter Devalldevī went to him and spoke:

179 Hammīra is referring here to Mahimā Sāhi's family and entourage.

180 Chieftain or king.

107: "Oh! Oh! Father! Why are you abandoning this kingdom on account of me? Can anyone [dare] damage even one nail of this palace?"

109: "If by giving me away to the Śaka king, the kingdom can live on forever, then [do so] because if a wish fulfilling stone can be protected by giving away a piece of glass, then why not the kingdom?"

112: "In any case you will gain a son-in-law like ʿAlāʾ al-Dīn and our piece of the earth will be protected. What else is there to say? We will remain chief!"

114: "Therefore pay attention to what matters and do things in a timely manner. Do not overturn my words! Send me to the Śaka king!"

118: "If the entire kingdom would be made happy by giving you away, then shouldn't one consider surviving by eating the flesh of one's own son?"

122: "O Daughter! Your suggestion that we would benefit from giving you away, is an expression of your childlike attitude!"

123: "It is perfectly clear that if I gave you away to this sinning, cow-flesh consuming Śaka, then, Oh! Oh! What kind of benefit would we gain?"

130: In the meantime, Ratipāla went quickly to Raṇmalla's home and said in an agitated tone:

131: "O Brother! Why are you so contented? We should think of escaping immediately because our king thinks that his dutiful servants like us are enemies! He is coming to take us prisoner!"

133: "The king will come with five or six men to your home in the evening. Mark my words!" Saying this he left for his own home.

134: Just like Ratipāla had forewarned [him], he saw King Hammīra approaching [his home]. He became alarmed. He escaped down the fortress and met up with the enemy.

135: When Ratipāla escaped down the fortress he fell at the Śaka King's feet just as someone who has fallen from high heaven tries to find refuge in hell.

136: After seeing this sort of behaviour [Hammīra] thought to himself: "A curse on the *kali yuga!*" He proceeded to ask the master of granaries, Jahāḍ, how much grain there was in storage.

137: Thinking to himself that by saying 'There is nothing,' he would create an alliance [with Ratipāla and Raṇmalla], out of a sense of greed he said: "[The granaries] are empty!"

139: Deeply troubled by this statement, King Hammīra returned to his palace and spent a sleepless night thinking about this until the last hour of darkness.

140: "If those two warriors whom I have paid such homage with incomparable honour and innumerable gifts can betray their master, then what fault do ordinary people with a lesser disposition have?"

141: "If traitors join hands with the enemy and then they tie me up and devour me on account of belonging to the same kin then this will be a grave irony!"

147: After this the king seated himself in the assembly hall in the early morning. He summoned Mahimā Sāhi in front of the gathering.

148: "We are ready to die for our birth land. The *dharma* of *kṣatriyas* will never ever end!"

149: "Only that person is *kṣatriya* who lives on even after he dies! King Duryodhaṇa was a clear example of [such a person]."

150: "You are a foreigner! Therefore, it is not good for you remain in a place of calamity! Tell me wherever you would like to go, I will transport you there!"

151: Listening to the king's words, Mahimā Sāhi fell unconscious as though his heart had been pierced by a spear. He grew enraged!

152: "So be it!" he said. He went to his home and slew his entire family with his sword and then [went back] and spoke to the king:

153: "Your brother's bride Illa Vilāsinī is eager to leave your kingdom as you suggested! She was overjoyed when she told me!"

156: "O Lord! [She said] if we leave without saying farewell to King Hammīra, then we will regret it! Please calm my wife down!"

157: Then King Hammīra set off honourably, arm-in-arm together with his brother Mahimā Sāhi.

158: The instant the king entered his home, he saw that the courtyard was like Kurukṣetra.

159: The heads of children and women bobbled in a pool of blood. The king fell unconscious to the ground.

160: The king awoke from the tears flowing from the eyes of Vīrama and other brothers. Hammīra embraced Mahimā Sāhi and began weeping!

161: "O Upholder of the Kāmboja Tribe! O Dwelling Place of the Glorious Tribe! O Person of Matchless Virtue! O Blessed Courage! O Bearer of the *kṣatriya* Vow! O beloved of humanity! Even if I sacrifice my life as your king, how will I ever repay my debt [to you]?"

162: "There is no one greater than you, and there is no one lesser than me! In my stupidity I never imagined you had so much affection for me!"

169: Then upon returning he [stopped] at the granary which was immeasurably full with grain. He asked the keeper of the store, Jahāḍ: "What is this?"

170: Then when [Jahāḍ] replied with foolishness, the king said: "The foolishness through which you have brought about the end of the clan, may a thunderbolt strike it down!"

171: Then following the law, the king showed the dwellers of the city the gate from which to exit. He then instructed his queens to enter the fire.

172: Then after he had worshipped Janārdan, made offerings and had become impervious to pain, he sat down for a brief moment at the banks of the Lotus Lake.[181]

173: In the meantime, Queen Āraṅgidevī who was wearing exquisite ornaments bathed there together with other austere-minded ladies. She bowed to the king and stood there.

181: King Hammīra was satisfied. He cut the finest locks of his hair and distributed them as articles of adornment.

182–183: He then embraced his daughter Devalldevī tightly and wept. He let go of her with much difficulty. Then he spoke to her: "If anyone should ever have a daughter they should be like you, who like Gauri has propelled her father to the pinnacle of fame!"

185: Then after he had placed his daughter in his heart, those doe-eyed [ladies] entered the funeral pyre in which terrifying flames soared.

187: Then King Hammīra summoned Jājdev who performed the last oblation for those ladies with water and sesame seeds. Then he quickly severed the heads of eight women and offered them as a sacrifice.

188: The king said: "What is this?" He replied: "Just like Rāvaṇa worshipped [Lord] Śaṃbhū, I too am worshipping you!"

189: "And, one head belongs to me! This way the Mleccha will have nine heads in his hands!" Saying this he beheaded himself.

191: [...] Then the king thought to himself: "Where should I hide the kingdom's treasure?"

192: Then in a dream the Lotus Lake spoke to him: "Hide all the treasure inside of me. The Mughals won't be able to retrieve it, even if they sacrifice themselves!"

193: "All the lowly warriors like Ratipāla and others have joined up with the Mlecchas, but these warriors and this fortress will not betray you!"

194: After the king awoke, he ordered the keeper of the store, Jahāḍ, to empty all the wealth of the kingdom into the lake. Then the king said: "Now what should I do?"

195: "Grant me permission!" said Vīrama. Upon receiving permission from King Hammīra he cut off [Jahāḍ's] head like slicing through a pumpkin.

196–197: After this on the sixth day in the light half of the month of Śrāvan on the night of Sunday, as though he was eager to see his fame traverse heaven,

181 During my conversations at the fortress, I was told emphatically that Hammīra was a devotee of Lord Śiva to whom he had finally offered his own head inside the small shrine where he would regularly worship the deity. In the text, however, both Hammīra and his father Jaitra Siṃha are portrayed as devotees of Lord Viṣṇu.

King Hammīra leapt into the battlefield together with chieftains who could materialize matter; nine warriors who were like *vīr rasa* itself.

198: "Hammīra has arrived!" Hearing these words, the brave Śaka king stood firm like an enemy in front of him with his army.

199: In front of Hammīra stood the best warrior, the one who is skilled at warfare, the chieftain of Champa, Vīramadev – just like the king of the Aṅga country, King Karṇa, stood in front of Duryodhana.

200: Within moments, the great Vīrama frightened the enemy army with his arrows and the sound of his bow.

201: Roaring like a lion, the warrior called 'Lion' scared the enemy army like a herd of deer. He adorned the sacrifice of enemies like a lion!

202: [The warrior called] Gaṅgādhar Ṭāk also stood by his name by slicing through the bodies of the enemy warriors with his gun.

203: The warrior called Rajada also stood by his name by demoralizing the radiant faces of the Yavanas.

204: The four mighty Mudgal warriors, Mahimā Sāhi and others, the four Pathan warriors were adorning the four bodied army of the enemy with an eagerness to live.

205: The Parmar king Kṣetra Singh dispatched thousands of enemies as guests of Yamarāj. He too proved the name of his royal clan.

207: "Who is the Lakshmī that resides in heaven that the king wants to marry me to?" As though desirous of seeing her, Vīramadev reached heaven before King Hammīra.

208: Many of his warriors who were excited to sacrifice their own lives reached heaven before their lord. Such was the disposition of heroes!

209: Seeing that Mahimā Sāhi had collapsed after being struck by arrows, Hammīra himself entered the battlefield.

211: Hammīra alone slaughtered hundreds of thousands of soldiers. With his sword he sliced off enemy-heads making the sky seem like a [vast] lake of lotuses.

212: Surrounded by Hammīra's blazing arrows, the Śaka fighters felt as though they had entered the sun's orb.

218: Hammīra cut through the bowstrings and the archers who were capable of competing with Arjuna.

220: The battleground that was littered with the heads of enemies severed by the king appeared as though death itself had harvested a field of sesame seeds.

223: This hero slaughtered enemies in such a way that the abode of Yamarāj was overflowing [with the dead].

226: The one who performs fearsomely in war, the jewel in the crown of the heroes' clan, wounded in every limb by the onslaught of enemy arrows, honoured by the entire earth, King Hammīra, thinking that the Yavanas would capture him, slit his own throat and carried on toward heaven becoming a guest of the gods!

Sarga 14

17: The son of Rādhā, [Karṇa] removed his body armour; King Śibi cut off his own flesh and King Bali offered up the entire earth; Jīmūtavāhana sacrificed half of his body. But none of them can compare to King Hammīra who unhesitatingly sacrificed his daughter, wife, all his followers and himself for the sake of Mahimā Sāhi who had sought refuge. Only his story is indestructible!

20: "One should not kill one's own kin." Keeping this injunction in mind, ʿAlāʾ al-Dīn captured Mahimā Sāhi. Mahimā Sāhi who was still alive was taken to the Mleccha king. He entered [the sultan's tent] [disrespectfully] showing him his foot. "Now that you are still alive, what will your behaviour toward me be?" Mahimā Sāhi retorted: "I will do to you what you have done to King Hammīra!" Who in the world can compare with the courage of someone like Mahimā Sāhi?

21: "O Ratipāla! You who struck King Hammīra's [fallen] head with your foot and upon ʿAlāʾ al-Dīn asking you: 'What mercies did the king bequeath upon you?' answered by describing all the kindness [he bestowed on you], it was appropriate that the Śaka king had you skinned [alive]! Otherwise, would not people betray their masters? Many would have!"

Appendix 2: Conversations at Ranthambore

The following passages are translated portions of conversations I had in Hindi during a fieldtrip to Ranthambore. They represent a remembrance of the fortress, its history and architecture, and the history of Hammīra and his allies and enemies from the perspective of the people I spoke with who have been associated with the fortress in one way or another for a considerable amount of time.[182] The narratives offered here sometimes merge and at other times diverge from the accounts found in some of the written sources discussed in the chapters of the book. Although certain details described ideally require one to be physically walking through the different awe-inspiring parts of the fortress, I hope that the reader can – with a little help of the imagination – visually walk through the tremendous edifice that the fortress represents in sheer material terms but more so in terms of a richly mosaicked memento of the past as it lives in the narration of people who reside on its grounds and nearby. This verbal record together with the many written narratives that have been presented in the main body of the text constitute the 'totality' of written and spoken records through which the 'reality' of the history of the fortress is imagined.

1 The Maze of Gates

In the following conversation the reader is taken through the many gates of the fortress, some of which are associated with a deity or deities that are 'stationed' at these gates. The gates are designed in such a way so as to make it difficult, confusing and almost impossible to penetrate the fort. The passages in the beginning also offer a story about how the location of the fortress was 'discovered' and when it was originally built, pushing back its history to the 5th century, and more importantly associating certain notable and powerful 'tribes' – the Bhīls and Minas or Bhīl-Minas – with its construction. Later on here – as in some of the other conversations – the person being interviewed also weaves autobiographical elements into the narrative. The present-past is thus constituted of lived experience and memory that is personal and non-personal or historical,

182 While these conversations cannot strictly be classified as 'oral narratives' *per se*, they do, however, constitute a verbal record of the history and significance of the fortress in a manner that is grounded in the materiality of the heritage site – its thick walls, gates, palaces, inner courtyards, temples, mausoleums, shrines, water bodies, trees and more.

https://doi.org/10.1515/9783110662795-013

but then the historical becomes personal by participating in an individual's experience.

Guide 1: Sages used to meditate here ... right on this hill. Two princes came by here while they were playing and so they met the sages. After speaking to the sages they realized [that the hills were special]. Otherwise they never knew that hills like these existed. They had not travelled around much. So they did not know about these hills. So the sages told them that there are such hills and that there are no other hills anywhere else. They told them everything. Ever since then the princes started thinking about constructing the fort here. It began from there.

Questioner: Who were these princes of the past ... was it not Hammīra [who built the fortress]?

G1: No, no ... this was far, far earlier. This incident took place before the 5th century. The princes' names aren't mentioned. It just says two princes. It's from here that we believe – they didn't construct it – but that is from here where it all started. The princes spoke about this and later on discussions continued. Kings discussed it and later on the foundation of the fortress was laid. Its foundation is believed to have been laid by Maharaj Jayant. But it is also believed that in 944 CE Sabalak Chauhan laid the foundation, and in addition to these [kings], there were tribals, and amongst them was King Hadda. [According to some] it was under his rule that this fort was constructed by tribals. This is mentioned in historical texts. According to the Archaeological Survey, it was constructed in 5th century by King Jayant, but before this even the Archaeological Survey put up a board here stating that Sabalak Chauhan laid the foundation of Ranthambore Fort in 944 CE. But three/four years ago they claimed that fort was established in the 5th century.

Q: So it's much older? Who were these tribals? Were they people of the Bhīl community?

G1: Bhīl-Mina.[183] Bhīl ... it was the Bhīl tribe. So the king [Hadda] belonged to the Mina community. He was the king, so under his command, this was [fort] built. He was a Mina king, and under his supervision, the tribals constructed this fort. The people were tribals, this fort has been constructed by them. This is one of the explanations. The other one I told you is of Sabalak Chauhan who constructed it 944 CE. Now since the past three years, the Archaeological Survey has attributed it to the 5th century. Just three years ago the same people used to attribute it to Sabalak Chauhan in 944 CE. [They claimed] that Sabalak Chauhan had laid the foundation of the Ranthambore fort in 944 CE. Later on when this was surveyed then they must have found something else so they now say this is to be associated with the King Jayant from the 5th century. So there are three views regarding [the construction of the fort]. It's not clear even today who constructed it and when it was constructed ... after crossing the first gate, you get the second gate and the ravine comes in front of you, if we close this then we get to the ravine, see here ...

Q: Oh yes!

G1: See how deep the ravine gets ... and see the gate number 3, the entire ravine emerges ... see how amazingly it has been constructed ... nobody can attack from here and also nobody

183 See Mayaram (2003).

can attack from there ... and this is the route and the highest chances of attack are from the direction of the route only ... so that was difficult from here ... it was difficult from here but there was no chance from here ... it was constructed in an amazing fashion ... it has been given a 90° angle ... This is the watchtower.

Q: What is this?

G1: The watchtower was for sending signals.

Q: Okay. A watchtower.

G1: If you notice in the forest, every 1 to 2 kms you will find this [kind of] umbrella. Many umbrellas have now been broken. And, this umbrella where we sat earlier, from there [the watchtower] was the first thing visible ... from the entire area that is can be seen, from 5 km to 10 km, 15 km, from there it was completely visible to the entire village.

Q: Very good.

G1: This umbrella has fallen ... but from this place they used to receive signals, from here to there, from here, to here to here ... so in this way the entire forest [was covered]. So they had definite codes, like showing a flag in the daytime to the next person ahead, who then in turn he would show it to the one ahead of him, and that person did the same thing, etc. At night by lighting the torches ... in this way there were definite codes ... since there were no mobile phones thus the SMS messages were sent across by the people [in this way]. The army of the king of Ranthambore ... I told you, there are four routes to reach the Ranthambore fort ... there is one hill ... the soldiers were stationed in the fort ... it was very difficult for the enemy to penetrate it.

Q: What is this?

G1: Padam Lake. This is Padam Lake ... yes, rainwater accumulates here. You can see ... this is how their signals were received.

Q: I see.

G1: These small installations were for the surveillance. These were not visible, there were many things that were not visible. Like when the signal arrived, the person here would see it, but the person there would not be able to see it. That means there were different ways of spying. So when spies roamed around, they used to be able to see them from that point. So that the enemy wouldn't know that the signal was sent, or that it has been received. [All these systems] were established after a thorough application of the mind. Yes, this is the idol of Lord Ganeśa and it was installed here by Hammīr Dev Chauhan in the 13th century to protect this gate. It is a natural statue which is six and a half thousand years old; it is natural and magical. It is Trinetri (having three eyes). The third eye is a symbol of wisdom through which we acquire knowledge. Riddhi and Siddhi are two wives and Śubh and Lābh are two sons. Lord Ganeśa is established here along with the entire family. So this is like a head office. All the other Trinetri [deities] in the world don't have what we have here. It has been installed here for the security of this gate. After crossing the first gate comes the Pañcdev [five deities], where you offered Rs 10 in the name of Lord Rāma. Pañcdev was installed there by Hammīr Dev Chauhan for protecting the first gate. It was installed by Hammīr Dev Chauhan. Pañcdev was installed for the protection of the Naulakha Pol of the first gate. Similarly, the idol of Lord Ganeśa was installed here for protecting the third gate.

Fig. 10: The shrine of Lord Ganeśa in the outer stone wall of the fortress

Q: Is there no idol installed on the second gate ...?

G1: There is none on the second gate. Ever since the time of Hammīr Dev Chauhan, a fair has been conducted here. A fair in the name of Lord Ganeśa has been celebrated here since the era of Hammīr Dev Chauhan, since around the 13th century. This fair is organized during around the month of August on Ganeśa Chaturthi *bhādra śukla pakṣa*. During Ganeśa Chaturthi, a huge fair is organized. 1,500,000 to 2,000,000 people pay a visit in less than 36 hours ... people come on foot while chanting the name of the god. 80 per cent of people come walking from a distance of 50 km, 100 km and [even] 500 km! They leave their home a month before in groups and they engage in dance and music and come pay a visit here. The [attacking] armies used to walk, they knew that they would attack but they used to walk fast, they knew where the gates were. If they did not know where the gates were and even if they walk fast then only ten or twenty out of a hundred would survive. The remaining would go and attack, but they used to get confused on coming here not knowing how to enter. While deciding [where to go] they would get killed. Such gates were constructed to confuse them.

Q: What is this? These windows?

G1: This was Safari Palace. When the kings used to go somewhere and when they returned, the queens would gather here to welcome them. It was called Main Gate, Main Dvar, Safari Palace. Flowers were showered [on them] from here. This was called by different names in different regimes. It is also known as the Bhul Bhulaiya[184] gate because if the enemy army was successful in reaching here then the King would order opening the second gate which meant that the king had accepted defeat and out of fear had ordered the gate to be opened. This made the enemy happy. They would celebrate with loud noises but then found the gate to be closed. There was a ravine ahead that was covered with grass and bushes. [The soldiers from the enemy army] would fall into that. These were the kinds of ideas that the kings possessed. There was an idol of the god ...

Q: Where?

G1: An idol of Lord Rāma was installed in the Raghunāth Temple. It was made up of some metal, it had gold polish. It was stolen earlier.

Q: The idol was stolen?

G1: Yes ... there is a pool in which the air was blown ... the air was blown using the pressure from the mouth, like the conch is blown using the mouth, so the pool used to be filled automatically with water. There is a pipe like thing ... when the air was blown into it, due to the air pressure, it used to get automatically filled with water. Anyhow, they had created a system, a system that allowed the pool to get filled automatically. I can't say anything about today but we have seen this 10 – 12 years ago. We came here during our school days as a group. We all tried hard and water really came up ... we witnessed that, now that was the [special] architecture. It was not made later, it was there since the beginning. It was there even before our country gained independence ... because the Raghunāth Temple is an old temple. There was an entire city established here earlier, all the trees that you can see, there were colonies here, it was a city and the houses were made of raw clay.

Q: This is Rani Pond?

184 = Maze or labyrinth.

Fig. 11: Gravestones in the inner precincts of the fortress

G1: This is Rani Pond. Now, let's see the court. The court of their period. It is also amazingly made. There was somebody called Sayyed Sadruddin Shah, he was an aged person. This is his grave ... these are graves ... of their family members ... this is what we are told.

Q: What is this?

G1: [Graves] of Khaljī, his family members.[185] This is what we've been told. [There are many other stories] but the majority opinion matches this idea. There was a lake all around the fort. There was a Tabara ... near each Bāvḍī.[186] Tabara was a structure that allowed people to sit in the shade, taking rest and leaving after drinking water. There are around 36 Bāvḍīs here and these used to be the source of drinking water when a war was going on. ʿAlāʾ al-Dīn Khaljī fought a war in around 1301 against Hammīr Dev Chauhan that went on for 18/19 years. The reason for the war was that even the uncle of ʿAlāʾ al-Dīn Khaljī, Jalāl al-Dīn Khaljī had also attacked this place. Jalāl al-Dīn Khaljī was the uncle of ʿAlāʾ al-Dīn Khaljī, he was the emperor of Delhi and he had attacked this place but wasn't able to conquer it. So what ʿAlāʾ al-Dīn Khaljī did was that he dethroned his uncle and became the emperor of Delhi and then he planned to conquer this fort. This was like a brotherhood, the other thing I will tell you, there was a war fought between Sardar Muhammed

185 This is an intriguing claim that the sultan and some of his family members burials are located in the precincts of the fortress.
186 = Water well.

Shāh together with Hammīr Dev [against 'Alā' al-Dīn], so it was a like a brotherhood. 'Alā' al-Dīn Khaljī wanted to conquer it but his uncle Jalāl al-Dīn hindered his ambitions. So 'Alā' al-Dīn killed him by poisoning him. 'Alā' al-Dīn then sat on the throne of Delhi. Now the story is that 'Alā' al-Dīn had three commanders named Ullu[gh] Khan, Nusrat Khan and Sardar Muhammed Shāh. Sardar Muhammed Shāh was in an illicit and illegitimate relationship with the wife of 'Alā' al-Dīn Khaljī.[187] 'Alā' al-Dīn came to know about it and he ordered the death penalty by hanging of Sardar Muhammed Shāh. The story behind the illegitimate relationship between Sardar Muhammed Shāh and Khaljīs wife was that once 'Alā' al-Dīn Khaljī and Sardar Muhammed Shāh went on a hunting expedition. 'Alā' al-Dīn Khaljī waited for the whole day but couldn't hunt anything down and got irritated. So he left Sardar Muhammed Shāh with his wife and moved further [into the jungle] in search of an animal to hunt. While that was happening, a tiger appeared and Sardar Muhammed Shāh hunted the tiger down. Seeing this, the wife of 'Alā' al-Dīn Khaljī became very impressed by him. So they started a relationship. When 'Alā' al-Dīn Khaljī came to know about it, he ordered the execution of Sardar Shāh. Sardar Muhammed Shāh ran away from there. He had heard that Hammīr Dev is the only king who can give him refuge. Because it was his duty, Hammīr Dev's father Jaitra Singh Chauhan had told Hammīr Dev right before his demise that offering refuge to the needy was his first duty ... even if it is your enemy. Sardar Muhammed Shāh knew about this. So Sardar Muhammed Shāh arrived here. And Hammīr Dev Chauhan provided him refuge. Following the instructions of his father, he gave him protection. 'Alā' al-Dīn Khaljī got to know about it. 'Alā' al-Dīn in any case wanted to fight the war, it was about the brotherhood, so fighting the war was already on the cards. His first assault happened in 1292. Earlier all this went on happening but in 1292, he launched an open assault. During this assault, his main commander Nusrat Khan got killed.

Q: Here?

G1: Nusrat Khan was killed here. Many soldiers too died but his main commander Nusrat Khan was killed. They retreated but attacked again in 1296. ['Alā' al-Dīn] attacked afresh but again faced defeat. In that battle, Hammīr Dev Chauhan's most important commander Bhīm got killed.

Q: Bhīm?

G1: Bhīm! He was the main commander of the army of King Hammīr Dev Chauhan. He got killed. His main commander got killed but still Khaljī had to face defeat. He retreated once more ... till Delhi. But he came again. 'Alā' al-Dīn was an amazing king, whatever he desired, he used to achieve it! See what he did, the first fort here is Chittorgarh, the second is Ranthambore fort. First of all he brought those under control due to which the smaller [rulers] would automatically run away out of dread. If he can conquer the [big] fort then the smaller [rulers] accepted his authority unconditionally. He first conquered the Ranthambore fort in 1301. In 1303 he won the Chittor fort. So this way battles kept going on and finally 'Alā' al-Dīn Khaljī came here. He had an army of one hundred and eighty thou-

187 This detail is in significant variance with the idea that the general mutinied against the sultan because of the unequal and exploitative manner in which the spoils of war were distributed amongst the so-called 'neo-Muslim' commanders of the sultan's armies.

sand soldiers at that time, after 1296 CE. He came with his entire army and set up the camp on all sides [of the fortress] for two to four years. When the draught hit these Bāvḍīs during that period ... he then dug new Bāvḍīs. There were a lot of soldiers. That's why you will find many Bāvḍīs in the entire forest. There is an area called Zone Number 3, it is known as Dudh Bāvḍī. Its water was like milk. Its name is Dudh Bāvḍī. And you will find many Bāvḍīs in the forest. I have seen many Bāvḍīs.

Q: Were they made by Khaljī?

G1: Yes, these were made by Khaljī. He had constructed the water source for the army. I will show you a Bāvḍī right now when we move further; there are two Bāvḍīs near the road, I will show you. Those are near the road. So he constructed many Bāvḍīs. Finally he surrounded the fort from all sides and sent three messages to the King Hammīr Dev Chauhan. The messages stated that if you accept my three demands then we will not fight a war. The first message stated that Sardar Muhammed Shāh is an offender and should be returned. The second message was that Hammīr Dev's daughter Padmāvatī be should married to ʿAlāʾ al-Dīn. Third message was regarding a pact that issues should be resolved through communication. Hammīr Dev committed some blunders while working [out the details] of the pact. Trusting his three main commanders Raṇmal, Ratipāl and Sāmant Bhojrāj, he sent them to communicate with ʿAlāʾ al-Dīn Khaljī. ʿAlāʾ al-Dīn Khaljī bribed them and told them that he wanted to conquer the fort only to capture Sardar Muhammed Shāh and punish him. Khaljī told them that he didn't need anything else. He further stated that he would make them (the commanders) the kings [afterwards]. The commanders got lured [into his plan]. They informed Khaljī about [Hammīra's] entire war strategy. They told him how the war would be fought, and that Chauhans would emerge victorious because [ʿAlāʾ al-Dīn] couldn't fight [Hammīra] face to face. They divulged all the secrets of Hammīr Dev to ʿAlāʾ al-Dīn. It is said that *baiṃsā* (heft or handle of an axe) is taken from *bāṃs* (bamboo). When we come to the forest to cut trees, we make a *baiṃsā* first. I am telling you the meaning of this proverb. So *baiṃsā* is taken from *bāṃs*. One meaning is that when we come to cut down the trees, the axe used to cut the trees has a *baiṃsā* made up of wood only. And that *baiṃsā* which is made of wood is taken from the tree only. The *baiṃsā* is therefore taken from the *bāṃs* (bamboo, implying the wood of a tree). And that is what is used on the tree to cut it. So this is from where the breach happens: it is from the *bāṃs* only, which means it is from insiders. Here *bāṃs* indicates the family. That means treachery happens from within the family. So just like the *baiṃsā* is made up of wood taken from the tree, similarly the treachery stemmed from the family of Hammīr Dev only. They [the commanders] told ʿAlāʾ al-Dīn the entire strategy – how the war would be fought, and that the Chauhans would win. Gunpowder had already been invented by the 13th century, i.e. by that time [of these events]. Hammīr Dev used to sell gunpowder for a long time. In order to avoid falling into the hands of enemies during those times – since there was extreme harassment and torture – armies would set themselves on fire and blow themselves up. Therefore, the king's palace was destroyed. The commanders divulged the entire strategy of how gunpowder was laid out in the palace, how the war would be fought and how the Chauhans would be victorious. They [told ʿAlāʾ al-Dīn] that they would raise the wrong flag and all the queens would set themselves on fire and Hammīra would not be able to bear this. He would be left alone: "You are very stubborn but he is more stubborn than you. He will kill himself, he will not be able to bear this". That is what exactly happened, he went to the Lord Śiva idol and chopped his head off. He had a boon from the god. His head joined back twice. At the third time, he spoke to Lord Śiva in anger, "*hey bhagwan, singh gaman, satpurush vacan, kadli phalae ek bar, tiriya tel Hammīr hatt, chade na duji baar.*" This means that if a brave man promises something, then he abides by it, he ensures it. The banana tree provides fruit only once in its lifespan. Then second plant emerges from the side and that will bear fruit in the future. However, the main plant will bear fruit only once in its lifespan ... *kadli phale ek bar.* This means the banana tree bears fruit just once. *Tiriya Tel*, when a child gets married in Hindu religions then the oil is offered just once, in many states, the oil is called *set*. The oil is offered. In wedding ceremonies, the barbers (male or female), they come home and the oil is offered for three days. So if the oil is offered once and if the other family takes a U-turn, then the relationship is over. So the relationship is severed. But if the oil is offered once and then they are made to marry each other, no matter what [they can't severe the relationship]. In Hindu religion, a man promises once, the banana tree grows fruit once, and the oil [for a wedding ceremony] is offered only one time. Similarly, if Hammīr has made up his mind for something then there is no looking back. "Just like the marriage happens once in the Hindu religion, [and] the oil is offered once, in the same way I have offered my head and I will not take it back." Therefore, he is popular by the name *Hammīr haṭṭ*. He had great control over Malwa, Maharashtra, and Gujarat. He was not an ordinary king!

We move in the forests in groups. There is a royal battlefield ahead. I have seen the battlefield. The soil is absolutely yellow in colour. You can't even imagine where can you find yellow soil on this hills. You only get it on the hill that is beside a battlefield fortress. There is a drain in between, and here is the battlefield. It is a flat area. It is the hill of the size of the fort, it is absolutely flat, and there is yellow soil in the battlefield. There is a Chashmabāvḍī there. Raṇ and 'baby' of Raṇ. Battles used to take place on the two hills. Raṇ was the main battlefield and 'baby' of Raṇ was the small part of the main battlefield, hence it was called as the 'baby' of the main battlefield. This is Chashmabāvḍī. No matter how extreme the drought, there is always water at this height. Sometimes you also encounter tigers there. Then there is Tapkan, There is a place on top of the hill and there is water dripping from that all the time. So Tapkan was a place where anyone used to go to drink water, especially in summers. It was always guaranteed that there will be water and those who were extremely thirsty, they used to go there to drink water ... it is because it was sure that one will find water there. If one sat down and was lazy then it was difficult to reach there.

Tigers are scared off by throwing rocks at them. Villagers move in groups ... in this one has to stay strong. Villagers cut grass from the Raṇ. The grass is for fodder. So villagers collect grass from there. We too brought a bundle of grass 10 – 12 years back. Many times the officials of the Forest Department used to come here and collect the grass. They used to set the grass on fire. We would run away, they used to set fire to the grass. There is a checkpoint, then a police station. Similarly, there was a small court. The first round of questioning [in a case] was done here. And, that was the main court. This one was small. See there, that is Balamji Khel. Balamji Khel ... that is a palace. That is an umbrella with 32 pillars. Here is a Jain temple.

Q: Is this the one?

G1: Earlier there were people living here. This entire area was populated. It was a very nice place, during those times – prayers were offered here and hence the entire forest used to reverberate. See the wall, this is how it was. This is the small court, you will see the big court ... Can you see the hill in front, after that comes our village. That is the last hill and after that came our village. All this was ruined. These were solitary hills ...

Q: What is that?

G1: Padam Lake. No, that is the Rajbag Lake, we cannot see the Padam Lake from here.

Q: And, after that?

G1: You can try to see the lake from here. If you see it from here, you will see the green trees and something shining, that is like water. See that path, that temporary path. That is going round like that, so there is a gap in between the trees ... something greenish, that is the Padam Lake. If you look, there is a green tree, a very heavy tree. Can you see there is something shining, that is water. It is slightly visible.

Q: Yes, yes, I can see it ... near the large tree.

G1: Yes, something is shining near the tree. That is the green tree. And, that is the lake. Malik Lake.

Q: Do you have any idea how it came to be called Malik Lake?

G1: Malik lake means ... there is nothing much in history regarding this.

Q: It's alright.

G1: It is known as Malik. Even today it is known as Malik. Villagers used to graze buffaloes. The people of our village even today graze the buffaloes. So Malik is somebody's name ... there is not much mention of its history. If there would have been any, then I would have been aware but there is not much mention.

Q: It must be someone's name.

G1: There is a pond named Padam Lake. The is the place where Hammīr Dev's daughter committed suicide. Now I told you about it yesterday. It is said that it is as deep as the length of seven cots. It is said that there is a drain on this side and when 'Alā' al-Dīn Khaljī attacked, he had many elephants and horses in his army. So there was a drain on the way and it was filled with filth ... it was filled with the excreta of elephants [and horses], anyhow it was full of [excreta]. So, King Hammīr Dev was in a risky position. What it they attack from this side?
So there was a *Soni* (goldsmith) in Kota, he was aware of the secret of this tunnel. He knew that if the tunnel was opened once, it would open into the drain. It is above the Padam Lake I was just telling you about. There is a drain near that. So it is said that Hammīr Dev Chauhan had given him the key. There was a *Soni* in Kota who was aware of this secret. So only he had the key to this tunnel. So when Hammīr Dev told him about the possible danger, he handed over the key to him. Then he (the *Soni*) said, "seven seas, nine hundred rivers, that much of water is there in it ... seven seas, nine hundred rivers, that much water! Just open the lock of the tunnel and then fight as much as you want, O King!" Which meant, open the lock, which further meant that lock which is holding the water in the tunnel, open that lock and then fight as much as you want ... *seven seas, nine hundred rivers, that much water and just open the lock of the tunnel and then fight as much as you want!* So as he opened the door, so as he opened the lock, a huge pile of elephant and horse excreta flowed out!

Q: Oh my god!

G1: Everything belonging to Khaljī got washed away. He [the *Soni*] claimed that there was so much water in it. The people of the village talk about how deep it was. According to them it was as deep as the length of seven turban cloths [7 × 6 m]. That is how deep it was. So there must have been something in it. The forefathers said that there must have been something in it. It must have refilled later on since many years had passed. Since it was not cleaned for years so it must have filled up again. When he said, "seven seas, nine hundred rivers, such huge quantities of different kinds of water, and just open the lock and then fight as much as you want," he meant that once you open the lock, you need not worry after that, just fight as much as you want. He opened the lock and that is what exactly happened ...

Q: So they used to sit here themselves? The King? Or somebody else used to come here.

G1: This was the court, so the court was where the justice was served during that era.

Q: So they used to come as well?

G1: This was the jail and this is where people were kept. The king used to announce the penalty and the culprit used to be jailed here. So all this was for the purpose of imprisonment. This was the jail. In the language of that era, it was known as the *kachheri* ... therefore, there was prison in every village, in every big village there was a prison. There is a jail in our village. So, the punishment was pronounced there. Since at that time there were no [transport] facilities available, walking was the only way, so if there is a case ongoing in the High Court, it was not possible to walk so often, so there used to be these jails in every village. The punishments were pronounced there only. So that is the *kachheri*, there is one in our village as well. It is known as *kachheri*. This used to be the court, in today's parlance, this was the office of the Collector. It used to be amazing. See this gate, how thick it is. See how amazing it is? I wonder if it will ever fall? How will it fall? No one knows if it will ever fall! It appears as if it will never fall. This is [real] work ... So if it is made into a hotel today, these gates are going to cause a lot of trouble. See what this is, it is shining a little, so if it is polished a little, it will look amazing. The voice also echoes in this, even a slight sound becomes loud here. A low sound also becomes loud since it echoes. See how marvellously this has been made ... See how brilliantly it has been made ... let's go on top of it once.

Q: Which place is this?

G1: This is *bakko*, the place where a dead soul [resides].

Q: Oh!

G1: Can you hear the strange of noises ... *hoon, hoon* ...
There is a pond inside here too ... We will get down here and there is a way that takes us to the temple of Sanjana Mata. If you want, we can go there.

Q: We can go ...

G1: [A person's soul] becomes a Jānd after death. If we don't conduct the last rites then it turns into Jānd and then there is a Jindal on top of 100 Jānds and on top of 100 Jindals, there is Jindalī Mātā. There is a temple of Jindalī Mātā here. I still remember what I was told. I am telling you what was told to me.

Q: Delhi Gate?

G1: This is known as Delhi Gate. We saw it on the map, the gate in the direction of Delhi is called the Delhi Gate. The government attempted to create a straight route through this ... from here going through the Delhi Gate ... but they couldn't succeed.
I will tell you about everything in one go. You can do the recording in the temple of Balaji, it is known as the Hanumānjī of Delhi Gate. And this is [the temple] of Mātājī, this is the one of Viṣṇujī and this is shrine of Bhairavjī.

Q: This is the shrine of Bhairavjī?

G1: Yes, this is the shrine of Bhairavjī. And, this is known as the Hanumānjī of Delhi Gate. This is Jindalī Mātā. The entire [city of] Sawai Madhopur is visible from here.

Q: From the top?

G1: Yes, but people don't come here. From here you can see ...

Q: Sawai Madhopur?

G1: You can see Sawai Madhopur, Bahadurpur. There was somebody called Bahadur, so Bahadurpur was established in his name. It is called Bahadurpur. It has *Bāvḍīs* and houses. Madhav Singh had come here. At that time there was King Hadda from Bundi. He betrayed Madhav Singh by provoking the local people of this place.

Q: King Hadda?

G1: There was a King Hadda in Bundi. The Bundi fort is [relatively] near this place ... once you reach Kota. So the local residents of this place were incited by King Hadda and the locals stopped paying taxes to Sawai Madhav Singh and hence his income stopped.

Q: Sawai Madhav Singh was the king of this place?

G1: Yes, he is the one who established Sawai Madhopur. [He] belonged to the Jaipur kingdom. So on the provocation of King Hadda, the local residents revolted!

Q: He was from Bundi?

G1: Yes, he was King Hadda. He ruled over Bundi. So he incited everyone here. He ran away from this place and took refuge in Taleti hill. People started troubling him [Sawai Madhav Singh]. So he developed the area. He is the one who established Sawai Madhopur. It was Madhav Singh who did this. This was established in the year 1763. Madhav Singh did that. Jagat Singh was the last king in 1810. This is the village and this is the hotel. These big establishments are hotels [now]. There are many hotels. There are hotels in hundreds. This is our village. This is part of our village. The land has been sold here. One *bigha*[188] costs Rs 40 lakhs to 50 lakhs.[189]

Q: That's a lot!

188 Measurement of land between 1/3 and 1 acre.
189 1 Lakh = 100,000.

G1: Really! All the farmers here are millionaires. But only if they sell their land, if they don't then they are poor. We did not sell any land of ours. I don't have much of a share of land, only seven/eight *bigha.* But I did not sell [the land]; we grow food on it and consume it. We have a guava orchard. We manage Rs 2–2.5 lakh from it and we do part-time farming ... and by doing different things we manage a business of around Rs 5–6 lakhs. My younger brother is an engineer. He is in Gujarat. He is a mechanical engineer in the railways. He is a government employee. And whenever I get little time, and as and when I get a call, I come here [to the fortress]. My expenses are met like this. From farming, funds come once in 12 months. So I have made this my source of daily living.[190] Let's go ... There is an umbrella consisting of 32 pillars. Hammīr Dev got the umbrella with 32 pillars constructed in the memory of his father Jaitra Singh Chauhan who ruled for 32 years. It was in his memory. For his remembrance. It was used as a 'conference room.' This was the *Divān-e-Khās*. All the 'VIP' meetings used to take place here. And there is a temple of Lord Śiva in it. You can pay a visit to the temple too. Hammīr Dev used to meditate for a long time in solitude.

Q: Inside here?

G1: Inside here. Hammīr Dev Chauhan was a devotee of Lord Śiva.[191] He came here so as to not get disturbed. It has been constructed in such a way ... see how cool it feels. There is air pressure coming in from the front. And, from inside it is absolutely cool ... Hammīr Dev established the idol of Lord Śiva in the memory of his father Jaitra Singh. He used to sit here and meditate in solace so that nobody could disturb him. [The shrine] is like Śivjī ... it always remains cool. The umbrella on top is made of 32 pillars symbolizing the 32 years of King Jaitra Singh's rule. Thus the umbrella made of 32 pillars has been erected in his memory. It has been given a code number of 32. Maharana Sanga had a wife named Rani Karṇavati. She ruled here from 1509 to 1527. So he made the [palace] for her. It is also known as Adhure Sapne (meaning 'unfulfilled dreams') because she suddenly left this place and went back to Chittorgarh. She had offered a *rākhī* to Humayun. She had a son named Vikramaditya. Humayun had promised that he would win back the fort of Chittor. So [he told her] to leave that [the palace in Ranthambore] and come to Chittor. So she left this place but by the time she reached there, she could not meet Humayun because he had died by then, and, therefore, it remained an unfulfilled dream. That's why it is known as the 'unfulfilled dream.' Humayun was the emperor; she had offered him the *rākhī* which means he accepted her as his sister. He considered her his sister. The queen had two sons, so Humayun said that he would win back the fort of Chittor for her sons. So she left behind everything and went there. But that dream of hers couldn't get fulfilled because Humayun had died by that time. Since Humayun had died, so he couldn't get her the fort as promised. That's why in history it has been called the 'unfulfilled dream.'[192]

---

190 The job of being a guide.

191 In the *Hammīra-Mahākāvya* there is no mention of the king being a devotee of Lord Śiva, rather it mentions that the king's father (and presumably also the king) was a devotee was Lord Viṣṇu.

192 Rani Karṇavati was indeed the wife of Rana Sanga. After his death while trying to defeat Babur together with a federation of Rajput armies in 1527, the queen solicited the help of the Mughal emperor Humayun whom she made a '*rākhī*' brother in defending the fortress of Chittorgarh from an assault by Bahadur Shah of Gujarat in 1535. Humayun did not die before he could

This is the king's palace. These were the courts of the kings. This is one of the seven locations. Three locations are on top and three/four are underground. They are underneath. In that era this used to be the garden of kings and queens ... now these people from the Archaeological Survey have made this into a garden and have been maintaining it. Here is the king's palace. The king had [many] queens ... around 1300 ladies committed *jauhar* here. I had mentioned earlier that gunpowder had been invented by that time. So the king had already hidden the gunpowder in the queen's palace. So it blew up and everything was shattered. The queen's palace ... it had 32 pillars ... the pillars are 32 in number. The umbrellas on each side are such that there are 4 in one and 8 in the other ... 4 multiplied by 8 equals 32. There are 32 [pillars]. There is a code with the number 32 in it. There is another umbrella that is further up ... that too has the same structure. That too has 32 pillars. Then when you go further up, there is a temple of Lord Śiva. This was their 'conference room.' See the view from here. It's very nice. This is the *Divān-e-Khās*.

Fig. 12: A *chattri* or umbrella with multiple pillars

This is the Padmavati Lake. This is where [Hammīra's queen became a widow]. The self-immolation of an unmarried woman is considered to be a sin in the Hindu religion. That is why she [Hammīra's daughter] committed *jal jauhar.*[193] Padmavati Lake is known by her

help the queen, rather he was occupied with a military campaign in Bengal and was unable to return to Chittor in time. Facing imminent defeat the queen and several other noblewomen committed *jauhar* while the Rajput men donned saffron attire and rode into certain death.

193 *Jauhar* by drowning.

name and the tunnel that I was telling you about, that runs beneath this lake. There is a tunnel here. And the drain which is also here, the battlefield is in front of it. The battlefield is ahead of the drain. There is a secret related to the tunnel. And this is the drain. So when this got full and the battlefield was over there ... this is a very deep drainage. It is 500 to 700 feet deep. I told you about the *Soni* from Kota, he had a key [for opening the gate to the drain]. He told the king: "Seven seas, nine hundred rivers! There is that much water here! Open the door with this key and then fight ferociously King Hammīr." It is believed that as he opened the door, all his enemies got washed away. And only when the drain levels increase did Hammīr Dev find relief.
Prithvi Raj Chauhan II offered a gold urn here at some point of time. These are statues of [the Jain deities] Śaṃbhunāth, Sumatināth, and Nemināth.

Priest: I am the priest here and perform prayers and serve the deities. I am an Agrawal Jain. There are two of us. [The temple] belongs to the era of kings and emperors.

Q: The kings used to come here?

Priest: Yes.

G1: This is [idol] of Nārāyaṇ or Lord Viṣṇu, Goddess Lakṣmī, Vāman Pothi are sitting on an eagle. There are three photographs, one is of Lakṣmī Nārāyaṇ, one is Lord Viṣṇu on top of an eagle. There is Lord Rāma, Goddess Sītā and Lord Kṛṣṇa.

Q: When were these established?

G1: This has been in existence since the past 800–900 years. The tiles and other things have been installed later on. There used to be a touchstone that used to turn [ordinary metal] into gold. So there was no shortage of wealth for them. It was easy to acquire wealth. All they had to do was [bring metal] in contact [with the stone]. They used to create wealth by making gold. Therefore, there was no shortage of wealth. When ['Alā' al-Dīn Khaljī] attacked ... all the queens committed *jauhar.* The [princess] tied the touchstone to herself and jumped into the Padmavati Lake. Later on when Indira Gandhi was the Prime Minister, then she stayed here for a night. In the past foreigners would come here. They knew about this, and so they would walk around with iron boots in a hope that they would come in contact with the touchstone and would get rich. These kind of stories prevail here. Indira Gandhi didn't find anything. The boon that was bestowed on Hammīr Dev, it ended with him. He had a touchstone. If iron was made to touch the stone, it become gold. The kings of that era were very rich. They are famous for the amount of wealth they possessed ...
Hammīr Dev's mother's name was Hirādevī. His wife's name was Kasturīdevī.[194] Hammīr Dev's horse's name was Ghansaha. Its name was Ghansaha because it used to walk on a circle of dots. That's why its name was Ghansaha.

194 The Sanskrit text states that the queen's name was Āraṅgidevī.

2 Ritual Landscapes

The following conversation takes place with a Sadhu (holy man) who is sitting next to the entrance of the inner sanctum of a temple dedicated to the Goddess Kali. While explaining how and when the temple was built, he also reaches into a lengthy explanation concerning the sacred potency of the fortress which he describes as a place that is abundantly conducive to tantric ritual practice and worship. The narrative he offers spans different time cycles and a shifting movement of expansion and contraction from one age to another. Thus he states that the temple was once – during the *dvāpara yuga*[195] – a fort which then became a temple in this age, i. e. the *kali yuga*. The history of the fortress is now pushed back or rather framed in a culturally significant conception of time that is invariably also the manner in which other sacred sites such as *tīrtha-sthānas*,[196] temples and narrative texts are understood to have originated. Underlying the current, historical and therefore 'visible' or 'tangible' past is an invisible, yet powerful, network of causes, event and actions that are knowable through a different set of esoteric 'sources' in the form of texts or through the insights of sages and holy men and women. The fortress is therefore not exclusively a 'historical' or 'material' object but also a sacred site for the reasons that the Sadhu outlines, including the fact that it is beneficial to tantric ritual practice but also because it is the location of many shrines and temples as well as the acts of long-gone kings. Here again, as in the case of the first conversation, the Sadhu interweaves autobiographical details into his account of the origin and nature of the fortress.

Questioner: When was the temple established?

Sadhu: This was established by Padma Ṛṣi ... There was king called Rāshidev. The idols were installed during his time. They were all here. The temple was once a fort. In the *dvāpar* era, it was a fort then it became a temple. When this fort was made then these *maṭhs* (temples) came into existence, as the kings ruled, they built *maṭhs*. The *maṭhs* which were inside ... so this is a tantric region. This entire area is blessed. All the gods and goddesses of Tantra are here; all the idols which are installed here have all been done so according to tantric [rules] ... All the prayers that are done to the deities are done according to tantric [rules]. This means that all rituals conducted for the deities are conducted according to tantric [rules]. So the tantric mothers are the *solhā mā* (16 Mothers); these are symbolized by sixteen Śivaliṅga. Lord Śiva is worshipped to acquire knowledge ... to free oneself from fear and to acquire knowledge; that is why Lord Śiva is worshipped ... Lord Śiva has different forms ... He has manifold forms so different things are offered to him

195 That is, the age that preceded the current one. The *dvāpara yuga* presumably ended with the devastating war of the Mahābhārata which then ushered in the *kali yuga*.
196 "crossing-places" = pilgrimage sites.

... So considering [all] these things and keeping these [things] in mind, the sages have dedicated years [reflecting and meditating] on these matters ... There is a gold idol of Lord Ganeśa there ... it is self-generated ... In tantric rituals, it is supreme ... in the tantric ritual system, Ganeśa is called a Guru ... and the Guru is supreme ... Therefore, it is the self-proclaimed and self-emerged idol of Lord Ganeśa ... In tantric rituals, he is considered as supreme. Considering this, the sages established him at various places. Now there are all ten Mahāvidyās, all three Mahādevīs, sixteen Śivaliṅgas. These belong to the old era established by the sages ... they offered the prayers ... and established all these [deities], the temples and the mosques were established later ... The one where we are standing was constructed later. So this fort was constructed after that, it is written on the fort ... As the kings started coming here, they kept establishing new temples.

There are many temples here. In addition to those, there are many more small temples in the entire region. First, there is the Śiva temple and then there is Trinetri [Ganeśa] ... In addition to that there are seven Śivaliṅgas in this forest. And all three Mahādevīs are there inside [the fort] and all ten Mahāvidyās are established outside it. Some have been popular as Kālī Mātā, while some [are popular as] Sītā Mātā. These are all the ten Mahāvidyās. They are all established in this region. It is a blessed region. Now when you go down, you will come across the other gate. Ahead of that gate, you will see in the side a roadway being build ... there is a kind of labyrinth system underneath it ... And all the gods which are present here, that are considered to be here, they can appear in front of you anytime. These are those kind of gods! And whatever you will desire, the fulfilment of all those desires will definitely happen! These are those kind of gods. They exist here. The sages have blessed this [region]. Our ancient Guruji poured life into this place. There was a forest, it all became a forest, after King Hammīr Dev [died], nobody else became a king here. Hammīr Dev was the last king. But now it is all over, there are no more kings anymore. So just like you, I am here. So people went to different places taking their religions along with them. This is the clan goddess of your Chief Minister Devi Singh. This goddess has been his clan goddess. His brothers and all keep coming here. Somebody comes from some corner of Ahmedabad, in Gujarat. Even today people visit this place. They ask about it. There are many powers (*śakti*) in this region. Bhairo is present here. Bhairo who belongs to all the castes is here. This entire region is blessed. There is an Ekliṅg [Śiva] here. Animal sacrifices were done here. They were done in the past. They were stopped suddenly in 1993. A *yajña* was performed and through prayers it [the goddess] was made quiet. Initially you could not look into the goddess's eyes. It was very scary even in the daytime. Even in daytime it used to look so scary that you couldn't look at it. And whosoever came here it was as if she had appeared. Yes, it was fearful at the entrance itself. Let alone sitting inside. I came here in the year 1975 for the first time. I am telling you of the time when I came here for the first time ... in 1975. At that time you couldn't look into [the deity's] eyes! If somebody offered money, even then you would see the brightness [inside the shrine] immediately. Therefore, it is *dakṣiṇamurti guru*. Therefore, it is south facing. So to interrupt it, to calm it down, prayers were offered. This is same with Ganeśa. If somebody performed tantric rites and wished negative things, it was worshipped with *pañcamakāra*.[197] That prayer could be offered only by a sage or by a

197 The so-called '5 Ms' used in Tantric ritual practice: *madya* (wine/alcohol), *māṃsa* (meat), *matsya* (fish), *mudra* (gesture) and *maithuna* (sexual intercourse).

person who has been given [special] powers (*śakti*). So only a person bestowed with [special] powers could worship her [the Goddess] or the sages could do it because they were bestowed with special powers. The kings who were there had their priests and sages and they [priest and sages] used to provide them [the kings] with special powers (*śakti*). They used to bestow them with special powers. They used to chant bhajans, offer prayers, and by doing this, they used to make them efficient so that by completing this 'power meditation' and prayers, they could move forward. To get into this 'power meditation,' it is important for one to already be powerful. Only then you can do the 'power meditation.' So when Lord Shankar empowered the Goddess Parvati by bringing her to [the practice of] *sādhanā*. Because Sati had already done *sādhanā*. Sati did *sādhanā* to gain Śiva. She had already done *sādhanā*. So this is the form Goddess Parvati achieved after *sādhanā*. So Lord Śankar has empowered her after their marriage. So when it [*śakti*] came in the *bāmaṅga* (left side of the body) was it called *dakṣiṇa*. Only when Goddess Parvati came in the *bāmaṅga* of Lord Śiva, was she called as *dakṣiṇa*. If the Goddess is called *dakṣiṇa kālī*, it doesn't mean that it was established in the south direction. So this Goddess is the *dakṣiṇa kālī* because she resided in the *bāmaṅga*. A man's wife is also *dakṣiṇa*. [She] is called *bāmaṅgi* (the one who sits on the left side). Today *bāmaṅga* is considered to be wrong. [But in fact] *bāmaṅga* is the *yoga* path which makes one free from all the things. One can win over all the ten senses[198] by entering into the *bāmaṅga*. Therefore, both husband and wife are initiated (*dikṣit*) so that they may continue with their *sādhanā* and may keep getting free from everything. Ganeśa also practices *sādhanā*. There is nothing wrong with *pañcamākari* [*sādhanā*]. If you practice it without being initiated (*dikṣit*) then it will have negative consequences. But if an initiated person does it, then they will gain these things, means it can't be destroyed ... And Tantra is for the betterment of the people. If I am doing *sādhanā* for myself, then it will not be a success, I will be destroyed. My family and my home will be destroyed. My clan will be destroyed. *Sādhanās* are practiced for the larger good of the people.

... There were kings [back then]. They had their priests and sages who used to provide them with special powers. They used to bestow them with special powers. They used to chant *bhajans*, offer prayers and by doing this, they used to make them capable so that by practising the 'power' meditation and prayers, they could move ahead. To get into the 'power' meditation, it is important for one to be powerful. Only then you can do 'power' meditation.

... If you make the gods happy through *sādhanā* – if you make them happy – then everyone around you will be happy. You automatically become auspicious for everyone. You will receive respect wherever you go. You will get everything [you want]. So it is the same as [performing] *vaśīkaran*. [Once you do *sādhanā*] then there will be no requirement of *vaśīkaran* at all. It is the misuse of such things. So whatever is happening these days, it is the misuse of it, whatever people are doing today ... and all the knowledge today is knowledge acquired through cramming. Knowledge is being used for business. The priests have knowledge and they are all business oriented. That is how they earn [their living]. But the *sādhanās* that existed there earlier, they used to be successful because they were done without any bias. There was no ill-intention brewing in people's minds. There was no greed, no lust, no consumption and there was no desire for anything at that time. Even if today you practice this, and if you are working to get your desires fulfilled, even then

198 ten senses = the meaning of this is unclear.

do it without greed. Then you will achieve it in this life. If you are doing it out of greed, attachment or fear then you will not be able to get its benefits in this life and you will only get [the benefits] in your next birth. Therefore, the *sādhanā* and rituals become unsuccessful. *Havan* and *yajña* venues catch fire today. It is because rituals are not being followed as they should be. People get things done on the basis of their income. You can take any example or take your own *sādhanā*, whatever the thing is, you collected all your money through your hard work, etc. So then bring it to good use; if you do this, you will never be destroyed. You will get [what you want], and you will get twice [what you want]. But if you use if for satisfying your lust, or for materialistic consumption, then you will be destroyed one day. So whatever name you have earned, whatever money you have earned, that will be destroyed one day. So therefore after [singing] *bhajans* you are either sent as a king or as a hermit [into the world]. So if you do *tapasya* in any era then you end up either as a king or as a hermit. The hermit will move ahead in life but the king will fail at last in his life. So if the head of the clan (king) is not *dikṣit* (consecrated, anointed) then he will fail. And, as a king, he will be arrogant and out of arrogance he will trouble his people, will misuse his money and enjoy everything and will run away ...

So these are the things, this entire region is pure! There is Eklingnāth [Śiva] over here just ahead of the graveyard. This region has everything that is needed for *sādhanā* and it is really helpful. This region has everything available like the Rajdwar, forests, hills, ruins, wells, Bāvḍīs, ponds, rivers and drains ... and also the trees, every kind of tree. *Chil* trees and *Pipal* trees. One may have to do the *sādhanā* of a *yakṣa* and *nāganīya* on any tree, and it has all the trees available making it a very suitable place for *sādhanā*. Sometime *sādhanā* has to be performed under a tree, or it has to be done by sitting on a tree. All these things are available here. So those things can be worshipped here and the *sādhanā* can be easily performed. So this region is known as the region of *sādhanā*. Due to the underground labyrinth system, you can achieve good and instant *sādhanā* here, and it is safe. This region is surrounded by forts from all the directions. And also by the Gods which have been established at different places. Therefore, in order to do *sādhanā* we to come to this region. So, there are no obstacles while doing *sādhanā* over here. Therefore, one becomes quickly successful if you do *sādhanā* here.

3 Into the Forest

In this third conversation, the speaker situates the fort in a narrative regarding the forest and lakes that surround it. The journey into the fortress begins so to speak with the large and dense forest at the foot of the hill upon which the fort has been built. This is a forest that is populated with wild animals including tigers and crocodiles, which inhabit the lake that is on the edge of the forest. The description suggests that this is a kind of magical forest in which animals, including dangerous predators, and the forest guard who works there are able to communicate and care for each other. The description of the forest then moves on to describing in succession the various gates, deities, shrines, mosques and *dargāhs* that saturate the inner and outer features of the fortress with historical, religious and ritual significance. Each material or architectural detail is amplified through a story or anecdote, gathering each together offers us an interlocking sequence of the 'present-past' that comes into existence when it is spoken and narrated. In this passage there is also a longer autobiographical portion that has not been edited since it vividly reveals the intersection between the 'personal' and the 'historical' and how these two seemingly distinct discourses begin to merge and flow into one another in the arena of the 'everyday' that is defined by struggle, hardship, aspiration and also success.

Guide 2: I am from Sawai Madhopur. In the Ranthambore [area], Sawai Manpur was named after King Sawai Man Singh. He was the king of Jaipur. So possibly, it was named after him. Ranthambore is 13 km from the railway station. In between, you will see Amaresar, Misaldara, Keshdhar. From then on, the forest entry gate starts. When enter into the forest, you will find yourself in Misaldara. Misaldara was earlier known as Gomukh and there you will see statue of a cow with water flowing through its mouth. Gomukh means where water comes from the mouth of cow. Beyond that there is the forest. And that's the area from where our Ranthambore national park starts. Ahead of that the area is known as Bahadurpur. So, there was a guard named Bahadur. The area was named after him. At that time, all the animals, be it tigers, bears and so on knew him by the smell of his body. He used to call out to them once, and they would come to him immediately. He was a *Harijan*, and was known as *Maliya Baghel.*

Questioner: When was this?

G2: I am talking about 1982.

Q: It's fairly recent, then.

G2: So, he was a guard and he used to roam around to check security [in the forest]. He was the only guard in the jungle and no one was there with him. Animals loved him so much that they would always accompany him. There were trees everywhere and he used to prepare his cot near some trees. The animals used to guard him. He used to feed them and if any of them got injured, he used to take care of that animal. For example, if a thorn pierced an animal's paw, he used to pluck it out and take care of it. He loved them like his own pets just as we love our pets and cattle and the animals loved him as well. So, [that location] was named as Bahadurpur. After it, comes Singdvar. It is called so because *sambhar, cheetal* and other deer used to shed their horns here. Then comes gate number 1, from there four/five paths branch off ... after that comes the uphill route ... the Morkund (peacock basin) comes before that ... Sorry, I forgot Adavaleji. That's the name of a temple. The uphill route starts from there and it goes down and then comes Bahadurpur. Singdvar comes after that. There comes an uphill route from Singdvar and then comes the *dargāh.* The *dargāh* comes only after the uphill route from Morkund. The *dargāh* is named after the Sufi Saint Fateh Sahab. There was another *dargāh* after the name of Kalushāh behind that ... then Amrāhi. That area is known as Amrāhi.

Q: Okay, which is up there?

G2: When we move uphill from Singdvar, after the second upwards slope from Morkund there is a small sewer. The *dargāh* is located after that. Its name is Fateh Sahab. There is another *dargāh* behind Fateh Sahab called Kalushāh. He too was a Sufi saint. After that comes the region of Amrāhi. The area is full of mango trees. Therefore, it's known as Amrāhi. As we move ahead from there, there comes the last uphill path ... the last uphill path ... after that as you go inside and there appears the Jogi Mahal of the police department. It is right ahead. There is a pond in front of the Jogi Mahal Gate where kings used to fight battles.

Q: The Jogi Mahal which is down there?

G2: Yes ... It goes toward the town ... Ranthambore ends here and over there ist he Jogi Mahal Gate which was a battlefield ... Battles were fought there ... If we start from there, the first gate that comes is called Naulakha Gate.

Q: Is the *dargāh* down there? The one that you were talking about?

G2: It has been left behind down there ... The *dargāh* of Kalushāh has been left behind down there ... You have walked uphill now ... You have come above Amrāhi ... Jogi Mahal Gate has come ... and then comes the temple of Lord Ganeśa. There is a big *Pipal* tree there and also a well in front of it. And as we go around, there is also an office of the Archaeological Department. It is known as the Foreman Department, Archaeological Survey Department of India, Ranthambore. After that we climb the twenty-two steps and take a turn. They make those turns because the elephants used to break the gates using their backs, so very fine nails were installed on the gate. So these gates were constructed in such a way that they didn't get damaged, and no attack could take place from Delhi. The gates used to be very heavy and 12–14 feet tall. Someone could try and ram them but the gate couldn't be broken. If they were able to break it, then the army had to be ready for war. As we go ahead, there are two rooms where the watchmen used to stay. Then further up, there is a temple of Lord Hanuman. There is an idol of Lord Hanuman, Lord Ganeśa and Goddess Pārvatī installed there. There used to be a mosque on that path earlier where people used to live.

Q: There was a mosque?

G2: Just a few moments ago, the place where we were visiting, there is a mosque by its side ... it is at a distance of around ten feet from the temple ... there is a minaret ... a pole, then as you move from there, we find the temple of Lord Hanuman. After that there is another place.

Q: Is the mosque presently there?

G2: Yes, the mosque is still there and it is a very old mosque. After that we shall enter the second gate. Its name is Hathipur. There is a skull there belonging to a person called Mingangdu. He used to go to the battlefield frequently. 'Alā' al-Dīn Khaljī's son Jalāl al-Dīn Khaljī had claimed that he was an absconder from Delhi. So he had asked for refuge. He was kept in the mosque. He was an absconder from Delhi. The king recruited him in his army. And he was put on duty at the gate. What Mingangdu did after that ... we will move on to that story later. Now we arrive at the third gate called Ganeśpur. There too the gate is in the opposite direction. If we go from the top, there comes the Andheri Gate and Tar Gate. This part of the fort has been constructed in such a way that it resembles the betel leaf. It is known as Supari Mahal (Betel Palace). An officer of the Archaeological Department stays there only along with a watchman and an office staff. Now if we climb the twelve steps, we come to the Raghunāth Temple. If we go on that side, there we will come to Mina Mahal and Rani Mahal that are just next to it. There is a temple of Lord Hanuman right in front of the Rani Mahal. Then there is a garden and as we take a turn from the garden, we arrive at the temple of Lord Hanuman. It is known as the Raj Mandir and near that is Jatuyan. This the location of 'an unfulfilled dream.' Rani Handi, the wife of Rana Sanga, had a desire to construct it, but it could not be constructed, and it remained 'an unfulfilled dream.' After that comes the umbrella (*chattrī*) of 32 pillars. There is a Śivaliṅga inside it. It is huge. The queens used to worship it by circumambulating it. All the pillars have been constructed in the memory of the ones who were martyred in the war. So whenever somebody got martyred, a pillar was constructed in his name. So that umbrella got the name 32 pillars. The women used to worship it by circumambulating it. There is a huge Śivaliṅga when you go inside. If we leave the route below the steps, and if we go straight, there comes Rani Mahal. After that comes Hammīr Mahal. The entire route from Hammīr Mahal to Rani Mahal is in ruins. This happened because the second gate of Hathipur had a watchman. As King Hammīr went to fight the battle, he showed the black flags which indicated that King Hammīr had lost the war. The queen was sitting in the Supari Mahal, she saw it and believed that they had lost [the battle] and that the King had died. She went to her Mahal and committed suicide. Hence it all turned into ruins. And all the queens who were sitting in the Padmavati Mahal came to know about it and they all died. There were many conflicts due to the *pāras* [stone], as its touch could convert iron into gold. So majority of the wars were fought because of the stone.

Q: Okay. They had it?

G2: Yes, King Hammīr had it. King Hammīr's daughter, Queen Padmāvatī, took the *pāras* stone and jumped into the pond. Hence it is known as the Padam Lake. Moving further, we come to the Annapurna temple. All the people who used to live nearby the Annapurna temple used to worship there during hard times. There is also a *dargāh* nearby in the name of those who have been martyred ... there are four-five *dargāhs*. Going further, there are plenty of Guṃtis constructed. That is the uppermost *morcha* (fortification), so if anyone attacked from the front, this wall used to stop them. It is a very thick wall on the side. The temple comes only after that and there is a shop alongside it. The people who now live there, only their grandfathers were allowed to live here earlier. There were four houses only for them. There are four-five quarters constructed in the front [of the houses] where the staff members of the Archaeological Survey of India reside. There is a Ganeśa temple and it is believed that Lord Ganeśa had appeared here.

Q: Oh ... on his own?

G2: Yes, on his own ... so the public started believing in him. Now the real idol is beneath and is known by the name Gajānand Pīr.

Q: Oh, Gajānand Pīr!

G2: Yes, Gajānand Pīr. The Madohi priests [residing there], Shuklājī and Madhubanijī, can tell you what it really is. Today there has been a proliferation of many smaller priests, the new youngsters have turned into priests. However, the ones who were there earlier are still here. There is a small temple where they sit. They are both very aged now. This is famous by the name Gajānand Pīr. It is beneath the temple; they know it is a *dargāh*.

Q: Oh, it is below.

G2: Yes, it is below ... There is a vault in which there is a *dargāh*.

Q: It is a *dargāh?*

G2: Yes, it is known as Gajānand Pīr. People having Hindu faith started believing in him so they established an idol and they began worshipping him as the Trinetra. And this region came to be known as Raṇbhom due to the battles that took place here.

Q: So when did he ... How did Gajānand Pīr come here?

G2: He appeared on his own. So he is known as Gajānand Pīr. A fair is organized in the month of September and people in their hundreds of thousands pay a visit to this temple. A fair is organized and food is offered to the people. People are served and the place is equipped with police and doctors and other things. Beyond that walls (*parkoṭā*) have been constructed. Thereafter is Gupt Gaṅgā. People living here used to claim that there was a great sage who used to meditate here at the Gupt Gaṅgā. As the army used to get ready for battle here, he used to release the water from Gupt Gaṅgā from above. Even today there is round the clock availability of water in the Gupt Gaṅgā. The city is established there, so he would make the water exit from there. They had an arrangement of bringing the excreta of donkeys and other animals and mud to the top, so the soldiers used to get washed away by the flow of the water. That water would exit from the Satpol gate. The Satpol gate is the gate just behind the temple. There are three gates named Satpol gate.

Q: Below the Ganeśa temple?

G2: There is a Śiva temple of King Hammīr just below the Ganeśa temple, so it is known as the Satpol gate. The water flow would flow from there and all the soldiers used to get washed away. It happened during the battles. There were furnaces built inside the fort where *ghee* was made. The people used to throw the canisters filled with *ghee* on the soldiers which used to make walking uphill difficult for them. There were plenty of furnaces and all the arrangements of weapons and gunpowder inside the fort. All their clothes were also kept inside the fort. Also there were many different idols belonging to them kept inside the fort. All the equipment of the ironsmiths to make weapons too was kept inside the fort. The places of gods and goddesses are there as well. There are two places, one of Dhumejī and other of Mātājī. The water used to flow from the Gupt Gaṅgā and it used to be an advantage for the king as the flow of the water used to wash away the enemy soldiers, bringing their morale down. As the black flag was waved at the Hathipol, the queens saw it. Seeing the black flag, they believed that they had lost. They went inside the fort and committed suicide. The daughter jumped in the pond. There is the *dargāh* of Sadruddin here. The King came here leaving Gupt Gaṅgā behind towards Ranihoud. He is known as Sadruddin Baba and was believed to have magical powers. When the king came here, he saw the flag in the market. So he thought that, we have not lost, we are all alive and the queen must have betrayed us. She has done something mischievous. The king took his soldiers and horses and proceeded so as to go and kill the betrayer. The skull idol has been installed in the memory of the killing of the watchman who was an absconder. The king then went ahead and the gate of Ganeśpol was shut. Everyone had asked, including the queen, to lock all the gates.

Hence the horses had climbed from Ganeśpol. Their marks are prevalent till date explaining that the horses had climbed. As the kings reached the palace, he saw all the queens dead. The daughter had jumped into the pond. King Hammīr was a devotee of Lord Śiva who used to serve Lord Śiva continuously. Hence, in order to take his own life, he went to the Satpol gate to that spot and cut off his head seven times using his sword.

Fig. 13: The shrine of Lord Śiva where Hammīra offered his head

Q: Seven times?

G2: Seven times! But his head used to join back to his torso every time. On the eighth attempt, his body fell on the floor. Hence an idol of the king was established. It is made up of seven metals and is placed inside the palace. It is known by the name of Hammīr Śiva temple. We are about to come to the [main] palace, but before the palace, there is the Dulhā Palace. This palace was meant for the wedding programs and ceremonies of the people living here. It is the Dulhā Palace and is situated nearby. When we take a turn here, the Raghunath temple comes first, then comes the Dulhā Palace which was for the purposes of marriage. There is a museum in front of it. It is an absolutely new building with objects placed inside it. Moving further, there is a *dargāh*. There is a *mazār* (mausoleum) in the front of it in the memory of all those who have been martyred. There is a pond in front of that named Ranihoud. The queens used to bathe in that pond. There is a well in front of that pond. The water in the Houd empties but the well never empties. It is known as Mūrti Kuān (well). There is a temple in front of Ranihoud. Sorry, it is a mosque.

Q: In front of the Rani Mahal?

G2: Ranihoud, a pond made in front of the *dargāh*. It is known as Ranihoud. There is a mosque in the front known as the Akbari Mosque. The *namāz* was offered in front of the pond only. The mosque is in the front; you may have seen it. When we go inside, there comes Badal Mahal. There was a commander named Badal, so he along with his entire army used to live here separately. Inside that, there, deep underneath, there is a pond named Badal. The responsibility of the maintenance and security of the entire palace (Badal Mahal) was with his mother. When he used to get ready for war, he used to begin moving along with his entire army from here. He was the most ferocious fighter known as Badal. Moving further ahead, there comes the Hammīr *kachheri* (court). Before that comes the Munśi Koṭ a place where the lawyers sit and you take a slip [ticket] from there to move further. Hammīr *kachheri* was established later. The Delhi Gate is behind Hammīr *kachheri*. There is a Lord Hanuman temple there. There is the site of Jind Bābā which has jasmine and frangipani trees near it. Both are believed to be in love which keeps them together. There is a lot of love and great friendship between Lord Hanuman and Jind Bābā. The Delhi Gate is behind that. There is also a way to go up there from the *dargāh* in Amrāhi but it has been closed. Walking along from there we come to the Mātājī Mandir towards the wall (*parkoṭā*). A few people, once or twice, went there after getting drunk. They either became blind, ran away or some became mentally unstable. There were special powers at that point of time. As a result, the people here started believing in it. There is also a Jain temple here. People from the Jain community too live there. People from the Jain community too served the temple. There is also a Lakṣmīnārāyaṇ temple on one side. As you enter, there is Lakṣmīnārāyaṇ temple, then Jain temple there and Mātājī temple here.[199]

Q: Have they also been established here from earlier times?

G2: All of them have been established here from earlier.

Q: Have they been here since the time of the king?

G2: As their family tree kept growing. Like we had Lallujī, he has sons. The sons too have sons now; this is how it has been going on. The four houses there belong to them only. Two are *bhāṇḍs*, one is a *bhāṇḍ* and he has two children. Both of them have shops on top of their houses. Here there was Gautamjī, right now there is Satyanārāyanjī. One is Indarjī and his wife has died. Mahesh and his brothers are five in all. There is one Piyush. All the shops belong to him and the priest of the temple used to serve him ever since the beginning. Both of them died. They died on the day of the [September] fair in the year 2007. Since then Devlaljī's Fair is organized.

Q: Whose?

G2: Ganeśjī's Fair is organized first and three days after that is the Fair of Devlaljī.

Q: Who is Devlaljī?

G2: In case of a snake bite, he ties some thread. He is known as Devlaljī and a fair is organized in his honour.

Q: Oh! Here itself?

G2: There is one more [shrine of] Deśdhan Amreśvar Mahādev. As we move from here, it is on the side of the road. One person who was known by the name of Nāth, his family members are worshipping and serving [the deity]. There are six or seven brothers so the turn

199 There are a multitude of different religious communities assembled inside the fortress: Hindu deities, Jain temples, mosques and Sufi shrines.

comes once in every year. Like this year, the second brother got the opportunity, the next year, other brothers may get the opportunity. So every year one brother serves and worships [the god]. It is a very good temple ... There is no history whatsoever of this fort as to which king made it or not.

Q: Really ... there is no such history?

G2: There is no history of its construction. There is no history regarding who constructed this till date.

Q: Is there no information on when and why the settlement was done here?

G2: This place was meant for getting ready for war and to attack. This was the place where the preparation for winning [wars] was made. Many [rulers] including Akbar, Humayun, Aurangzeb, King Hammīr, 'Alā' al-Dīn Khaljī, Babar came here. People used to construct many houses here. But when 'Alā' al-Dīn Khaljī ruled, he destroyed [instead of building]. Now there is not even a single house left. Everything has turned into ruins. Even today, though, there are trees and herbs on top of the fortress that are useful. For example, there is a tree called *athsote* that is used to make gunpowder.

Q: Athsote?

G2: Athsote ... As we move further, we get a place of a deity called Jora-Bora. Then again there is an umbrella with 32 pillars. And it is known as Surajpol. There is a gate there as well at Surajpol. There were two granaries ... rice, wheat or whatever it may be, these were stored in the storage houses ... and after that comes the Phansighar (place where people were hanged).

Q: Phansighar?

G2: When we return from the route behind the Raghunāth temple, that is where Phansighar is situated. There is also a Hanuman temple. In the past when somebody was attacked or if some people engaged in quarrels, etc., amongst themselves, the king used to pronounce judgement in the court regarding hanging, so the Phansighar is where they were hanged.

Q: Over there?

G2: Over there. The soldiers would take the accused from Amerkachi. There is a Phansighar.

Q: How did the *dargāh* get there? You are saying Sadruddin ... what was the name?

G2: He too was a martyr?

Q: He was also martyred?

G2: Obviously. Everyone was martyred in the war.

Q: Alright. That was the reason ...

G2: Now when the gate opened the king charged ahead, destroyed everything and returned. 'Alā' al-Dīn Khaljī launched an attack on him [Hammīra].

Q: Alright. It happened back then ...

G2: What could he have done; the king died there. The gate remained open and the queen died. He then captured it. Much later Rana Sanga came and he fought and won it back.

Q: There are many people [who tried to conquer the fortress].

G2: They kept coming. Rana Sanga had a wife called Queen Handi. She once had to suddenly return to Chittor. That's why it remained her unfulfilled dream near the umbrella of the 32 pillars. It is in front of the garden and is known as 'the unfulfilled dream.' Those pillars are empty and the top corners are made a little like this. Only god knowns what is there on its top? Beside it is the Raj Mandir (royal temple). There is also a Hanuman temple. It has so many powers. The place gets very crowded at the time of the fair that nobody knows from where these people come. They keep coming and it gets crowded and the arrangements that are made are huge. People go to the Sawai Madhopur Railway Station on foot while around 30 – 40 buses are functional and the taxi services are also available. All those who stay here get the parking facilities, they walk from here, get free food, and nobody in any shop will charge even a single penny. You will have to pay for cigarettes and tobacco but food is free. There are at least fifty places on the way from Sawai Madhopur to this place which offer free food to the people.

Q: That is very good!

G2: It is very good. Doesn't matter what you may think, but I am a Muslim and I have earned a lot of money through the blessings of Ganeśjī situated in the fortress. In fact, my house was constructed using that money.

Q: Very nice!

G2: I am there since 1985. I remained there till 2007. I have also worked in it.

Q: In the temple?

G2: No, in the Archaeological Survey Department. I had also joined the course. I just did not pay attention at that time and today even my case is ongoing in the Archaeological Survey Department.

Q: What?!

G2: That's how it is. All the dates [for court cases] have come and gone. I have a knowledge of each and everything including which officer was there and who is there now. Even if I go there today, the permanent staff of that department will treat me with a lot of respect.

Q: That is very good!

G2: They are also scared of me. Like if somebody known to me was troubled, then I got them [the other person] transferred ... the officers listen to me because I used to do a lot for them. There was an [officer] from Delhi. Whenever he would come, he used to inform me in advance and I used to arrange a vehicle for him. At that time, the vehicles were very few in number. During my time, there were only 15 buses that were functional. So when a train arrived, one bus used to transport ten people. The ticket used to cost Rs 1 to Rs 1.5.

Q: That's all?

G2: It was nothing ... As the passenger count increased from 10 to 15, they were made to sit in the bus and the bus was made to leave. Those were the mini buses similar to the city buses running on the roads these days. I have worked in those as well either in the city bus or at the [bus] stand. I used to coordinate 15 buses from here and used to bring the buses from there as well. I used to take the passengers from here and used to bring back the same number of passengers. I used to ensure that nobody sat in the other bus. If that would happen then the passengers would fall short in numbers and the owner used to shout at me. If I took 20 passengers, then I used to come back with the same number of passengers. It should not be less; however, if it was less, the passengers would share the extra burden of 2 to 5 rupees amongst themselves. Then the bus would start. All the owner wanted was the money from 20 passengers. After that the taxi union was established as more and more buses caused problems on the uphill path.

Hence the government, the RTO (Road Transport Office) and the police banned big buses. After that taxis became functional. Taxis were given permission and they started [plying the route]. At that time, I used to get the passengers for Rs 5 if somebody wanted to see a tiger or wanted to go into the forest. I used to take Rs 5 on the spot. There were two/three pickup cars including my relatives' [cars]. I used to load people in those and take them. Fathers and brothers – everyone – would go into the forest. [My] brothers and other [relatives] used to [do the job] of guides [for tourists]. At that time, everyone used to do this. I used to take one passenger by charging Rs 5. I used to take them there, show them a tiger and bring them back. It started spreading amongst the public gradually. There was one person called Fateh Singh. He died due to snake bite. He constructed that park.

Q: I see. Fateh Singh?

G2: The place was bordered from all sides for the safety of the animals. He sought the help of the police by seeking ban on the grazing of cattle and other animals in the forest. The animals should not be allowed to graze inside – whatever the case – they must be kept outside. So he constructed a boundary from all sides. He also constructed a checkpoint and placed a guard there. There are many names here like Bahadurpur, Rajbagh, Kamaldar, Guda and all. There are houses constructed inside as well and the visitors used to come on foot from there and despite being on foot, no animal was harmed. Fateh Singhji is the one who made this forest.

Q: Did he belong to this place only?

G2: Although he was not from here, he worked in the forest. He did the most work for the creation of this forest. Whenever he saw a tiger with an injured paw, he used to tie a goat so as to feed the tiger. He carved out the path using the help of people telling them that if they walk like this then the path will be formed like that. The tiger can be seen from here also as there is a pond there. It can come to drink water. Since there was no arrangement for water during the rainy season, he used to construct ponds and small pools. The animals used to come there for drinking water during summers. He used to get these ponds and small pools of water filled using his [water] tanks. When the ponds dried up, where would the animals go? So at that time, he used to construct a pool and used to put water in that, which the animals used to use for drinking water. This means that he served the animals. When he used to drive there with his vehicle, the animals automatically knew that someone who cares for them has come. Their fortune changed at the time of that guard only. I am talking about that time [long ago]. So both of them [Fateh Singh and the guard] did a lot of service. It was like they had fallen in love [with the animals] while looking after them. [The forest] kept expanding.

Gradually the [general] public started coming to visit it. Ticket prices started from Rs 5 to Rs

15 and then became Rs 25, Rs 30, Rs 60, Rs 120, Rs 150 and today it is Rs 600 – 700! At times it is Rs 5000 or Rs 3000 including [the use of a] Gypsy [off road vehicle]. Gradually as the public interest increased, it started becoming more and more popular. And, finally it was named a National Park. At times somebody came from abroad and gave a donation. People used to donate money for making checkpoints [the forest] inside for safety [and security]. They used to ask them to make two to four sheds, make buildings and they would give them donations for this. There were a lot of donations pouring in. Bhale Sir used to come from Delhi, and there were many foreigners who came and other new people who would transfer donations to the government before they returned [home]. Sometimes when a politician or officer visits, the maintenance of the building and the entire forest is re-done. Therefore, this National Park [gradually] became famous.

Q: This is a very good thing.

G2: This area is such that only one animal (group of animals) can live here. Another animal will not come here. And if any animals like monkeys come here ... in the case of monkeys, if there are 40 female monkeys then there will be 1 male monkey. You can see the Jogi Mahal Gate from here. All the monkeys at the Naulakha gate under the shed and on top of the wall ... If the monkey below sees the other at the top of the wall of Ganeśpol, then he will run away. It will not come into its boundary and if it goes there, then the other monkey will fight it. If this one monkey gets old and loses the fight against the other, then the other monkey becomes their king. It is the same game of kings and queens wherein the one who wins the war gets the opportunity to serve all the queens. So wherever the male monkey goes, the female monkeys will follow. They have made groups – like when you go to the temple, you will only find the male monkeys there, you will not find the female monkeys there.

Q: Yes, there are many monkeys.

G2: You will not find even a single female monkey. All are male monkeys. All of them are very fat and they can't beat the one ahead of them. If the king engages a fight and if some other monkey wins in it, then he gets to keep all the female monkeys. All the monkeys live according to themselves in their defined areas. Their system is ongoing ever since the time of the kings. You see, this is how the system is!

Q: That's great, very good. So you worked as a guide here earlier?

G2: I used to work as a guide. I told you that I have been here since 1985. As I worked as the agent of the bus, I came here. Then I got into the taxi business. I left that as well and got into the work related to parking. It was contractual work. I used to go from here and if, in between, there were no passengers, I used try something else. If it was two o'clock and the gates were closed, and if anybody came, I used to show him the place. They used to come telling me that they didn't want to hear anything. They just wanted to see things. Gradually I started telling them the stories as well, so somebody used to give me Rs 20 or Rs 10 sometimes. It kept on going like this ... then it rose to Rs 60, then Rs 150. After that I left this too. My home is at a distance of 22 kms from there, so I used to go on a bicycle.

Q: Oh my god ...

G2: Although I use to run too. I have riden bicycle for 22 years but all those working with the bus and Jeep used to ask me not use the bicycle. They asked me to go comfortably.

That's how I used to go. Now the times have changes and the place remains crowded and the goods and items for the shops are also transferred there. Ten to twelve people also stay there in groups. After I stopped going, there was a Gujjar milkman who used to go there to supply milk from the village. He used to carry the dung on top. He used to supply milk. Slowly he learnt what I used to do. So all these [guides] are the ones who started this [job] after me. The *palke* (?) system was introduced by me.

Q: Naresh is also here?

G2: Yes, Naresh.

Q: You must be knowing him ...?

G2: Yes, Naresh Gujjar ...?

Q: Yes.

G2: The one from down there? They all started after me. He came started only after me. He does things the way he likes. Ask him about me some day. Ask him if he knows Wahid Muhammed of his taxi union. Everyone started after me. He goes there often to supply milk and used to take Rs 10 commission each time. He used to carry the load of the wheat sacks, *makhane* sacks, sugar sacks, gram flour sacks – each weighing 50 kgs. He used to carry that load initially and he used to earn Rs 1.50 per kg load. He used to make Rs 20 for each sack he used to carry up there. The distance up the hill distance was 1.5 km. It was none other than me who got the price increased from Rs 1.50 per kg to Rs 2 per kg by asking the shopkeeper. The shopkeeper now gives Rs 100 for a sack of 50 kgs. He used give Rs 5 for a canister so now it was raised to Rs 10 for a canister. Later on from Rs 10 I got it increased to Rs 15 and then Rs 20. Today a 15 kg canister pays Rs 20. Therefore, people there know me and I have also done all the work there [that there is to do]. Gradually, I came here and left everything. Then I got entangled in the case. I worked from 2002 to 2007 in the Archaeological Survey of India. I have been the one to get the digging of all the buildings done here by the labourers. All the sections you see here were once ruins. There were big trees growing in them; the buildings had sunk. The officers used to come from Delhi and I used to get the visits coordinated. I used to send a message to them that they will find a boy who will show them everything. The building that was getting broken used to get surveyed first and from there the budget used to get approved. I used to write that such things were happening. It is in danger as there are so many guests coming from outside and this is the situation here. It is good, since the place of deity is there, etc. So I have written to them on multiple occasions. So from there the budget was approved. The officers used to live in Delhi.

Gradually, the budget started getting approved from Delhi. Gradually if any wall of the Raghunath temple got damaged then it needed repairing as well. A monkey may come and kick it in and then it will fall on people. Hence the work of the entire building from bottom to top is my work. I have got it completed. And the colour was perfect ... There is a *geru* (red colour) which is mixed it with cement, lime and *bajri* (gravel) and with my skills, you will get a perfect 'combo.' But what I used to do in the morning used to appear like it was not done in the morning. In the morning it would appear as if it was done 20 years ago. Although it is newly repaired but it should appear as it if was done earlier. As we used to pour water on it on the third or fourth day, there used to be a shine on it. The officers used to get very happy with this thinking, who is this boy? They praised the artistry and how I managed to cover over everything. The mixture doesn't retain at all on that design on the stones that you can see. I used to scrape off all the mixture using a broom so that nobody could judge that there was mixture in it. One rock used to be placed on the other rock in such a way that the repair work appeared old. [While the] name is Archaeological Survey Department, but the repairing work was newly done. However, the work used to be such that when the officer visited on the third or fourth day to see how the budget had been utilized, then they used to get extremely happy on seeing it saying: "Let's leave this and move ahead with the palace and let's go to Dulhā Mahal, Badal Mahal, Raghunāth Temple, Raj Mandir, Mataji Temple, Jain Temple!"

Slowly and gradually the budget started getting approved. It kept on going. Even today the work is going on. The top of Supari Mahal is turning into complete ruins, hence the trees there have been tied back and that work is going on. That is the last task. All the remaining work related to the walls is over. I have got the work completed until Surajpol, but the walls are still broken and its construction has still not been completed. The animals like panther, bear, etc., come there. They come during the night-time over the walls as there is no guard in the front. They are also in danger, so I said to them that if you are going out at night then the animals may come anytime. I used to take along the cement and concrete trolley with me and I was the one who used to get half the trolley unloaded as it [was too heavy to] climb uphill. The remaining material was then carried using donkeys after which the material was carried on labourers heads. I was the one to start the donkey system so for that I got hold of three/four donkeys. Today there is an owner of donkeys there who is there permanently. He has the contract and it is given to him only. He charges less and his donkeys are very nice and strong. He has five donkeys. So he has been made the permanent carrier of the concrete material, cement, limestone, etc. His donkeys live in the palace. Sometimes other donkey owners complain that only his donkeys are contracted, they too should get the opportunity. So the forest officers wrote to them asking them to take their donkeys to the village. Here they say that work is unavailable. So they go to Jaipur and get it in writing and the work of the donkeys resumes.

There are many types of problems sir! What does one not do for small earning? Now see, I used to travel 22 km for a very small earning. It was my compulsion and earning is also important. Where else is the business? So I used to wake up in the morning and used to depart at 6 am and reach fort by 8 am. I was the one who used to prepare tea and serve it to the officer. All the staff from the village that used to work there used to reach after me. Somebody reached by 9 am while somebody else by 10 am. If ever there was shortage of anything, like if there was a fair or anything and the officers used to visit, then I was the one to look after all the arrangements. It was because all the taxi owners were known to me so the taxis used to charge less. They used to charge Rs 60 or Rs 80 instead of Rs 150. It so happened that the entire staff and the officers started knowing me. So they asked to work there only, to which I replied that what to do with working for Rs 2200 only. I am already earning this much here. My officer compelled me a lot to got to Kota within eight days. He said that he would register my name and that I would only have to sign there. I said that I am earning well and who would go to do the labour work for Rs 2200? He said that you don't need to do anything, just get your name registered in the store. If my name would have been registered in the store at that time, my salary would have been Rs 4200. But I did not go since I was earning here. Greed is bad sir. I thought what would I do with Rs

2200 salary as I was sometimes earning Rs 100 in a day, sometimes Rs 200? There was time when I started earning Rs 250 and sometimes also got Rs 4000. Sometimes such clients come who pay that much. Sometimes when we go to the Ganeśa Temple, they give Rs 10,000, asking me to bring such clients for them more often so that their business can flourish. There are certain shopkeepers of shops like tea shop, idol shop, all those used to be very happy with me as people did not used to go directly to them. The *prasād-wālās* used to request me to ask the visitors to buy *prasad* worth Rs 51 for Rs 100 from them. This is how I got to know everyone.

Q: Very good!

G2: Gradually I stopped coming by bicycle.

Q: It is very far.

G2: Then I got into the hotel industry. Although I can still go but things are not the same. God is kind enough to bless us with bread and butter. I stay here 24 hours.

Q: Okay, you live here?

G2: I stay here day and night. Once in a week I go there [to the fort]. If there is any work then I go there. Nobody stops me. Now I have been here for a year ever since the hotels, the properties began to be constructed ... it is a lonely place, long grass, the snakes and scorpions are moving around but I live here. I live on this terrace only.

Q: There were snakes here?

G2: Yes, all the big ones. There was no light and water, it created a lot of trouble. Now if there is nobody living in a building, animals are bound to breed there. This gate was closed so there was a gate made at the back for entry and exit. I used to live here alone by just praying to God. Then gradually it was auctioned and the bank took it away and then it was auctioned again and the God also blessed them. The building came into their possession ... God also heard their prayers. If one works hard then it will bring earnings. Today this is absolutely right. Because things happen due to hard work. Our hotel is in the city.[200] There is a gate called Meru Darwaza that is on the way when we travel from Sawai Madhopur Hospital to Saritapur. It is known as the Blaken (?) temple in English. It is in the name of Kala-Gora [Bhairu]. It is a very nice place belonging to the deity. It used to be completely surrounded with ponds. Earlier there was only water here. However, there was a Rani Ka Jhula, a building in front of the 'Rassa Tut' from Rajbag, and there is a checkpoint, we call it Jhumarbāvḍī.

Q: Badbāvḍī ...?

G2: Jhumarbāvḍī ... the palace where her (the queen's) king was. The palace is still in the name of the king and is called Jhumarbāvḍī ... it is the red coloured building there on top near the hill. The rope [for the swing] was made there. The rope broke and the queen fell into the water then the water was made to flow out from the door. Hence even today, every year it is celebrated as the day of the queen. It is near to our place and is called Ranihoud. She used to enjoy the swing and even today it is celebrated as her day. She was from the

200 The guide is talking about the hotel in which he now works.

family of the Diya Kumari Ji who is the Member of Parliament. She has recently become the MP. So slowly this village got settled. Initially there were 2–4 people but today entire Sawai Madhopur has been settled. People kept moving in boats for years and during the rainy seasons, the boats used to drown. Now the small bridge has been constructed. The traffic has started across the bridge. Here there is Indergad Mātājī, which is also a nice place belonging to the deity. Then there is Jot ka Parwada, she is also Goddess and this is also a special place of the deity. Then there is Isvardah, that is the place of Lord Śiva which is also a special place. The fairs are organized at the different places accordingly. You please come in September sometime later.

Q: Okay. Are many fairs organized?

G2: You will be surprised to see it as you will not have it witnessed anywhere ... you will line up in the afternoon and your opportunity will come in the evening and the pushing and pulling will be out of control ... the entry will be different from the exit ... The queue used to start from Sawai Madhopur to that place ... there is no other way ... it was so crowded that it surprises us when we see it ... It is unknown from where the public comes ... I used to carry disadvantaged people like kids, some old women, and pregnant women or those who had brought some fruits, or a bag of clothes on my bicycle when things were closed at that time. The garlands used to be taken from here, and I used to carry it on my bicycle. I used to park my bicycle on the Misaldara gate. Then I used to place the garlands on my head and then used to take it on my bicycle. Then I used to carry it upstairs. This is [what is called] greed. Earned in the afternoon but what to do at night? So I used to carry the garlands at night so that I can earn the extra money while also enjoying the fair at night. In the temple I used to get Rs 200–250 to Rs 400. One round used to fetch Rs 250 so sometimes I used to make three rounds and sometimes four rounds. Sometimes somebody forgot his briefcase, so I used to carry that also and he used to give me Rs 50–100. It used to continue for the whole night. It was only to make small earnings. The food was free and there was no tension regarding being hungry and making a decision as to where to eat. Free food was on offer at all the places. You can eat anywhere. This is the thing sir!

4 Jogi and Pīr

The following conversation centres around the 'Jogi Mahal' and the manner in which both Hammīra and 'Alā' al-Dīn use the supernatural abilities of a Jogi and *Pīr* toward gaining victory and consolidating their political and military power. The Jogi Mahal which was built for a Jogi who assisted Hammīra in performing an elaborate ritual (*yajña*) by virtue of which he achieved dominion over 32 kingdoms. The Jogi Mahal or Jogi Palace is also visited, perhaps more so that the fortress itself, by successive royal princes, queens, Bollywood actors, prime ministers and presidents.

Guide 1: Someone told me that according to the *Akbarnāmā*, Jahangir visited once and he told the Prime Minister of this place that accommodation was not comfortable, [so] he should build another place. So, the Rajbagh Palace, which is about one hundred metres away from the Jogi Mahal, within the ambit [of the fortress] was built later on. But [Jahangir] unfortunately, never returned.

As far as I know about the Jogi Mahal, there was a Jogi, just like there are *Fakirs* who do not care about this world.

Questioner: Yes, yes, *Fakirs*.

G1: Yes, like a *Fakir*. So, he [the Jogi] performed a *yajña* here. He performed a *yajña* for Hammīr so that he could successfully defeat 32 kingdoms and win all his battles. He prayed a lot [for the king's success]. Indeed, Hammīr emerged victorious, and therefore he constructed the Jogi Mahal in memory of the Jogi. It can be seen from up there ... the most beautiful place. Not just the building, but the whole environment, it's lovely. It used to be a hunting reserve and hunting lodge later on and also a tourist lodge when this became sanctuary for tigers. There were not many places around here, not many hotels, before 1970. Maybe after 1973 [hotels were built], and I am telling you about much earlier than that ... Tourists would stay there. It contains only four rooms, four suites. All of them used to stay there, but later when they realized [probably] for conservation purposes [they stopped staying here]. Even Rajiv Gandhi stayed there in 1986. He stayed there with Priyanka and Rahul Gandhi. Yes, they were kids. There are many photographs of them as well. And Amitabh [Bacchan] also came here to join them. They stayed here for seven days.
Rajiv Gandhi spent seven days at this place and it's only subsequently that Ranthambore became famous. And an even bigger [tourist] boom was seen after Clinton visited here.

Q: Clinton also came here?

G1: Yes, Clinton [came here] in 2002, [when] he was the President. After that there was a boom [in visitors]. They came by helicopter, visited [this place] for couple of hours and the forest for tigers and flew back to Jaipur.

Fig. 14: The Jogi Mahal

There is a huge banyan tree in front of it. From up here, you can see its crown. That is the second biggest banyan tree in Asia. The largest one is in Kolkata, in the National Botanical Garden. Once its crown was measured, it was found to be about 377 sq. metres with thousands of aerial roots. It is the second largest. This is the other reason why it is famous, [because it has] one of the oldest banyan trees.

A Bollywood film was also shot there. Sanjay Dutt starred in *Daud*. An entire song for that film was shot there, under the banyan tree. It's a huge tree.

Q: So, was there any connection between the Jhumarbāvḍī and the fort? Did some other king make it?

G1: No, the fort does not have any link with the Jhumarbāvḍī. The Jhumarbāvḍī is a recent construction. It was built by Gayatri Devi (Maharani of Jaipur) and others. It was recently built. We cannot say it is completely new, but in comparison to the fort it is very recent, because it was a private hunting reserve. Ranthambore was a private hunting reserve of the Jaipur Maharajas and Karoli Maharajas. They used it to hunt tigers and other game as well. And they did that for six weeks in a year only. They ensured that animals would get enough time to increase their population. That's why they fixed a certain period for hunting. For example, they said that we will hunt the animals only between such and such a date, and if an animal is hunted and killed during this time-period then it's fine, otherwise we won't hunt them. They also would to invite outsiders for hunting. They had a concern for conservation as well.

Q: Is that true about Queen Elizabeth [that she visited]?

G1: There are photographs [of her visit].

Q: She was invited [here].

G1: Yes, Queen Elizabeth came here once ... along with Gayatri Devi ... and they shot a tiger and some photograph are still there in the Taj Hotel.

Q: That means, it happened before the forest was declared a sanctuary?

G1: It happened before it was declared a sanctuary. So, the tiger was laid out on the ground and all of them are standing around the tiger with guns.

Q: Yes, the tiger was on the ground in front of them.

G1: This was the symbol of pride for these kings.

Q: That's why tigers are [almost] extinct now. They killed most of them.

G1: Then they used to make carpet from its skin or hang it on the wall. And some of them were preserved by using chemicals. For many years, I have worked in the Jungle. I observed all these things about nature and wild animals.

Q: What's that inside the central portion of the fort. The section which is closed off. What was that actually?

G1: Actually, that is the Hammīr Palace.

Q: It is closed and locked?

G1: It is closed because things have been kept inside.

Q: What kind of things?

G1: Things such as cannons, etc. [They are kept inside] so that no one can damage them. Some time ago, lots of gunpowder was also kept in there. Then they shifted it out. A huge amount was transferred from here. Ranthambore is now under world heritage as well. Budget allocation [for conservation] was started recently, once it came under world heritage status. Otherwise, condition of the fort was very pathetic.

Q: Many parts are still in bad condition!

G1: But the main sections have been repaired. Local people do not care about its history and importance, they only come here for the Ganeśa Temple. They come here to visit the Ganeśa Temple. Not only local people, but people from outside also come here to visit the temple. You will not find a three-eyed Lord Ganeśa anywhere else except in this temple. People have tremendous faith. In fact, I would say that during the big fair that is organized during rainy season millions of people come here. You won't find any free space during that time, and there are long queues.

Q: So, this Ganeśa Temple was also constructed during the time [of Hammīr]?

G1: It was constructed later.

Q: There is a Jain temple and a *dargāh* as well?

G1: Sadruddin Aulia's *dargāh*.

Q: Was he a *Pīr?*

G1: Yes, he was a *Pīr*; a very famous one. There is also a story related to him. 'Alā' al-Dīn Khaljī was not able to seize Ranthambore fort, then Sadruddin Aulia ...

Q: Was he from Delhi or from here?

G1: No, he was not from Delhi. Though he came with 'Alā' al-Dīn Khaljī – he was a holy man – but he belonged to a nearby place called Bundi. 'Alā' al-Dīn had heard that he [the *Pīr*] did not care about the world and that God would grant him anything he would request. 'Alā' al-Dīn was told to go to [and meet] this holy man. When 'Alā' al-Dīn failed to [capture the fort] in two attempts, he went to Bundi. He requested the holy man to tell him a way to win this fort. The holy man said [it's good] that you've come to me, but there is a man in your army who is even more well-connected to God! Then 'Alā' al-Dīn asked "How will I be able to identify him?" The holy man told him that on such and such date there will very bad weather and storm, and during that storm you will discover that in one of the tents [in your camp] a lamp is still burning despite the forceful storm and then you will know that it is him. 'Alā' al-Dīn waited for the day and when the foretold storm started, he searched for that tent and found the tent where lamp was burning despite of the storm. 'Alā' al-Dīn bowed down touching the feet of the saint. The saint asked the king to explain how he got to know about him. 'Alā' al-Dīn told him whole story. The saint then cursed that holy man and said that after the holy man dies, donkeys will wander on his grave till eternity. And, even today when people visit the grave of that holy man, they see donkeys walking over his grave.

Q: When I was there, I saw four donkeys as well!

G1: Yes, that's because of the curse.

Q: Yes, they were either donkeys or mules.

G1: Yes, he cursed him that donkeys will wander on his grave. Even now, whenever you will visit his grave, you will see donkeys there – standing or rolling on his grave. The saint then prayed for 'Alā' al-Dīn and finally in the third attempt, he won the fort.

5 Ranthambore

In this fifth and final conversation the narrator focuses on the prior and later history of the fortress by referring to Hammīra's famous ancestor Pṛthvīrāj Chauhan, but also to later Rajput kings such as Maharana Pratap and his conflict with the Mughal emperor Akbar who ruled in the 16th century. At the end of the narration the speaker describes the origin of the fortress and how it is linked to the discovery of the hill upon which it is built by two brothers who were princes. Several different names for the fortress are mentioned each signifying a different etymology that in turn suggest varied origins. The name for the fortress, as is its history, is thus shifting and changing depending on the context in and from which it is being narrated.

Guide 1: This is the Raghunāth Temple. It used to be polished with gold and some of that polish you can see even today on the sides. Let's go a little further ... now see these ruins ... see ... see this ... now there is no idol ... earlier there was a huge idol of Lord Rāma. ... It sounded like a cannon firing. We heard the sound continuously, like four/five times. I asked the old and elderly people about it ... they said that it was like a war was [still] being fought there ... as if cannons were being fired and a battle-wind (*raṇvāyu*) was blowing through the battlefield. *Raṇvāyu* means that there is a war going on in the battlefield. Sometimes, at night, it seems as if there is war going on!

Questioner: Even today?

G1: Yes, even to this day. Our old aged and elderly people take the buffaloes to [the area of] this battlefield during the rainy season to feed them. The buffaloes stay there during rainy season. So what happens is, sometimes a *raṇvāyu* starts during night. It appears as if there is a storm going on and sounds come from all the directions, like *hee-haa-huu*. It seems as if a war is going on. This was mentioned in the *chaturved* (four Vedas). That if a person drinks water by bending and bowing down then snakes appear everywhere in that place. This was especially told to me by my uncle who I am very is very close to. Once, we washed dirty utensils there and then snakes appeared all over the place. We then folded our hands and apologized, that saved our life ... snakes appeared all around. The elderly people, they know about it, and scientists also know about it but they do not admit it. You have already visited this building. You have already seen one or two floors from inside ...

Q: Is this the palace?

G1: This is the palace, the main palace. This used to be the main palace.

Q: How many floors are there, three more?

G1: Three floors are above the ground level and three or four floors are underground. There is a small tunnel that goes from inside and ends at Kandharpur. It is around 7–10 km long. Food was brought through the tunnel using donkeys. It used to come directly from Kandharpur.

Q: Where is this Kandharpur?

G1: Kandharpur is after these hills. *Dar* is there, and here is the *Kandhar Potli*. There is a tunnel here, so food used to reach here with the help of donkeys. This was their system.

People believe that all these palaces were constructed during the time of Hammīr Dev Chauhan. Since his father ruled for 32 years and after him Hammīr Dev Chauhan ruled from 1282 to 1301. So most of the development took place here during the era of Hammīr Dev. Veer Narayan came here at that time. Veer Narayan, and then came Govind Deo.

Q: When did they come?

G1: A battle was fought in the foothills in 1192. Pṛthvīrāj Chauhan fought against Muhammed Ghori. In 1191 it was the second last [battle]. The final battle was fought in 1192. In that battle, Muhammed Ghori defeated Pṛthvīrāj Chauhan. After defeating Pṛthvīrāj Chauhan, Muhammed Ghori plucked his eyes out. Pṛthvīrāj Chauhan's poet, Chandbardai Sevak, told Muhammed Ghori that the Chauhan forgave you 16 times, so please forgive him at least once. To which, Ghori replied, "I am not a fool like Pṛthvīrāj Chauhan. I cannot

spare my enemy when he is right in front of me. If you would have killed me before, this situation would not have arisen at all." To this, Chandbardai Sevak said, "It is all right, king. You plucked out his eyes, but I would like to say that he is an archer of great calibre and such archers are rarely seen in the world. He can, despite being blind, target the eye of a goat." To which Ghori replied, "You are praising him despite him being blinded. Let's see how he can shoot arrows with blinded eyes." To which the Sevak said, "He can take a shot but the bow has to be his own." Ghori had his hands on the bow of Pṛthvīrāj Chauhan who was tied up in iron chains. Ghori got the Chauhan unchained. And, in anger, he said "You can aim at me. If you can hit a target even when blinded, then aim at me!" So then what happened Muhammed Ghori sat high up with his shield to protect him. So Chandbardai Sevak recited a poem:
Char Bans Chaubis Gaj Angul Asht Praman, Ta Upar Sultan Hai,
Tir Mar De Sene Par Ab Mat Chuke Chauhan

Which means, the sultan is sitting at a height equal to 4 bamboos (earlier 12-foot bamboos were used), i.e. 24 yards (*sic*), and *Angul Asht Praman* means you can add 8 fingers space more to this – 4 bamboos, 24 yards, and 8 fingers. He wanted to tell the Chauhan that Muhammed Ghori was sitting at such and such height, and that now Pṛthvīrāj should pierce his chest and shouldn't miss this chance. He finished off Muhammed Ghori by piercing the latter's shield. You probably know that the grave of Pṛthvīrāj Chauhan is situated in today's Afghanistan. They buried him ... despite the fact that he was a Hindu, they buried him. Although he didn't die because of them. He died on his own. Chandbardai Sevak told him that we are under Mughal rule now, and they will torture us badly. So, please kill me! Chandbardai was very intelligent, he did not want to say that you kill yourself and kill me as well. No! He said "Please kill me. We are under their rule now. They will now torture us endlessly. So, I request you to kill me, my lord!" He pleaded like this. He said "You kill me first. As soon as you chop my head off, you hand over the sword to me. Then, I will kill you!" This is what happened, and, the Mughals could do nothing but witness it. They both killed themselves. This angered the Mughals, so what they did was they made a grave for Pṛthvīrāj in Afghanistan which exists even today. People walk on it with their shoes and sandals on so as to disrespect him, even today. It became a political matter. So Pṛthvīrāj was a very powerful king!

Now, there were kings like Uday Singh Rana, Maharana Pratap. All these have been very powerful kings of Rajasthan. Now see, Uday Singh Rana. He had two sons: Hariram and Maharana Pratap. Uday Singh Rana had two wives. One day as Uday Singh Rana entered his palace, he found his wife in a very distressed state. To which Uday Singh asked her, "Hey queen, why are you sad?" The queen said that she was not sad, but later she said to Uday Singh that, "I will tell you the reason, but first you have to promise me ..." Uday Singh promised her that he will grant her whatever she would ask for. Then she said "O king, you have lived your life ..." Uday Singh Rana was very powerful and Maharana Pratap was the son of his first wife. She said "Maharana Pratap is powerful and very active too ..." Just like when we say things about our children that "they are active, and they will lead their life comfortably." She continued, "But what will happen to our younger son, Hariram?" Hariram was her son. Uday Singh knew about her plan when he promised her to fulfil her desire. He said, "He will be our successor (he had already decided it). He will be our successor."

Q: Hariram?

G1: Yes, Hariram. So they made Hariram their successor. After that, in 1556 Akbar became the king of Delhi. Akbar tried bringing all the Hindu kings under his control. He was consolidating his own empire. There was a king of the Jaipur *Darbār*, named Man Singh. He gave his daughter to Akbar, his very own daughter. King Akbar did everything, either by hook or crook and that is why he was so successful. As he surged ahead from Delhi bringing all the kingdoms under his control, he reached Chittor. So what happened there? Hariram was the king of Chittor and a war took place between them.

Q: Akbar started the war?

G1: Yes, Akbar did. After the war, Hariram chose to be under the reign of Akbar. But despite choosing to be under the rule of Akbar, Akbar killed 30,000 [of Hariram's) people. This infuriated Maharana Pratap. That he didn't fight didn't mean anything – it was his kingdom after all, as he was the elder son. He was the true successor of the throne. So when he got infuriated, he took up arms and fought the battle of Haldighati against Akbar, who defeated him as well.[201] Ever since then the people of that place saw Maharana Pratap as their king. They considered Maharana Pratap as their king. After the war he took shelter in the Aravalli Hills. He was not afraid of death. He didn't hide from death. He [hid] so as to defend, to defend the citizens of his kingdom. He knew that they would make a comeback sometime. He knew that if he died then there would be nobody to protect his people afterwards. He loved his people. He engaged in wars only for his people. Otherwise, he had no greed or lust unlike other [rulers] had ... for women, or for having a large number of queens, or his own rule. He never thought about such things. He just wanted to serve the people of that region. For that he even ate *rotis* made of grass growing in the forest. There is also a poem regarding this which I cannot recall right now. The essence of the poem is that he asked for the *roti* made of grass and a cat ate that *roti*. But he wanted to make a comeback, and therefore he took shelter in the forests of the Aravalli Hills. There have been plenty of kings like Maharana Pratap. Veer Narayan was one such king here at that time. After Veer Narayan, his son Govind Deo became the ruler. So, Veer Narayan ruled here as well. Qutubuddin Aibak once invited Veer Narayan and by deceit he poisoned his milk. This killed Veer Narayan ...

Q: He was the king of this place?

G1: Yes, he was the king of this place [too]. His wife became *sati* ... You can see the umbrella there; so that umbrella that you can see there was erected for the *sati*. When she got to know about her husband, she became *sati*. She immolated herself. Then Govind Raj took over the governance in 1192. So, Govind Raj was [Hariram's] son. But he had an uncle named Hariraj. Hariraj was the uncle of Govind Raj. Hariraj staunchly opposed Govind Raj and therefore he had to vacate the fort. Hariraj was his uncle. From the 12th century, Pṛthvīrāj Chauhan's dynasty has ruled this place.

201 The battle took place between the forces of Maharana Pratap and Raja Man Singh I of Jaipur who was a vassal of Emperor Akbar. Maharana Pratap was defeated but survived the battle and escaped to live in the nearby hills and forests.

After Govind Raj there was Jaitra Singh Chauhan and after Jaitra Singh Chauhan there was Hammīr Dev from 1282–83. I am telling you about the era prior to this. Then came Bagvat and then came Narayan Govind Dev, then Narayani Devi, Ballahan Dev, Nahar Dev. Their dynasty ruled this place. Hariraj organized a *yajña* here. The umbrella was constructed here at that time. This umbrella was constructed by Hammīr in fond memory of his father Jaitra Singh. There was also a *jauhar-kund* here, where 1300 queens committed *jauhar.*

This place is called Ranthambore, because as you can see the hills in the front of here, that is the battlefield ... and battlefield means *Raṇbhūmi* in Hindi ... the fort is called *thaṃb*, because it has been made on a single hill ... there is no other hill adjoining it ... it is standing straight like a pillar ... pillar is known as *thaṃb* in Hindi ... *Raṇ* means *Raṇbhūmi* (battlefield) plus *thaṃb* (pillar). Between the outer wall and here there is a 500–700-ft-deep drain. This is called *Bhanwar* ... hence *Raṇ* plus *thaṃb* plus *bhor* ... joining these three words together gave birth to the name of this place, i.e. Ranthambore. In 1972, this place was declared as the site for the Tiger Project. In 1982, it was given the status of the National Park, before that it was also known as *Ranat-bhanwar-gad.*

Q: *Ran* ...?

G1: *Ranat-bhanwar-gad.* It was believed that Ranat and Bhanwar were brothers and princes, so *Ranat-bhanwar-gad* was also named after both of them. Later on when it was declared to be the site for the Tiger Project, it was named as Ranthambore Fort. It was done because they extracted the meaning: battlefield means *Raṇbhūmi* or *Raṇ* in Hindi, which is a battle place, and *thaṃb* or pillar because the fort was made on a single hill and the hill is standing straight like a pillar, as you have already seen ... Therefore, it is called a *thaṃb* in Hindi plus *Bhanwar,* as there is a drain passing between these two. So *Raṇ* plus *thaṃb* plus *Bhanwar* ... adding all three of them, gave this place a name, i.e. Ranthambore. I was talking about this drain – this hole that you can see, it is *Padmāvatī Tālāb.* The hole was opened to fill the drain and when the pond filled, then it was opened again. It was cleaned then. Now it is again full and deep.

Q: What were the names of the brothers again?

G1: Ranat Bhanwar, Ranat and Bhanwar were two brothers. You can find all this written in history. It's from their names the fortress gained its name, i.e. *Raṇthaṃban.* It is also known as *Ranat-bhanwar-gad.* There was also a king, named Raṇthaṃban Dev. Ranthambore is also known by his name, Raṇthaṃban Dev. So there are three to four such reasons it seems [for naming the fortress].

Q: Oh, I see!

G1: Yes, it has different names from the beginning. This is known as *Ranthamban Dev, Ranat-bhanwar-gad,* and then *Ranthamboregad.* This has been changing [again and again]. At that time, the commanders of the armies were known as Sardars. This was the mansion of the commander Sardar. This was the VIP colony of that period. It was known as Satpol because there are seven gates in succession to reach that mansion. The commander, the Sardar, used to live here. The symbol that you can see there, the white symbol on the mansion. This was the national symbol of the Chauhan dynasty.

Bibliography

Ahmed, Aziz. 1963. "Epic and Counter-Epic in Medieval India." *Journal of the American Oriental Society 83*, 470 – 476.

Anver, Javed. 2018. *A History of Ranthambore*. New Delhi: Intach.

Appleby, Joyce, Lynn Hunt and Margaret Jacob. 1994. *Telling the Truth about History*. New York: W. W. Norton & Company.

Asad, Talal. 1993. *Genealogies of Religion*. Baltimore: Johns Hopkins University Press.

Asher, Catherine B., and Cynthia Talbot. 2006. *India before Europe*. Cambridge: Cambridge University Press.

Assman, Jan. 2011. Cultural Memory and Early Civilization: Writing, Remembrance and Political Imagination. Cambridge: Cambridge University Press.

Assman, Jan and John Czaplicka. 1995. "Collective Memory and Cultural Identity." *New German Critique* 65, 125 – 133.

Bandyapadhyaya, Brajnath. 1879. "Hammīra Rasa or a History of Hamir, Prince of Ranthambore." *The Journal of the Asiatic Society of Bengal* 48, 186 – 252.

Baranī, Ziyaʾ al-Dīn. 1967. *Tarīkh-i-Firūz Shāhī*, trans. A. R. Fuller and A. Khallaque. Calcutta: Pilgrim Publishers.

Barthes, Roland. 1986. *The Rustle of Language*. Oxford: Basil Blackwell.

Baudrillard, Jean. 1994 [1981]. *Simulacra and Simulation*, trans. Sheila Glaser. Ann Arbor: The University of Michigan Press.

Bayly, Susan. 1990. Saints, Goddesses and Kings: Muslims and Christians in South Indian Society, 1700 – 1900. Cambridge: Cambridge University Press.

Bednar, Michael Boris. 2007. Conquest and Resistance in Context: A Historiographical Reading of Sanskrit and Persian Battle Narratives. PhD Dissertation. Austin, Texas: The University of Texas at Austin.

Bednar, Michael Boris. 2017. "Mongol, Muslim, Rajput: Mahimāsāhi in Persian texts and the Sanskrit *Hammīra-Mahākāvya*." *Journal of the Economic and Social History of the Orient* 60, 585 – 613.

Bhatnagar, V. S. 1991. *Kanhadade Prabandh*. New Delhi: Aditya Prakashan.

Blackburn, Stuart. 1985. "Death and Deification: Folk Cults in Hinduism." *History of Religions* 24, 255 – 274.

Blitz, Mark. 2016. "Mark Blitz on Heidegger." *Great Thinkers*, YouTube, 21 October. https://www.youtube.com/watch?v=IS9WAOmDoO8. Accessed on: 18 February 2020.

Bly, Robert. 2004. *Iron John: A Book about Men*. Cambridge (MA): Da Capo Press.

Borges, Jorge Luis. 1964. *Labyrinths*. New York: New Directions.

Bowie, Malcolm. 2008. "Remembering the Future." In *Memory: An Anthology*, A. S. Byatt and Harriet Harvey Wood eds., 13 – 28. London: Vintage.

Boyarin, Daniel. 2016. "Thrēskeia; or, the Lexical Absence of Ancient Religion." Paper presented at *Max-Weber-Kolleg for Advanced Social Science Research*, 14 December.

Briggs, John. 1981 (1829). History of the Rise of Mohammaden Power in India through the Year A.D. 1612, 4 Vols. New Delhi: Oriental Books Reprint.

Bronner, Yigal, David Shulman and Gary Tubb, eds. 2014. *Innovations and Turning Points: Toward a History of Kavya*. New York: Oxford University Press.

https://doi.org/10.1515/9783110662795-014

Buchta, David and Graham Schweig. 2010. “Rasa Theory.” In *Brill’s Encyclopedia of Hinduism, Volume Two: Sacred Texts, Ritual Traditions, Arts, Concepts*, Knut Axel Jacobsen ed., 623–629. Leiden: Brill.

Carr, David. 2014. Experience and History: Phenomenological Perspectives on the Historical World. New York: Oxford University Press.

Chakrabarty, Dipesh. 1995. “Modernity and Ethnicity in India: A History for the Present.” *Economic and Political Weekly* 30, 3373–3380.

Chandra, Ramesh. 2003. *Nayachandra Sūrikrit Hammīramahakāvya ka Samikshātmak Adhyayan*. Ghaziabad: Akash Publishers and Distributors.

Chandraśekhar. 2002. *Hammīr Haṭṭ*, trans. Ātmārām ‘Aruṇ’ Sharmā. Delhi: Bhāgyavanti Prakāśan.

Chattopadhyay, Brajadulal. 1998. Representing the Other? Sanskrit Sources and the Muslims (8th to 14th Century). New Delhi: Manohar.

Collingwood, Robin George. 1994. *The Idea of History*. Oxford: Oxford University Press.

Deleuze, Gilles. 1994 [1968]. *Difference and Repetition*, trans. Paul Patton. New York: Columbia University Press.

Deliege, Robert. 1985. *The Bhils of Western India*. New Delhi: National Publishing House.

Doshi, S. L. 1978. “A Sociological Analysis of Political Unification Among Scheduled Tribes of Rajasthan”. *Sociological Bulletin* 27, 231–244.

Dumezil, Georges. 1973. *The Destiny of a King*, trans. Alf Hiltebeitel. Chicago: The University of Chicago Press.

Eagleman, David. 2019. “The Incredible Time-Bending Power of your Brain.” *BBC Ideas*, 13 June. https://www.bbc.co.uk/ideas/videos/the-incredible-time-bending-power-of-your-brain/p07d07d3. Accessed on: 22 June 2019.

Elliot, Henry Miers and John Dowson. 1871. The History of India as Told by its own Historians: The Mohammedan Period. London: Trübner and Co.

Fazl, Abul. 2015/2016. *The History of Akbar (Akbarnama)*, trans. Wheeler M. Thackston, *Murty Classical Library of India*. Two Volumes. Cambridge (MA): Harvard University Press.

Flood, Finbarr B. 2009. *Objects of Translation: Material Culture and Medieval “Hindu-Muslim” Encounter*. New Jersey: Princeton University Press.

Gadamer, Hans-Georg. 1960. *Wahrheit und Methode: Grundzüge einer philosophischen Hermeneutik*. Tübingen: J. C. B. Mohr (Paul Siebek).

Ghosh, Manmohan, trans. 1950. *The Natyasashtra*. Calcutta: The Royal Asiatic Society of Bengal.

Gilmartin, David and Bruce Lawrence, eds. 2000. *Beyond Turk and Hindu: Rethinking Religious Identities in Islamicate South Asia*. Gainsville: University Press of Florida.

Gonda, Jan. 1969. *Ancient Indian Kingship from a Religious Point of View*. Leiden: E. J. Brill.

Grimm, Brüder. 1994. *Kinder- und Hausmärchen*. Stuttgart: Reclam-Verlag.

Habib, Muhammed. 1931. *Khazā ‘inul Fuṭūḥ of Hazrat Amīr Khusrau*. Bombay: D. B. Taraporewala, Sons & Co.

Handelman, Don and David Shulman. 2004. *Śiva in the Forest of Pines: An Essay in Sorcery and Self-Knowledge*. New Delhi: Oxford University Press.

Hardiman, David. 1987. “The Bhils and Shahukars of Eastern Gujarat”. In *Subaltern Studies V: Writings on South Asian History and Society*. Ranajit Guha ed., 1–54. Delhi: Oxford University Press.

Harlan, Lindsey. 1992. *Religion and Rajput Women: The Ethic of Protection in Contemporary Narratives*. Berkeley: University of California Press.

Hartog, François. 1996. "Time, History and the Writing of History: The Order of Time." In *Kungliga Vitterhets Historie och Antikvitets Akademien Konferenser, XXXVII*, Rolf Torstendahl and Irmline Veit-Brause eds., 95–113. Stockholm: The Royal Academy of Letters, History and Antiquities.

Heesterman, Jan C. 1985. *The Inner Conflict of Tradition: Essays in Indian Ritual, Kingship and Society*. Chicago: The University of Chicago Press.

Heidegger, Martin. 1954. *Was heisst Denken?* Tübingen: Max Niemeyer Verlag.

Heidegger, Martin. 1967. *Sein und Zeit*. Tübingen: Max Niemeyer Verlag.

Heidegger, Martin. 1976. *What is called Thinking?* trans. J. Glenn Gray. New York: Harper Perennial.

Heidegger, Martin. 2001. *Poetry, Language, Thought*, trans. Albert Hofstadter. New York: Harper Collins.

Herodotus. 1987. *The History*. Chicago: The University of Chicago Press.

Hiltebeitel, Alf. 1990. *The Ritual of Battle: Krishna in the Mahabharata*. Albany: State University of New York.

Hiltebeitel, Alf. 1999. *Rethinking India's Oral and Classical Epics: Draupadi among Rajputs*. Chicago: The University of Chicago Press.

Husserl, Edmund. 1990. *On the Phenomenology of the Consciousness of Internal Time* (1893–1917), trans. J. B. Brough. Dordrecht: Kluwer.

Inception. 2010. Movie directed by Christopher Nolan. https://en.wikipedia.org/wiki/Inception. Accessed on: 18 July 2019.

Jinavijaya, Muni ed. 1968. *Hammīra-Mahākāvya*. Jodhpur: Rajasthan Oriental Research Institute.

Jodhārāj. Vikram Saṃvat 2006 [1949]. *Hammīrrāso*, trans. Śyāmsundardās. Kāśī: Nāgarīpracāriṇī Sabhā.

Jodhārāj. 2007. *Hammīrrāso*, trans. Kṛṣṇbīr Singh Chauhān. Jaypur: Granth Vikās.

Juvayni, Ala al-Din Ata-Malek. 1958. *The History of the World Conqueror, 2 Vols*, trans. John Andrew Boyle. Cambridge (MA): Harvard University Press.

Kayasth, Heera Nand. n.d. (18th century). *Tariq-i-Quila-Ranthambore*, trans. R. K. Saxena. Jaipur: Sanghi Publication.

Keller, Helen. 2016. *The Story of My Life*. Noida: Om Books International.

Keller, Mary. 2002. *The Hammer and the Flute: Women, Power, and Spirit Possession*. Baltimore: The Johns Hopkins University Press.

Kermode, Frank. 2008. "Palaces of Memory." In *Memory: An Anthology*, A. S. Byatt and Harriet Harvey Wood eds., 3–13. London: Vintage.

Kolff, Dirk H. A. 2002. *Naukar, Rajput, Sepoy: The Enthnohistory of the Military Labour Market of Hindustan 1450–1850*. Cambridge: Cambridge University Press.

Koselleck, Reinhart. 2004. *Futures Past: On the Semantics of Historical Time*, trans. Keith Tribe. New York: Columbia University Press.

Kulke, Hermann and Dietmar Rothermund. 2016. *A History of India*. London: Routledge.

Lee, Seu-Kyou. 2001. *Existenz und Ereignis: Eine Untersuchung zur Entwicklung der Philosophie Heideggers*. Würzburg: Verlag Königshausen und Neumann.

Lincoln, Bruce. 1991. *Death, War and Sacrifice: Studies in Ideology and Practice*. Chicago: The University of Chicago Press.

Luhman, Niklas. 1980. *Gesellschaftsstruktur und Semantik.* Frankfurt: Suhrkamp.
Malik, Aditya. 1993. *Das Puṣkara-Māhātmya: Ein religionsgeschichtlicher Beitrag zum Wallfahrtsbegriff in Indien.* Stuttgart: Franz Steiner Verlag.
Malik, Aditya. 1994. "The King, the Boar and the Waterhole: An Oral Narrative about the Recreation of Pushkar". In *Art: The Integral Vision: A Volume of Essay in Felicitation of Kapila Vatsyayan.* Baidynath Saraswati, S. C. Malik and Madhu Khanna eds., 281–288. New Delhi: D. K. Printworld.
Malik, Aditya. 2005. *Nectar Gaze and Poison Breath: An Analysis and Translation of the Rajasthani Oral Narrative of Devnarayan.* New York: Oxford University Press.
Malik, Aditya. 2016/2018. *Tales of Justice and Rituals of Divine Embodiment: Oral Narratives from the Central Himalayas.* New York/Delhi: Oxford University Press.
Malik, S. C. 2020 (1989). *Modern Civilization: A Crisis of Fragmentation.* New Delhi: D. K. Printworld.
Mani, Chandra Mauli. 2009. *A Journey through India's Past.* New Delhi: Northern Book Centre.
Mayaram, Shail. 2003. *Against History, Against State: Counterperspectives from the Margins.* New York: Columbia University Press.
Mukherjee, Sujit. 1999. *A Dictionary of Indian Literature: Beginnings – 1850.* Hyderabad: Orient Longmans.
Narayana Rao, Velcheru and David Shulman. 2005. *God on the Hill: Temple Poems from Tirupati.* New Delhi: Oxford University Press.
Narayana Rao, Velcheru, David Shulman and Sanjay Subrahmanyam. 2001. *Textures of Time: Writing History in South India 1600–1800.* Delhi: Permanent Black.
Nayachandra Sūri. 1879. *The Hammīra Mahākāvya of Nayachandra Sūri*, ed. Nilkanth Janardana Kirtane. Bombay: Education Society's Press, Byculla.
Olivelle, Patrick. 2013. *King, Governance and Law in Ancient India: Kauṭilya's Arthaśāstra.* New York: Oxford University Press.
Pamuk, Orhan. 2006. *Nobel Lecture.* https://www.nobelprize.org/uploads/2018/06/pamuk-lecture_en.pdf. Accessed on: 11 February 2020.
Pandey, Bhupendramani. 2005. *Hammīr Mahākāvya kā Samālochnātmak Adhyayan.* PhD Dissertation. Jhansi: Bundelkhand University.
Pollock, Sheldon. 2006. *The Language of the Gods in the World of Men: Sanskrit, Culture and Power in Pre-Modern India.* Berkeley: University of California Press.
Prakash, Devi. 1980. *Hammīra Mahākāvya kā Ālochanātmak Adhyayan,* PhD Dissertation. Aligarh: Aligarh Muslim University.
Raine, Kathleen. 1991. *Golgonooza: City of Imagination.* New York: Lindinsfarne Press.
Rathore, L. S. 2009. *The Glory of Ranthambore.* Jodhpur: The Thar Bliss Publishing House.
Ricouer, Paul. 1984. *Time and Narrative.* Chicago: The University of Chicago Press.
Rilke, Rainer-Maria. n.d. *A Walk*, trans. Robert Bly. https://www.poemhunter.com/poem/a-walk/. Accessed on: 22 March 2020
Roche, David. 2001. "The 'Dhāk', Devi Amba's Hourglass in Tribal Southern India." *Asian Music* 32, 59–99.
Roghair, Gene H. 1982. *The Epic of Palnadu: A Study and Translation of the Palnati Virula Katha, A Telegu Oral Tradition from Andhra Pradesh, India.* Oxford: Clarendon Press.
Rorty, Richard. 1989. *Contingency, Irony, and Solidarity.* Cambridge: Cambridge University Press.

Rosenfield, Israel. 1992. *The Strange, Familiar and the Forgotten: An Anatomy of Consciousness.* New York: Knopf.

Satchidanandan, K. 2018. "Alternative Ramayana Narratives". *Sahapedia Interview.* 19 September. https://www.sahapedia.org/k-satchidanandan-alternative-ramayana-narratives. Accessed on: 11 April 2020.

Shashtri, Nathulal and Madhukar Trivedi. 1997. *Hammīra-Mahākāvya: Hindī Anuvād.* Jodhpur: Rajasthan Pracyavidya Pratisthan.

Shulman, David. 1998. "The Prospects of Memory". *Journal of Indian Philosophy* 26, 304–334.

Shulman, David. 1999. "Dreaming the Self in South India." In *Dream Cultures: Explorations in the Comparative History of Dreaming,* David Shulman and Guy Stroumsa eds., 43–73. New York: Oxford University Press.

Shulman, David. 2012. *More than Real: A History of the Imagination in South India.* Cambridge (MA): Harvard University Press.

Shulman, David, and Guy Stroumsa eds. 1999. *Dream Cultures: Explorations in the Comparative History of Dreaming.* New York: Oxford University Press.

Singh, Upinder. 2008. A *History of Ancient and Early Medieval India: From the Stone Age to the 12th Century.* New Delhi: Pearson Longman.

Smith, John D. 1991. *The Epic of Pabuji: A Study, Transcription and Translation.* Cambridge: Cambridge University Press.

Sontheimer, Günther-Dietz. 1987. "The Vana and the Kṣetra. The Tribal Background of some Famous Cults." In *Eschmann Memorial Lectures*, Gaya Charan Tripathi and Hermann Kulke eds., 117–164. Bhubhaneshwar: The Eschmann Memorial Fund.

Sontheimer, Günther-Dietz. 1989. *Pastoral Deities in Western India,* trans. Anne Fedlhaus. New York: Oxford University Press.

Spira, Rupert. 2016. *Presence, Volume II: The Intimacy of All Experience.* Oakland (CA): New Harbinger Publications.

Stevens, Wallace. 1972. *The Palm at the End of the Mind: Selected Poems and a Play,* Holly Stevens ed. New York: Vintage Books.

Taylor, Charles. 2007. *A Secular Age.* Cambridge (MA): Harvard University Press.

Thapar, Romila. 2003. *The Penguin History of Early India: From the Origins to 1300 AD.* Delhi: Penguin Books India.

Thapar, Romila. 2005. *Somnath: The Many Voices of a History.* London: Verso.

The Usual Suspects. 1995. Movie directed by Bryan Singer. https://en.wikipedia.org/wiki/The_Usual_Suspects. Accessed on: 11 March 2020.

Tod, James. 1920. *Annals and Antiquities of Rajasthan.* London: Oxford University Press.

Traut, Lucia and Annette Wilke, eds. 2015. *Religion, Imagination, Aesthetik: Vorstellungs- und Sinneswelten in Religion and Kultur.* Goettingen: V & R Academic.

Vatsyayan, Kapila. 1996. *Bharata: The Nāṭyaśāstra.* New Delhi: Sahitya Akademie.

Venkatesananda, Swami. 1985. *The Concise Yoga Vasistha.* Albany: State University of New York.

Vinzent, Markus. 2019. *Writing the History of Early Christianity: From Reception to Retrospection.* Cambridge: Cambridge University. Press.

Vonnegut, Kurt. 2005. *A Man without a Country.* New York: Seven Stories Press.

Warder, Anthony Kennedy. 1972. *An Introduction to Indian Historiography.* Bombay: Popular Prakashan.

White, Hayden. 1980. "The Value of Narrativity in the Representation of Reality." *Critical Enquiry* 7, 5–27.

White, Hayden. 1984. "The Question of Narrative in Contemporary Historical Theory." *History and Theory* 23, 1–33.

Wittgenstein, Ludwig. 1958. *Philosophical Investigations*, trans. G. E. M. Anscombe. Oxford: Basil Blackwell.

Žižek, Slavoj. 2002. *Welcome to the Desert of the Real:* London: Verso.

Authors

Adams, Robert 81
Ahmed, Aziz 46–50
Asad, Talal 75
Assman, Jan 21, 53

Bandyapadhyaya, Brajnath 54, 65 f., 68
Baranī, Ẓiyā' al-Dīn 10,12, 13, 14
Baudrillard, Jean 76, 99 f.
Bayly, Susan 115
Bednar, Michael 11, 51
Bhāṇḍauvyās 11
Blake, William 39–43, 185
Bly, Robert 57
Borges, Jorge Luis 31, 33, 79 f., 87, 89, 95, 99, 112
Bowie, Malcolm 4, 28
Boyarin, Daniel 52, 55
Bronner, Yigal 72
Buchta, David 74
Bühler, Georg 14

Candraśekhara 11
Carr, David 24, 28, 30, 38
Chakrabarty, Dipesh 18 f.
Chattopadhyay, B.D. 9
Collingwood, R.G. 109–112

Deleuze, Gilles 87
Deliege, Robert 61
Descartes, René 40

Eagleman, David 24

Fazl, Abul 46, 116
Ferishtah 13
Flood, F.B. 8 f.
Fuller, A.R. 12
Fuller, Buckminster 34

Gadamer, H.G. 23, 37
Gonda, Jan 115
Grimm, Brüder 57

Habib, Muhammed 12
Heesterman, J.C. 115, 120
Heidegger, Martin 24–26, 37, 42, 56, 73, 82 f., 90, 92–98, 100–102, 105 f., 111, 115
Hiltebeitel, Alf 119
Hölderlin, Friedrich 94 f.
Husserl, Edmund 31, 37

Jinavijaya, Muni 20, 22 f.
Jodharāja 11

Keller, Helen 132
Keller, Mary 75
Khallaque, A. 12
Khusrau, Amir 2, 10, 46
Kirtane, Nilkanth Janardane 2, 9, 14 f., 20–22, 45 f., 50–52, 134
Kolff, Dirk 72
Koselleck, Reinhart 28
Krishnamurti, J. 33
Kulke, Hermann XV

Lee, Seu-Kyou 102
Lincoln, Bruce 119

Malik, Aditya 6, 11, 14, 21, 33, 40, 45, 59 f., 74, 80, 134, 163
Malik, S.C. XVII, 41
Mann, Thomas 28
Mayaram, Shail 61 f., 155
Mueller, Friedrich Max 14

Naipaul, V.S. 18
Narayana Rao, V. 21, 31, 85, 123
Nietzsche, Friedrich 100 f.

Olivelle, Patrick 115

Pamuk, Orhan 69
Pollock, Sheldon 72

Raine, Kathleen 39 f.

https://doi.org/10.1515/9783110662795-015

Rilke, Rainer-Maria 96
Roghair, Gene 21
Rorty, Richard 35

Schweig, Graham 74
Sharma, Dasharath 21
Shulman, David 21, 41, 59, 70, 72, 74, 81–85, 123
Smith, John 6, 21, 74
Sontheimer, G.D. XV, 59, 80
Stevens, Wallace 107
Sūri, Nayachandra 3, 7, 14–16, 19, 21, 31, 48 f., 54, 56, 69, 72, 74 f.
Szymborska, Wislawa 36

Taylor, Charles 74
Thapar, Romila 8, 10, 50, 52
Tod, James 14 f.
Tubb, Gary 72

Vatsyayan, Kapila 74
Vinzent, Markus 32
Vonnegut, Kurt 4, 33, 131

White, Hayden 90, 109
Wittgenstein, Ludwig 29, 35, 52

Yeats, W.B. 34

Žižek, Slavoj 100

Subjects

Afghanistan 2, 8, 192
Agency 75, 78, 112
– human 75
– idea of 75
– of God 75
Agni-kula 6, 54
Akbari Mosque 177
Akbarnāmā 116, 186
'Alā' al-Din Khalji
Ala-uddin 56, 64 f, 68
Alchemist's stone 58
– pāras 122, 128, 175
– Pārasmani 128
– Pāras stone 128, 175
– Philosopher's stone 58, 128
Alexander 11
'already-always' 26, 37
Amir 2, 8, 9, 10, 11, 46
Andenken 101 f., 111, 113, 115
– and *Denken* 101, 102, 111
– and *Gedächtnis* 101
– and History 111, 115
– and imagination 113
– as memento 112, 115
– as the gathering together of remembrance 102
Anecdote 15, 173
Annamayya 85
Apsara 56, 145
Āraṅgī Devī, wife of Hammīra 2, 135, 151, 166
Āraṇya 59
Archaeological Survey of India 123, 128, 175, 183
– Archaeological Department 126, 128, 174 f.
– Archaeological Survey 62 f., 155, 167, 180, 184
– Archaeological Survey Department of India 126, 174
Arjuna 13, 137, 146, 152
Artefact 86, 112 f.
– mind-born 41, 81, 112
Artha 140
Authoritative 24, 26
Autobiographical details 169
Awareness 26, 81 f., 90

Babar 63, 179
Bahadur Shah 166
Bamboo 143, 161, 192
Banyan tree 117, 188
Barbarian 9
Battle 2, 7, 10, 15, 19, 22, 49, 52, 54, 115 f., 121, 123, 126, 128–130, 134, 137 f., 140, 142, 144–147, 160, 162, 174–176, 187, 191, 193 f.
Battlefield 13, 67, 111, 116, 118, 120 f., 123, 126 f., 141 f., 152, 162, 168, 174, 191, 194
Befindlichkeit 73
Begriffsgeschichte 37
Being
– and imagination 35, 38, 40, 41, 43, 79, 83–85, 88, 106, 112, 132
– as the source of all possibility 39
– at the effect of 42 f.
– born 15, 35, 45 f., 50, 54 f., 64–66, 81, 84, 88, 115, 122, 134, 142
– coming into 62, 90, 106, 132
– divine 39 f., 67, 75, 118, 145
– historical XI, 44
– human and field of experience 25
– human 24, 25, 26, 94 f., 102, 104, 108, 131
– inner 33, 42, 64, 84, 92, 95, 100, 112, 122, 124, 137, 154, 159, 169, 172
– -in-the-now 39
– -in-the-world 26, 92
– -in-time 39
– language, thought and time 92
– lost and alone 56
– -ness 41, 98, 104
– of a human being 25
– -ness of a person 25
– possibility of 24–26, 40, 43, 77, 82, 90, 92, 97, 104, 106, 132

https://doi.org/10.1515/9783110662795-016

– remembrance of 75, 92, 102, 113, 154
– sentient 42
– separate 25, 59, 80, 94, 132, 146
– state of 8, 33, 41, 71, 78, 92, 104, 131, 137
– temporal 24, 27–29, 33, 35, 38, 40 f., 53, 91, 97, 103–105, 109 f., 123
– thinking that emerges out of 83
– unbounded 41
– well- 54
Benares 134
Bhairava 118
Bhajan 120, 171 f.
Bhārat 22
Bhāva 73
Bhil 55 f., 61
– Bhīl-Mina 62, 154 f.
Bhoja, younger brother of Hammīra 49, 134 f.
Bhṛgu 54
Big bang theory 30
Bijapur 13, 46
Bilhana 7, 14 f., 71
Block universe theory 30
Blood of Śakas 50
Boar and waterhole 58, 59
Body 11, 25, 28, 31, 35, 39–42, 49, 53, 56, 59 f., 63 f., 70, 79 f., 83–86, 116, 119, 122 f., 125, 130, 132, 138, 145, 153 f., 171, 173, 177
Brahmā 6, 45, 55
Brāhman 83
Bundi 117, 165, 190

Causality 29–32, 44
– historical 30
– idea of 32
– meaningful 44
– retroactive 31
– reverse 27, 29, 32, 48, 71 f.
Cause 2, 31 f., 38, 43, 53, 55 f., 78 f., 85, 91, 107, 115, 135, 164, 169
– and effect 31 f., 78, 91
Cavalry 12, 135, 141
Celestial canopy 12
Central Asia 22, 53
Champavat 60
Chandbardai 191 f.
Chattri 167
Chauhan 6 f., 9 f., 16, 48, 53–55, 134, 156 f., 159–161, 163, 166, 168, 191 f., 194
– Chahamana 7, 141 f., 144, 146
Chittor 11, 160, 166 f., 180, 193
Christ, gospels of 19
Circular Ruins, The (short story by J.L. Borges) 79, 82, 87 f., 95, 112
Clearing 42 f., 56, 105 f.
– *Lichtung* 42, 56
– lighting 42, 106, 156
Clinton, Bill 116 f., 187
Collective identities 19
Concealment and unconcealment 108
Conceptual edifice 29
Conceptual world 42, 87
Consciousness 18, 27, 40, 70, 74, 132
– and dream 106
– and William Blake 40
– historical 18
– of something forgotten 132
Constantinople 3, 19
Context 6 f., 18–21, 23, 27, 29, 31 f., 37, 41–43, 46, 53 f., 82, 85, 102, 104 f., 109, 111, 113, 116, 190
– and language 32, 109
– as framework for the occurrence of content 104, 105
– as not cause 31
– as prior to content 105
– as representing a possibility that lives in the future 38
– cultural 42
– for events, situations, political configurations 31
– future 31
– hidden 30, 32, 79, 102, 116, 118, 122, 140, 167
– historical 4
– historiographical 19
– of existence 37, 43, 85
– political 31
– pre- and post-independence 21
– present as 29, 105
– situational 109, 111

- social 18, 20–22, 26, 30f., 33, 51–54, 64, 72f., 86f., 93, 106, 113f., 116, 119, 131
Context free 51
Conversation 23, 28, 34, 37, 46, 58, 61–63, 67, 105, 114f., 118, 120–123, 130, 151, 154, 169, 172, 186, 190
Corporeality 88
Cosmopolitanism 45, 51
Counter-epic 46
Court 7, 10, 46, 49, 52, 54f., 67f., 71, 115, 134f., 141f., 159, 162–164, 167, 178–180
- kacchheri 164, 178
Creation, Vedic conceptions of 20, 28, 39–42, 63, 70f., 78–80, 82f., 88, 99, 104, 108, 112, 122, 131, 181
Cultural memory 53

Dakṣina kālī 171
Darbār 193
Dargāh 116f., 122, 126, 128–130, 172–179, 189
Das Sein 102
Das Sichentziehende 94
Deccan Sultanate 13
Delhi 4, 10, 12, 14, 19, 22, 51, 65–67, 117, 126f., 135, 140, 159f., 165, 174, 178, 180, 182f., 190, 193
Delhi Sultanate 6, 9, 11, 15, 22, 72
Denken 83, 90, 92f., 96, 98, 101f., 111
- and *Andenken* 101, 102, 111
- and *das zu-Denkende* 101, 102
- and *Sein* 102,
Desertification 101
Desert of the real 100
Desolation 79, 100f.
Deutungslos 94f.
Devalldevī, daughter of Hammīra 2, 135, 148, 151
Devnārāyaṇ 6, 21f., 33, 80
Dhārādevī 135, 138, 139, 145
Dharma 20, 54f., 134, 140, 150
Die Verwüstung 100f.
Die Vorstellung 83, 98, 104
Difference 8, 85, 87f.
Digvijaya 7, 11, 116, 134
Dikṣit 120, 171f.
Dilli 140, 142, 144
Disembodied person 75
Divān-e-Khās 166f.
Division 30, 119, 131
- of perceiver and perceived 131
- of subject and world 30
Donkeys 117f., 129, 176, 184, 190f.
Doppler effect 38
Dream 3–5, 7f., 16f., 21, 43f., 53, 69–71, 74–82, 86–88, 108, 128, 131, 136, 151, 166, 175, 180
- and agency 75, 112
- and buried knowledge 70
- and experience 70
- and freedom to create 79
- and imagination 69, 70
- and memory 70, 74
- and Nayachandra Surī 3, 7, 21, 74
- and non-dream 79
- and Sanskrit poetry 8, 21
- and Śiva 81, 82
- and *The Circular Ruins* (short story by J.L. Borges) 79, 80
- and the non-real 75
- and the real 112
- and Viṣṇu 137
- and waking reality 78
- as instrument of creation 88
- as legitimizing 3
- as objective fact 70, 75,
- as perfect simulacrum of the real world 78, 88
- as symbolic 69
- king's 4, 54, 57, 59, 61, 65, 75, 81, 116, 139, 141, 143f., 149f., 161, 166f., 187
- -like invention of social or physical worlds 86
- of a beating heart 80
- poet's dream 3, 5, 16f., 69f., 75f.
- shared 18–20, 77f.
- state 14, 38, 50f., 53–55, 58, 63–67, 69f., 72–74, 76, 78, 86f., 90, 92, 96, 102, 123, 162, 168f., 192
- unfulfilled 128, 166, 175, 180
- world of 88
Dreaming 3, 8, 74, 78f., 88

Dreamworld 70, 78f., 86, 88
Duryodhana 150, 152
Dvāpara yuga 119, 169

Earth 12f., 25, 34, 48, 50, 59, 101, 112, 132f., 142f., 146–149, 153
Eisenhans 57
– Iron John 57, 59f.
– Iron Man 57
Embodiment 75, 83f., 144, 147
Emotion 24, 73, 77
Empiricism 114
Emptiness 23, 35, 84, 105, 132
Empty sign 94, 96
Enchanted forest 56
Entity 24f., 37, 69, 80, 88, 95
Epic 6, 19, 21f., 45f., 48–50, 52f., 72, 74
Epistemic connection to the now 98
Ereignis 94, 98, 102
Eternity 39f., 43, 118, 190
Exile 57, 59, 67f.
Existence 19, 23–26, 28, 33–37, 41–43, 49, 55, 58, 62, 65, 70, 79, 81, 84–87, 90–92, 96, 99, 104–113, 119, 132, 168f., 173
Experience 23f., 28–32, 35, 37–39, 41–44, 53, 57, 59, 70, 73, 75–77, 79, 86f., 91f., 94, 97f., 100, 103f., 106, 108f., 112, 123, 131, 154f.
– and experienced 131
– and experiencer 131
– direct 3f., 29f., 46, 75, 82, 104, 110, 118
– of self 51, 96, 122
– of world as an occurrence 104

Factuality 3
Fakir 116, 187
Fantasy 35, 70, 88, 99, 112
Fiction 16, 31, 69f., 76, 99
Field of attention 103
Field of experience 24–26, 40
Fieldwork 19, 67, 114
Fire worship 47
Firoz Shah Tughlaq 15
Firuzpur 15
Fluid boundaries 18
Folklore 21
Forgetting 33, 59, 83, 132
Formation of 7, 27, 29f., 71
Fourfold nexus of time, thought, language and subject 26
French revolution 30
Friendship 18, 20, 22, 45, 51, 73, 123, 178
Future as that which is being lived into 103, 104
Future past 28
Future-present 30

Gajānand 122
Gajānand Pīr 116, 122f., 129, 175f.
Gandhi, Indira 58, 168
Gandhi, Rajiv 116f., 187
Ganeśa 116, 119, 122f., 126, 128–130, 156f., 170f., 174–176, 185, 189
– Chaturthi 157
– Trinetra 122, 129, 130, 156, 170, 176
Ganeśpol 130, 176, 177, 182
Gates 123, 126f., 130, 154, 157, 164, 172, 174, 176, 182, 194
Gaur Brahman 54
Gayatri Devi 188f.
Genre 3, 5, 27, 46, 76
Ghaznavid dynasty 8
Golconda 46
Goludev 58–60
Gujarat 6, 9, 48, 61, 135, 162, 166, 170
Gumti 128
Gunpowder 63, 130, 161, 167, 176, 179, 189
Gupt Gaṅgā 129, 130, 176

Hallucination 71
Hammīra 2, 4f., 7–11, 13–16, 19f., 22f., 27f., 46, 48, 50–56, 62, 64, 67, 69, 71, 75f., 115f., 119, 122f., 134–137, 139–153, 155, 161, 167, 177, 179, 186, 190
– Hambira 8, 9
– Hamira 8
– Hamīr Deo 13f.
– Hammīr Dev 48, 156f., 159–161, 163, 166, 168, 170, 191, 194
– Hamvira 8
Hammīrahaṭṭa 11

Hammīra-Mahākāvya 2–7, 10 f., 13–15, 19–23, 27 f., 33, 45 f., 48–50, 54, 64, 74, 134, 166
– Hammīr Kavya 48
Hammīramardana 14
Hammīra Rāso 11
Hammīrāyan 11
Hanuman 126–128, 148, 174 f., 178–180
Harijan 122, 125, 173
Haṭṭa 4, 75
Hemachandra 50
Here and now 23, 44, 97, 147
Heroic age 51
Hindu 5, 9 f., 13, 20, 22, 45–51, 53, 55, 64 f., 67, 76, 80, 115 f., 122, 129, 162, 167, 176, 178, 192 f.
Historical knowledge 23, 70, 110, 112 f.
Historical narratives 3, 19, 32
Historical thought 109
Historiography 5, 10, 22, 48, 70
History 3, 5, 15, 18, 20 f., 23–28, 31–33, 42–44, 47 f., 51, 54, 61, 63, 75, 86, 90, 97 f., 106, 108–112, 114, 116, 121, 123, 132, 154, 163, 166, 169, 179, 189 f., 194
– and causal, linear imagination 43
– and notion of autonomous individual 75
– and time 3, 25, 37, 41, 84, 91 f., 108 f.
– and written texts 109
– as alienation 108
– as *Andenken* 113
– as appearance 44
– as a way of knowing the past 109
– as function of imagination 43
– as possibility 25, 83, 106
– as re-enactment of the past 111, 112, 113
– as simulacrum 90
– as structuring of time 43
– as study of the past 33, 91, 97, 106, 108
– as ultimate codified truth 109
– construction of 33, 63, 75, 87, 118, 155
– heroic 2–4, 6, 10, 16, 21–23, 46, 48 f., 52, 54, 71, 73 f., 136
– idea of 11, 24 f., 30–33, 37, 40, 42, 44, 52, 64, 75, 87
– language and thought 23, 92
– of Hammīra 5, 9 f., 14 f., 20–23, 26 f., 31, 44, 48, 50 f., 53 f., 58, 60 f., 68 f., 75, 114–116, 122, 136, 147, 152, 154
– of the fortress 1 f., 4, 13, 19, 55 f., 60–63, 114, 116, 118, 120, 123, 135 f., 144, 148, 154 f., 157, 159, 161, 169, 172, 179, 187, 190
– personal 9, 15, 18, 26, 39 f., 42, 57, 70, 123, 131, 154 f., 173
– purpose of 15, 20, 108, 131, 164, 177
– question of 8, 27, 37, 62, 78, 85, 87, 94 f., 97, 105, 108
– retrograde and forward movement of 31,
– subaltern 51
– thinking about 29, 62, 90, 92, 96–98, 102, 104, 111, 149, 155
Honour 5, 12, 20, 66, 76, 137, 149, 178
Horizon 26, 30, 37–39, 53, 76 f., 107, 145
– interpretative 76
– of knowledge 30, 39, 42, 77, 98, 109–111
– of manifestation 26, 86
– primary 19, 39, 98
– secondary 37
– temporal 24, 27–29, 33, 35, 38, 40 f., 53, 91, 97, 103–105, 109 f., 123
– two-fold 38
Human being 24–26, 30, 34, 38, 43, 73, 76, 79, 93–95, 102, 104, 108, 131
– and being human 77, 94, 95, 97, 102, 131, 132
– and being-in-the-now 39
– and field of experience 24, 25,
– and point of view 29
– and that which has withdrawn itself 93, 94, 95, 98, 108
– and thinking 35, 72, 98, 102, 138
– as meaning-less sign 95,
– as sign 94, 95, 96,
– being-ness of 24 f., 104
– being of 25, 41, 95
– forward leaning of 104
– unlimited nature of 25
Huna 9
Hunting entourage 56
Hyperreal 99 f.

Illusion 71, 76, 85, 88, 100
Illusory thickness of the world 84
Imagination 1, 5, 16, 18, 21, 23, 27f., 33–36, 38–43, 69f., 78–86, 88, 97–100, 102, 106–108, 110, 112f., 118, 131f., 147, 154
– absence of 99, 107
– and arising of world X, 98, 131, 132
– and Being 8, 14, 25, 43, 56, 105, 113, 134
– and being-ness 41
– and Consciousness 40
– and creation and freedom 79
– and creativity 101, 107
– and *die Vorstellung* 83, 98, 101
– and emptiness 23, 35, 84, 132
– and experience 24, 27, 34, 37, 44, 109f.
– and folklore 21
– and history 16, 29, 33, 42, 112
– and hyperreal 99,
– and image 99, 102
– and imaging 99
– and its progeny 88
– and language 26, 92, 103, 110
– and love 82, 122
– and magic 80
– and memory 37, 113, 154
– and mind 23, 40, 41, 42, 80, 81, 84, 112, 113
– and non-imagination 34
– and positivist scientific ideology 41
– and reality 78, 82
– and solidification 132
– and the collapse of past, present, future 115
– and the dream 88
– and the presence of the real 70
– and thinking 35, 72, 98, 102, 138
– and thought 25, 27, 42, 80, 84, 90, 101
– and visible world 79, 84
– and William Blake 39, 40, 41, 42
– as active faculty 41
– as generative language 38
– as mental act 42
– as original source 40
– as prior to the real 82, 83
– as the source of all things 42, 108
– as world of eternity 39, 40, 43
– being, existence, remembrance 2, 4f., 7, 9–11, 13, 24–26, 28, 34–36, 38–44, 47, 49, 54, 56f., 59–61, 64f., 67, 69, 73, 75, 77, 80, 82–85, 87f., 92, 94–110, 112f., 115f., 120, 122, 131f., 134f., 137, 139, 145, 152, 154, 166, 170–172, 181, 186, 190–192
– causal 28, 43, 91, 105
– circles of 15
– effortless effort of 78
– end of 97, 107, 134, 141, 150, 190
– fierce, tough acts of 59, 85
– historical 3, 5f., 13, 15–23, 26–28, 30f., 33f., 42, 44, 46, 48f., 53, 62–64, 69f., 72, 76, 93, 110, 114–116, 121, 123, 154f., 169, 172f.
– human 25, 31, 37, 39f., 43, 51, 57, 64, 67, 75, 77, 79–82, 88, 92, 94f., 97, 102, 106, 118, 122, 131f.
– intertwined realms of poem, dream and revelation 16
– in Vedic thought 41, 42
– layers of 26f., 59, 83f., 109, 112, 118
– meaning of 16, 26, 31, 43, 52, 73, 92, 96, 101, 103, 141, 161, 171
– objects of 110, 114
– phenomenology of 44
– plasticity of 38
– political 8, 13, 18–22, 26, 28, 31, 33, 46, 52, 61, 67, 72f., 87, 109, 111, 113–116, 131, 186, 192
– realms of 16, 33, 41, 69f., 72, 80
– scaffold of 79
– substratum of 22, 26, 37, 131f.
– withdrawing of 94, 131
– world of 8, 32, 35, 39–41, 43f., 75, 78, 81, 83f., 86, 88, 96
Imagine 2, 21, 27, 31, 41, 79, 81–83, 98, 100f., 162
Imperialism 19f., 22
Inception (movie) 5, 75, 77f., 86–88, 94f.
Individual 2, 21, 24–26, 31, 37f., 40, 42, 53, 61, 64, 71, 75, 78f., 93, 115, 132, 139, 142, 155
– autonomous 75
Indra 55f., 63, 142, 147

Inert savoir 107
Intentionality 23, 77, 79, 86, 109
Interpretation 25–29, 37, 74, 95, 108 f.
Interpretative possibilities 114
Intertextuality 28, 72
Inventiveness, unhindered 79
'I' or 'me' as linguistic entities 37
Ivan and Bhuvan 58

Jāgar 59
Jaina 7 f., 14, 45 f., 50, 53, 65–67, 116
Jain deities 168
Jain temple 117, 162, 178, 184, 189
Jaipur 117, 125, 165, 173, 184, 187 f., 193
Jaitra Siṃha, father of Hammīra 49, 136 f., 151
Jalal al-din Khaljī 46, 49
Janārdan 151
Jal jauhar 167
Jauhar 2, 48, 135, 167 f., 194
Jayasiṃha Sūri 7, 15 f.
Jimūtavāhana 153
Jogi 115 f., 186 f.
Jogi Mahal 115 f., 126, 174, 182, 186–188
Judaism 52

Kabul 68
Kākaṭīya 67
Kalidāsa 7, 16, 59, 71
Kalinga 59, 135
Kali yuga 58 f., 137, 147, 149, 169
Kāma 140
Kāñcipuram 81
Karṇa 137, 152 f.
Kāvya 5, 7, 16, 20, 22 f., 31, 50, 72
Keyser Söze 2
Khaṇḍobā 80
Khazāʾin al-futūḥ 2, 10, 12
Kinaesthetic experience 92
King Bali 153
Kingdom 3, 9 f., 47, 52, 54, 57–59, 67, 116, 134–137, 139, 141, 143, 147, 149–151, 165, 186 f., 193
King Hadda 62, 155, 165
King Jayant 62 f., 155
Kingship 114 f., 120
Knowledge 10, 15 f., 23, 25, 29, 39, 43, 53, 66, 70, 76 f., 82 f., 99, 103, 105–107, 110, 112, 114, 119 f., 122, 143, 156, 169, 171, 180
Kota 163, 165, 168, 184
Koṭi yajña 7, 11, 134
Kṛṣṇa 168
Kṣatriya 2, 6, 54, 138, 141, 143 f., 147, 150
Kṣetra 59, 118, 123, 152
Kushana 9

Labyrinth 158, 170, 172
Lakṣmī 137, 168
Lakṣmīnārāyaṇ 168
Lakṣmīnārāyaṇ temple 178
Language 3, 5, 7, 9 f., 15, 23, 27–29, 32, 34–38, 45 f., 48, 51 f., 54, 71 f., 92, 108–110, 113, 131 f., 164
mystery of 132
Laterne der Reflexion 96
Listening 21, 34, 37, 104, 141 f., 144, 150
Loyalty 2 f., 10, 20, 22, 45, 51 f., 73, 123

Mahābhārata 145, 169
Mahādevī 170
Maharana Pratap 190, 192 f.
Maharana Sanga 166
Maharashtra 15, 61, 162
Mahāvidya 119
Mahāvīra 45, 65
Mahimā Sāhi 2, 13, 22, 135–137, 141 f., 145 f., 148, 150, 152 f.
Mahmud of Ghazni 9
Malik Lake 163
Maliya Baghel 122, 125, 173
Malwa 11, 49, 162
Mango kernels 4
Manifestation 26 f., 38, 78, 84, 86, 88, 104
Map 99 f., 165
Martin Luther 30
Martyr 179
Materiality 112, 154
Matrix, The (movie) 76 f., 85, 100
Mazār 177
Meaninglessness 23, 39,
Measurability 26, 40

Melā 122
Memento (movie) 32, 111, 115, 154
Memory 21, 27–30, 33, 37, 39, 53, 59, 70 f., 74 f., 91 f., 97, 101 f., 106, 109, 111–116, 123, 128, 130, 166, 175–177, 187, 194
– and experience 24, 27, 34, 37, 44, 109 f.
– and forgetting 59
– and history 16, 29, 33, 42, 112
– and Mnemosyne 101, 112
– and multi-sensory experience 91, 92
– and past, present and future 91, 131
– and person 24, 36
– and the dream 88
– and time 3, 25, 37, 41, 84, 91 f., 108 f.
– as a gathering together of what already desires to be thought upon 102
– as *Andenken* or memento 111, 115,
– as a remembrance of Being 102
– as gathering together of remembrance 101, 102
– cultural 8, 13, 22, 26 f., 37, 42, 46, 51, 53 f., 72, 109
– figures of 8, 53, 64, 134
– forward and reverse looking 28
– goddess of 101, 119, 142 f., 169 f.
– historical 3, 5 f., 13, 15–23, 26–28, 30 f., 33 f., 42, 44, 46, 48 f., 53, 62–64, 69 f., 72, 76, 93, 110, 114–116, 121, 123, 154 f., 169, 172 f.
– karmic 74
– of God 12, 47, 75, 113, 130, 170, 176
– of the poet 16, 54, 69 f., 75
– of the region 81, 118
– primary and secondary 37
– residual 77
– tradition of 5, 21, 47
Mimicry 72
Mind 4, 23, 28, 34, 39, 41 f., 47, 50, 70 f., 73–75, 80–85, 98, 103, 110, 112 f., 119 f., 133, 137–139, 145, 153, 156, 162, 170 f.
Mir Gabru 56, 64, 67
Misapprehension 12, 42 f., 132
Misrecognition 42
Mleccha 6, 9, 141, 144 f., 151, 153
Mnemo-history 21
Mnemosyne 100 f., 112 f.
Möbius 86, 116
Modernity 18–22, 75, 99
Modernization 18
Mongol 9 f., 20, 46, 49, 51, 61, 64
Mosque 47, 119, 122, 126 f., 170, 172, 174, 177 f.
Mudgal 10, 52, 140, 152
Mughal 9 f., 143, 151, 192
Mughal Emperor 19, 116, 166, 190
– Akbar 19, 63, 179, 190, 193
– Aurangzeb 63, 179
– Jahangir 116, 186 f.
Muhammed Ghori 6, 10, 191 f.
Muhammed Shāh 2, 13, 22, 64, 67 f., 135
– Sardar Muhammed Shāh 160 f.
– Sardar Shāh 160
Multan 48, 68
Multi-verse 27
Muslim 6 f., 9 f., 20, 22 f., 45 f., 48–51, 64, 115, 122 f., 134, 140, 180
– Mohammedan 53
– Musalman 67
Mutiny 11–13, 135

Namāz 177
Narrative templates 21
Nasik 15
Nationalist 5, 19 f., 31
Nation state 18, 21, 31, 33
Nāṭyaśāstra 73
Naulakha Gate 126, 174, 182
Nayahaṃsa 15
Nemināth 45, 168
Neo (main character from the movie *The Matrix*) 100
Neo-Muslim 10, 14, 19 f., 51, 135, 142, 160
Non-utilitarian cause 74
Non-visibility 83
Nothing 24, 27, 30, 35, 37 f., 52, 76, 83–85, 104, 106, 131, 149, 163, 171, 180, 192
– Nothingness 104, 131, 132
– No-thing-ness 43, 96, 104
Nusrat Khan 11, 12, 135, 143, 144, 160

Object 23–27, 33, 36f., 40–42, 47, 57, 78, 82f., 99, 101–105, 108–110, 112, 114f., 119, 131f., 137, 144, 169, 177
Objective 26, 70f., 73f.
Ontological category 25
Oral narratives 6, 21f., 80, 154

Pābūjī 6, 21f.
Padam Lake 115, 122, 128, 156, 163, 175
Padam Ṛṣi 56, 63f., 118f.
Padmavati Lake 167f.
Pañcamakāra 170
Pandu 138
Parasnāth 65
– Parśvanāth 65
Past, present, future as entangled temporalities 3–5, 8, 17, 20f., 23–26, 28–31, 33f., 36–39, 42–44, 53, 62f., 70, 72, 75, 90–92, 94, 97f., 101, 103f., 106–112, 114–116, 118, 131, 154f., 168–170, 179
Pathan 143, 152
Perception 22, 29, 32, 34, 90, 110, 132f.
Periya Purāṇam 81
Persian 3, 5, 9–11, 13, 46–48, 52, 76
Phenomenal world 40, 42f.
– as an 'as if' world 43, 44
– as appearance 44
Phenomenology XI, 44
– of History 3, 18, 22f., 28, 43, 44, 92, 98, 115
– of imagination 42f., 69, 84f., 88
Pipal tree 126, 172
Pīr 115–117, 122, 186, 190
Plain sense of things, The (poem by Wallace Stevens) 107f.
Plato 40, 76
Plato's Idea 104
Poem 3–5, 7f., 10, 14–17, 19f., 22f., 31, 35f., 45, 53f., 69–75, 85, 95, 107, 134, 192f.
Poetry 7f., 20f., 46, 53, 69–71, 86, 101f., 112
Poet's dream 3, 5, 16f., 69f., 75f.
Point of view 24–26, 30, 44
Possession 12, 15, 58, 75, 185
Possibility 26, 28, 31, 38f., 42f., 83, 103–106, 108, 132
Possibility of possibility 104
Possibility of the impossible 77
Post-heroic age 74
Potentiality 76
Prākṛta-piṅgala 11
Prejudice 29, 108
Presence 12, 29f., 33, 37–39, 46, 57, 69, 74f., 95, 97–99, 103, 105f., 108, 122, 145
as space 105
Present as replicating the past 103, 112
Present-now 23f.
Present-past 154, 173
Primordial connection of language, thought and world 132
Protention 23, 31, 37f.
Pṛthvīrāj Chauhan 7, 54, 134, 190–193
Pṛthvīrāj III 10
Pṛthvīrāja-rāso 10
Pṛthvīrāja-vijaya 10
Psychological 24, 46, 91, 101
Psychologie 101, 104
Pūcalār, devotee of Śiva 81f., 112f.
Puruṣa 64, 119
Pushkar 6, 11, 58–60
Puṣkara-Mahātmya 6

Quantum physicists 84
Quasi-historical narrative 114
Queen Elizabeth 188f.
Qutb al-Din Aibak 6

Rādhā Devī 134
Raghunāth Temple 128, 158, 175, 179, 184, 191
Raja Man Singh I of Jaipur 193
Rajasthan 2f., 6, 11, 14, 19, 22, 45, 54, 58, 61, 70, 74, 140, 192
Rajasthani 3–6, 11, 19, 21, 73, 76
Rajput 2, 4, 6–11, 13, 15, 19–21, 23, 46–49, 51–56, 61, 64, 72f., 125, 146, 166f., 190
Rāma 52, 75, 85, 137, 156, 158, 168, 191
Raṇbhūmi 120f., 123, 194
Rani Karṇavati 166

Raṇmalla 136, 141, 147–149
Ranthambore 2f., 10–13, 19, 49, 55f., 58, 60, 62f., 67, 114f., 117, 121, 125f., 134f., 143f., 147, 154–156, 160, 166, 173f., 187–190, 194
– Raṇasthaṃbapura 19
– Ranat-bhanwar-gad 121, 194
– Raṇthaṃban Dev 121, 194
– Ranthambor 55
– Ranthanbhūr 13, 14
Rao Jeyat 56, 61
Rasa 7f., 16, 23, 48, 71, 73, 134, 152
Rāṣtra 22
Rāṣtrīya Mahākāvya 23
Ratipāla 49, 135, 140f., 145, 147–149, 151, 153
Rāvaṇa 15, 137, 148, 151
Ravana and Basava 56, 61
Real and unreal 83
Reality 27, 30, 34, 41, 43, 69, 76–79, 85–88, 99f., 109, 112, 135, 154
– and experience encoded in writing 109
– and hyperreal 99, 100,
– and interlocking of dream, imagination, truth 82
– apparent 30, 34, 42f., 53, 132
– as a function of social agreement 27, 30
– 'as if' 43f.
– as residing in the imagination 34
– basic 52, 54, 70, 74, 99
– computer generated 100
– dimensioned 41
– dream 3–5, 7f., 16f., 21, 43f., 53, 69–71, 74–82, 86–88, 108, 128, 131, 136, 151, 166, 175, 180
– empirical 5, 99, 110f.
– everyday 17f., 25, 39, 43, 53, 65, 76f., 88, 173
– everyday experience of 39, 69, 84
– faithful copy of 99,
– imagining 12, 18, 20f., 27, 31, 41, 43, 85, 88, 99, 102, 106, 111f., 114f.
– physical 34, 64f., 70, 78, 86, 88, 96, 103, 111, 119, 131
– reality as a tissue of mentation 82, 85
– representation of 98f.
– simulated 76
– waking 78, 86f.
– world as a simulacrum of 77, 78, 86
Real world 78f., 86
Rebel general 10, 19, 22, 64
Recollection 37, 92
Re-enactment as intentional galvanization of the imagination 112
Religious affiliation 9
Religious fundamentalism 18
Remembering 4, 21, 23, 101, 112–114
Representation 18, 52, 69, 99, 109, 116
Resemblance 72, 87, 92
Residual memory 77
Resistance 9, 23, 46, 48, 50f., 53
Re-telling 27, 53, 123
Retention 23, 37f.
Retroactive 27–29, 31
Retrospective 28, 53
Ṛg Veda 54
Ritual of battle 119
Ritual practice 114, 118f.
Road Transport Office (RTO) 181
Ṛṣi Padam 56, 63f., 118f.

Sabalak Chauhan 62f., 155
Sacrifice 2, 6, 21f., 51, 71, 74, 114, 119, 121, 145, 150–152, 170
Sacrificial foundation 60
Sādhanā 118, 120, 171f.
Sadhu 118f., 169
Sadruddin Aulia 117, 189f.
Sage Padam 56, 63f., 118f.
Śaka 9f., 13, 137f., 140–144, 146–149, 152f.
Śakti 55
Śakuni 147
Sāma Veda 54
Śaṃbhunāth 168
Sanskrit 2, 4–11, 14–17, 19–21, 23, 39, 45, 53, 55, 59, 61, 63, 71f., 118, 128, 134, 168
Sanskrit Cosmopolis 72
Sanskritized 8f.
Sāraṅgadhara-paddhati 11
Sarga 2, 4, 6f., 13, 45, 50, 69, 134, 136f., 140, 143–145, 153
Sati 2, 50, 171, 193

Satya yuga 58
Sawai Madhopur 125, 165, 173, 180, 185 f.
Scientific knowledge 110
Secularization 18
Self and world 131 f.
Self-generation 83
Self-reflexive 16, 27, 72
Sensory reality 99
Śeṣ Nāg 143
Shadow world 43
Śibi 153
Siege 2–4, 10, 12 f., 19, 49, 67, 135
Significance 5, 15, 19 f., 22, 29 f., 37, 39, 52, 87, 109, 154, 173
Silence 23 f., 83 f., 107, 131
Simulacrum 43, 76–78, 86–88, 99, 108 f.
– of reality 41, 74, 95, 99
Simulated worlds 69
Sītā 168, 170
Śivaliṅga 119, 123, 169 f., 175
Śiva Purāna 50
Social agreement 27, 30
Soni 163 f., 168
– Goldsmith 163
Space 3, 10, 16, 18–20, 25, 34, 37 f., 40–43, 51–53, 64, 70, 79, 84–86, 104–107, 109 f., 131, 189, 192
– as clearing 105, 106
– as emptiness that surrounds objects and beings 105
space-time 30
Śrāvan 151
Subject 3, 10, 16, 25–28, 30, 40, 43 f., 54, 72, 75 f., 102, 105 f., 139, 141
Subjectivity 38, 77
Sufi 115 f., 122, 126, 173 f., 178
Sultan 3–6, 8, 10–14, 19 f., 22, 47–49, 51, 64, 67, 115, 153, 159 f., 192
Sumatināth 168
Supari Mahal 128, 175, 184
Surjanacarita 11
Sultan Mehmed II 3, 19
Sword 2, 13, 46, 55, 68, 130, 138, 145, 148, 150, 152, 177, 192
Symbols of infidelity 47

Tantric ritual 119, 169 f.
Tapasya 120, 172
Taʾrīkh-i Fīrūz Shāhī 10 f., 13
Temporal anchoring 24
Temporality 25 f., 28, 37, 40, 43, 53, 91, 103 f.
Testimony 110
Thinking 13, 34, 39 f., 77, 81–83, 90–94, 96 f., 101 f., 104, 108–113, 145, 147–149, 153, 184
– as distinct from thought 90, 91, 111
– interior 82–84, 114
– worthy of 60 f., 71, 92–94, 97, 101 f., 108, 113
Thought 2, 23–26, 29–34, 37–42, 45 f., 60, 66, 69, 76 f., 79–84, 87, 90–94, 101–108, 110–112, 130–132, 138, 147, 149, 151, 176, 184, 193
– as dividing seamless totality of experience 132
Thought-provoking 92 f., 97 f.
Thrown-ness 25
Tiger Sanctuary 115, 123
Time 3, 5–7, 9, 13–16, 21, 24–34, 36–44, 46 f., 49 f., 53, 57–60, 62–66, 70–72, 75 f., 78, 83 f., 86 f., 91 f., 97 f., 105–108, 110, 112–115, 118–121, 123, 125, 128, 130, 132 f., 137, 141, 145, 148, 154, 157, 161 f., 164–171, 173, 175, 177 f., 180–186, 188 f., 191, 193 f.
– and history 16, 29, 33, 42, 112
– and memory 37, 113, 154
– and not-time 25
– and the field of experience 25, 26
– and the possibility of the subject 26
– arising of 26, 37, 92, 132
– as psychological construct 24
– awareness of 25, 28, 31, 72, 131
– circular 24, 34, 79, 88, 100
– and dead ends 29
– experience of 23–25, 27–30, 37, 74, 76, 100, 104, 108, 114
– future 3–5, 8, 25, 28–31, 33 f., 37–39, 42 f., 58, 70, 72, 91 f., 97 f., 101, 103 f., 106–108, 131, 162
– historical 3, 5 f., 13, 15–23, 26–28, 30 f., 33 f., 42, 44, 46, 48 f., 53, 62–64, 69 f.,

72, 76, 93, 110, 114–116, 121, 123, 154f., 169, 172f.
- imagination and history 27
- inception of 3
- in chronological sequence 32
- islands of 53
- lived 38, 45, 55, 80, 103f., 154, 192
- loops 29, 34, 71
- movement in 38, 91
- mythical 62
- past 3–5, 8, 17, 20f., 23–26, 28–31, 33f., 36–39, 42–44, 53, 62f., 70, 72, 75, 90–92, 94, 97f., 101, 103f., 106–112, 114–116, 118, 131, 154f., 168–170, 179
- possibility of 24–26, 40, 43, 77, 82, 90, 92, 97, 104, 106, 132
- present 5, 8, 15, 21, 25, 28–31, 33f., 37–39, 42–44, 68, 70–72, 74, 77, 79, 87, 91f., 97f., 103–109, 112–115, 123, 131, 137, 170
- simultaneity of 28, 31, 33
- suspended from 53
- two-fold horizon of 38
- vanishing points 29
- zigzag 29
Tīrthaṅkara 65
Tīrtha-sthāna 169
Tirupati 85
Tomara 7, 19, 53, 71
Tribal communities 61, 118f.
Truth 3, 16, 26, 34, 58, 61, 69f., 74f., 79, 82, 108–110, 132f.
Turk 9f., 20, 47f., 51f., 61, 64

Ullu Khan 49, 134f.
Undifferentiated nothingness 131f.
Unhistorical works 48,
Urvashi 63f.
Uzbekistan 2

Vaideśika 2
Valmiki 85
Valour 6, 21f., 71
Varāha 59
Vaśiṣṭha 54
Venkateśvara 85
Verbal narrative 114
Vikramaditya 14, 166
Vikramāṇka-carita 14
Vikramāṇka-kāvya 14
Vīrama 7, 71f., 135, 141, 145, 148, 150–152
Viṣṇu 45, 58f., 81, 136f., 151, 166, 168

Wahid Muhammed 183,
Waking reality 77, 86
Warangal 67
Watchtower 156
Wells 114, 172
- bāvḍī 159, 161, 165, 172
'What is' 30
Wilderness 57, 59f., 85
Word
- and language 26, 92, 103, 110
- as speech 38, 84
- keeping or honouring one's IX, 4, 20, 22, 51, 53, 60, 74, 138
- spoken 21, 27, 154, 173
- written 27, 154
World 8, 11f., 18, 22f., 26, 29f., 35–38, 40–43, 52, 63, 71, 74–79, 81, 83–86, 88, 90–92, 96, 99f., 104, 108, 113, 116–118, 120, 131f., 137, 153, 156, 172, 187, 189f., 192
- and self 6, 21, 28, 119, 132, 170
- and subjective experience 76
- as simulation 76
- of imagination 42f., 69, 84f., 88
- reality of 77
Worldly vs. spiritual power 115

Yajña 6, 115f., 120, 170, 172, 186f., 194
Yakṣa 172
Yamarāj 13, 152
Yavana 9, 13, 138, 140–143, 145, 152f.
Yoga-Vāśiṣṭha 85
Yuddhiṣṭhira 52, 75

Zeitgeist 108

www.ingramcontent.com/pod-product-compliance
Lightning Source LLC
Chambersburg PA
CBHW071739150426
43191CB00010B/1636
9783111356020